fast light boats

fast light boats
A CENTURY OF KIWI INNOVATION

GRAHAME ANDERSON

Wellington
Te Papa Press
1999

Museum of New Zealand
Te Papa Tongarewa

First published 1999
Text © Grahame Anderson 1999
Images © the copyright owners

This book is copyright. Apart from any fair dealing for the purpose of private study, research, criticism, or review, as permitted under the Copyright Act, no part of this book may be reproduced by any process without the prior permission of the Museum of New Zealand Te Papa Tongarewa.

ISBN 0-909010-67-6

Designed by Walter Moala
Digital imaging by Jeremy Glyde
Edited by Anne French
Copy-edited and indexed by David Cauchi

Printed in New Zealand by Brebner Print

Published by the Museum of New Zealand Te Papa Tongarewa
PO Box 467
Wellington

Contents

Foreword
by Graham Mander vii
Acknowledgements viii

Chapter 1
    Beginnings 3

Chapter 2
    The advent of P, Z, I, & X 29

Chapter 3
    Stepping on the stones 43

Chapter 4
    Technology transfer 77

Chapter 5
    Innovation and interweaving 101

Chapter 6
    Small boats writ large 127

An illustrated checklist of small fast light boats 164
Glossary of sailing terms 176
Notes 178
Index 180

Foreword

To bring together all the factors that, over such a long period, have contributed to the high regard with which New Zealand yachtsmen are held is no small task.

Grahame Anderson, with his architectural background, and his strong sense of history as evidenced by his research into the exploits of Abel Tasman, has managed to portray in a well-balanced way a good record of the near and distant past in such a way that readers will be able to respect the achievements of our yachties both old and new.

His position as crew member for Barney Scully in various *Windhovers* representing Wellington from 1953 until winning the Moffat Cup in 1955, confirm that he has been there and done that, so that he was able to bear witness to much of what I consider was a wonderful era in centreboard yachting.

My interest in yachting history has recently allowed me in turn to respect the earlier pre-war generations of yachties who built boats, and sailed them hard, using as we did the materials and fittings available at the time.

It is to be hoped that younger readers will understand that present knowledge and skills are built on the efforts of those who came before, and that they in turn will add their contribution to progress in the sport we all enjoy.

Having been through the mill, so to speak, of sailing at national level in the major classes of my era, my fondest memory will always be that of getting my heavy old Taka *Surprise* up on to the plane. I am sure the youngsters of today continue to get the sort of buzz I did then.

Nevertheless, having suffered the disciplines of one-design yachting, I much enjoyed the freedom of designing and building R-class boats, which also gave immense sailing pleasure. Clearly yachting has many facets which we can all enjoy. I am sure readers both young and old will have a greater understanding of New Zealand yachting after reading this book.

Graham Mander
Christchurch
22 September 1999

Acknowledgements

This book began back in 1945 when I first sailed a P-class in Balaena Bay. Ever since that first nervous experience, mostly as a crew member and only occasionally as helmsman, I have been an enthusiastic sailor. To be that way in Wellington calls for an acceptance of frequent strong winds, and I have come to love racing when it is like that. Racing in small boats in such conditions means planing often, and learning to do so with skill and energy if winning is the aim.

Most Kiwi sailors learn that planing was invented in the UK by Uffa Fox in 1927 when he designed and sailed an International 14. But since the late nineteenth century, Kiwi sailors have been competing in boats that planed, which means that there has now been more than a century of such activity in New Zealand.

When people interested in sailing hear that a story is being written about the achievements of New Zealanders, they invariably provide information and support when asked for it. We are very grateful to Peter Mitchell, of Review Publishing, the proprietors of *Sea Spray*, for access to and use of the magazine's 50 years of printed and pictorial material – without which access this book would simply not exist.

Thanks are also due to: A & C Black (Publishers) Limited for permission to reproduce the extract from *The Symmetry of Sailing* by Ross Garrett; Gary Baigent, for permission to use extracts from his unpublished manuscript 'The Light Brigade'; Joan McCracken, Pictorial Reference Service, and Marian Minson, Curator, Paintings, Drawings and Prints, at the Alexander Turnbull Library; Barbara Spiers, Pictorial Collection, The Auckland War Memorial Museum Te Papa Whakahiku; the *Bay of Plenty Times*, *Daily Telegraph*, *The Evening Post*, *Evening Star*, and *The New Zealand Herald*, for permission to use photographs; Graham Brandon and Ross Giblin for permission to use photographs; Pat Sherratt (one of Alf Harvey's daughters), for allowing the use of photographs and information from her unique scrapbook about her father and the early days of the Idle Along class; the Worser Bay Boating Club, for permission to use photographs and other material from the club records; Robin Elliott, for his interest in what I was writing and his willingness to share information about the early days of sailing in New Zealand.

Special thanks are due to long-time sailing friends Bill Hayman, Graham Mander, Barney Scully, Hugh Poole, and Bob Williamson, all of whom willingly provided material from their personal collections of photographs and sailing memorabilia. To Hugh Poole I owe particular thanks, for access to his collection of *Sea Spray* and also for his generous and understanding hospitality while researching them at his home. At the very last minute, and to our delight, Brian Anstis of Piper & Co Ltd, Napier, provided us with photographs of the elegant lightweight Patiki class, the boats which started it all here late last century. I owe him special thanks.

My thanks are also due to the following: to Tim Walker, formerly of Te Papa, whose research and ideas for the **Parade** exhibition at Te Papa was the springboard for this book; to Anne French, Publisher at Te Papa, whose enthusiasm for sailing equalled mine and whose absolute determination to have this book published drove me to match it. Without that determination, the publication date would have been about the time of the next New Zealand America's Cup defence. Thanks are also due to graphic designer Walter Moala and copy editor/indexer David Cauchi, for their enthusiasm and skill in accurately and elegantly putting the material together on the pages; to Diana Minchall, Editor at Te Papa, whose patience never ran out despite my demands on it, and to Jeremy Glyde and the photographers at Te Papa for digital imaging under tight deadlines.

Sailors are notorious fault-finders when it comes to reading about their sport, and some will have a field day with this book, I am sure. But I hope the ideas and attitudes expressed in it will outweigh the occasional error, though any errors will be my own fault. This book will, I hope, go some way in enlarging our understanding of the history of sailing here in the midst of the Southern Ocean.

Grahame Anderson
Nelson
22 September 1999

Copyright sources

Te Papa Press has made every effort to obtain permission to reproduce the images in this publication but would like to hear from any copyright owners with whom we have not been able to make contact. Many unsourced photographs have been made available by *Sea Spray*.

Auckland War Memorial Museum Te Papa Whakahiku: pages 10 both (Neg. Nos. C.26068 top, and 8136 bottom), 19 (Neg. No. 9405), 32 (Neg. No. 9154), 35 (Neg. No. 9623), 39 bottom (Neg. No. 9192). *The Bay of Plenty Times*: pages 42-3, 57. Graham R Brandon: pages 54, 122. *The Daily Telegraph*, Napier: pages 39 top, 112. *The Evening Post*, Wellington: page 63. *Evening Star*, Dunedin: page 124 top. Ross Giblin: cover, pages 79 bottom, 85 top, 105, 123 top. Museum of New Zealand Te Papa Tongarewa: page 8 (Neg. No. B.037720). *The New Zealand Herald*: page 132 top. *Sea Spray*: pages 12, 14 top, 32 bottom, 33, 55 right, 56 top, 61, 66 top, 72, 73, 78 bottom, 81 both, 84, 86 bottom, 93, 98, 103, 114 right, 115 right, 118, 125 bottom, 135 bottom, 139 left, 142, 157 left. Alexander Turnbull Library, National Library of New Zealand Te Puna Mātauranga o Aotearoa, Wellington: pages 7 both (Neg. Nos. D-PP 0106-001 top, and D-PP 0106-002 bottom), 9 bottom (Zak Collection, Neg. No. F.135778-1/2), 11 top (Neg. No. F.2052), 18 (Neg. No. F.31905-1/2), 31 both (Neg. Nos. F.66293-1/2 top, and F.13578-1/2 bottom), 40 (Neg. No. F.140122-1/2), 41 (Neg. No. F.135776-1/2), 71 both (Neg. Nos. F.2314-1/2 top, and C.24055-1/2 bottom).

fast light boats

The 20 or more men sailing this big boat are doing so in small boat fashion, from the crew members on the weather rail to the way they are feeding information to the helmsman. The darker sail areas are Kevlar, and the complex rigging system necessary for such boats is visible in the cat's cradle of lines showing between *Fisher & Paykel's* mainsail and mizzen mast. Fisher & Paykel Ltd. are major whiteware manufacturers based in New Zealand.

Chapter 1
Beginnings

The enthusiasm for designing, building, rigging, and racing small sailing boats capable of speeds which made them exciting to sail, and to watch, had its true origins in New Zealand a century ago. In the years since, that attitude to sailing has spread far and wide, not only within New Zealand but also to the countries where competitive sailing thrives.

This idea of fast light boats comes, in the main, out of the maturity phase of New Zealand's colonial immigrant era – when Jack was as good as his master. Though there were class distinctions in the accommodation and customs aboard the immigrant ships which brought the colonists here, an egalitarian attitude flourished on arrival, and in due course it found an expression in recreational sailing. (In this book, those who sail are called sailors or crew, though quotes remain uncorrected, and those who hold the tiller, the use of wheels being unrecorded in small boats, it seems – are called skippers.)

Until World War I, yachting in New Zealand largely followed the customs inherited from England, Europe, and the US. Yachts tended to be big and expensive, and most of their owners were relatively well-to do. Their helmsmen (since many owners did not helm themselves) often had a considerable reputation for their sailing abilities and were paid accordingly, but they were considered to be of a lesser breed than their owners. The rest of the crew were usually keen sailors who could only afford to sail for someone else.

But in the 1920s, the advent of smaller, simpler yachts that could be made to a standard design made building and owning them much cheaper. As yachting became affordable for men of modest means, competition in centreboarders began to take hold.

Nonetheless, professionalism did not end all at once. Attracted by the widespread interest and even-handed competition that the new centreboard yachts engendered, many wealthy owners had their centreboarders professionally built and crewed, to the consternation of the less well endowed.

A disregard for such class distinctions soon became one of the tenets of small-boat sailing in New Zealand, though it has not been so evident in bigger boats, where costs are such that money still matters.

Nonetheless, yachting in New Zealand still suffers from the fallout from class antagonism – especially amongst those who don't sail and who think all those who do must be wealthy. The recent rise of professionalism in big-boat yachting is an altogether new phenomenon.

Massive sponsorship, made possible by television coverage, has made it possible for those who sail and crew the big boats to be paid for doing so. This is especially true of the America's Cup contestants, but is by no means confined to that competition.

The story of sailing in New Zealand is one small part of a much larger story, and a brief summary of the more significant events in the development of world sailing is a necessary part of its telling.

So here it is, followed by some evidence about the beginnings of fast light boats in New Zealand.

More speed under sail

Ever since sailors first hoisted something for the wind to push against, they have competed with each other – at first in trade and war, and later in races just for the enjoyment of it. Over the centuries, influenced first by developments in sails, spars, and hull shape, and later by construction techniques which retained strength while reducing weight, their boats got faster and faster.

For many years, the increased speed came from increases in size as much as from design, but at the beginning of the twentieth century there was what could be called a quantum leap in the way boats were designed, built, and sailed. Designers learned how to build strong, light hulls, and to arrange more efficient sails and rigs, and by these means boat speeds were increased dramatically.

The quantum leap came from the development of what became known as 'planing' hulls. As their speed increased, the lighter hulls lifted partly out of the water and began planing, skimming over the surface of the water rather than pushing their way through it. Planing came about in power boats at almost the same time as it did in sail boats, and further advances in one type were incorporated in the other.

Nowadays, the fastest single-hulled sailing boats are the Australian 18-footers, seen racing on Sky Television. They are capable of reaching planing speeds all the way round the course, both upwind and down, which no other sailing boat can yet do. (Multihulls and sailboards are excepted – but their equally significant quantum leaps lie outside the bounds of this book.) These photogenic, high-speed boats are the descendants of the 18-footers which once competed in what was grandly called the World 18-Footer Championships, which in fact usually involved only Australia and New Zealand, joined on occasions by Fiji. The Australian boats carried huge spreads of sail, and the New Zealand competitors seldom won.

▲ More recent developments in the Australian 18-footers can be seen on Sky TV but this picture of *Aussie*, hard on the wind in the class world championships, illustrates the trapezing and balancing techniques required of skipper and crew, both in light conditions (as here) and in strong winds.

▲ Eighteen-footers like *Rank Xerox* make dramatic pictures, even in black and white, with their sharply defined geometric patterns, lettering, and trapeze harnesses. Bright sunshine in this picture emphasises the sharpness. The big spinnaker halyard load is spread from masthead to upper crosstrees by a wire loop.

Nowadays also, big boats (as against the small ones which are the essence of this book) are designed, built, rigged, and sailed as near to the 18-footer ideal as can be contrived. America's Cup and Whitbread Round the World competitors are no exception. Hulls and spars are light and strong, sails are made and controlled in complex ways, and the crew spends a great deal of time sitting along the side helping to keep the boat upright. What began as a design revolution in small centreboard yachts has spread to racing yachts of all kinds.

Since well before the turn of the century, many New Zealanders, amongst them Frank Bethwaite, one of the famous Bethwaite family whose younger members conceived the current breed of Aussie 18-footers, have been at the forefront of the design revolution. Many New Zealanders continue to lead the world in its development.

In December 1990, the New Zealand yachting magazine *Sea Spray* celebrated its 45th year by listing '58 Famous People & 41 Famous Boats Who Had Made a Difference' to the development of New Zealand yachting. Since fast light boats came about as the result of innovation in both types, its lists include both powerboats and yachts. The names and achievements listed by *Sea Spray* are of the very essence of the country's sailing story, but this extract (below) concentrates on sailors who have been involved in some way with the story of fast light boats. The magazine's choices proved to be prophetic in several cases, though there are some notable omissions. It leaves out, for instance, Graham Mander, the only New Zealander to win all four national championships in the PZIX series.

David Barnes	Roy & Chris Dickson	Peter Lester	Geoff Smale
Jock Bilger	Richard Dodson	Don & Heather Lidgard	John Spencer
Peter Blake	Bruce Farr	Logan family	Chris Timms
Leo, Chris, & Tony Bouzaid	Richard Hartley	Helmer Pedersen	Hal Wagstaff
	Harry Highet	Ralph & Clive Roberts	Paul & Penny Whiting
Russell Coutts	Ron Holland	Tom Schnackenberg	Jim Young
Laurie Davidson	Bruce Kendall	Rex Sellers	

▶ The *Zeehaen* is the closer of the two three-masted, square-rigged ships in this copy of a seventeenthth-century drawing by Isaac Gilsemans, the Merchant and coastal illustrator on Abel Tasman's voyage to New Zealand. The *Zeehaen* was narrow beamed when compared with her square-sterned companion ship *Heemskerck*, anchored nearby in the drawing, and faster through the water. Though they could not sail to windward, the two ships nevertheless crossed what is now known as the Tasman Sea in nine days, achieving more than 200 nautical miles per day on several occasions as they did so.

▲ On several abortive occasions while on the New Zealand coast, Tasman's ship's boats were sent out to explore possible anchorages and to bring aboard fresh water. One of the small boats used for such tasks was sloop-rigged, the other had only oars. Their form is well illustrated in this Gilsemans view of water being obtained in barrels floated ashore from the Tongan coast. They look much like more modern wooden dinghies, with planked topsides, oarsman's thwarts, and all.

The origins of recreational sailing

The history of sailing terms gives some clues about what sort of sailing was done and where. The word *yacht* comes from the Dutch. As it happened, small Dutch boats, equipped with both oars and sails, were to be seen in New Zealand waters in 1642–43, some 200 years *before* the first wave of settlers arrived in New Zealand and were rowed to shore in ships' tenders.

Though Abel Tasman's ships' boats were too small to have been called yachts, they looked much like modern clinker-built dinghies in illustrations of the voyage. (One of them had sails which he described as a 'sloop', another sailing word which comes from the Dutch. The word *dinghy* comes from Hindi, and not Dutch, however.) The Dutch reserved the term *yacht* for a much larger vessel. One of Tasman's ships, the 100-ton *Zeehaen*, was listed as a 'war-yacht' in records of the voyage.

Although Tasman never came ashore in New Zealand, his ships' boats were used for a variety of tasks on the New Zealand coast. They were rowed out from the ships to sound out an anchorage near the shore in Golden Bay, to tow his ship *Heemskerk* away from the breakers in a calm off the entrance to Kaipara Harbour on New Year's Day 1643, and they were also used in an attempt to get water at the Three Kings Islands, off the Northland coast, a week later.

Early yachts, though not originally used for racing by the Dutch, were nevertheless smaller, swifter, and lighter than other sailing craft then afloat, and were employed both in commerce and by the Dutch navy. By the time of Tasman's voyage, owning one was a sign of affluence and social importance in the Dutch Republic and, for the well-connected affluent, 'yachting' became the fashionable thing to do.

Charles II brought both yachts and the custom of yachting to England when he returned from exile in a series of fast passages by yacht to become King of England in 1660. English yachts were subsequently adapted to English sailing conditions, which were very different from those of the shallow waters off the coast of the Netherlands.

The word *regatta* comes, not surprisingly, given the wetness of the city, from Venice. It refers not only to activities involving boats powered by sails but also to those propelled by engines and oars. The original participants in regattas were oarsmen, before boats with sails broadened the definition.

The first French sailing regatta took place at Le Havre in July 1840 – right at the time of the settlement of Wellington, the eventual capital city of New Zealand – though in England the Royal Yacht Squadron, membership of which largely involved the king and his wealthy yacht-owning friends, had been formed seven years earlier.

Some of the small boats used to service visiting ships at anchor in New Zealand waters had sails as well as oars, as did some local craft. No doubt there were occasional challenges between their crews which resulted in races of sorts. In a letter quoted in *Fresh About Cook Strait* and written by Edward Catchpool to a relative in England in November 1840, the year Wellington was first settled, there is a vivid description of a southerly squall causing havoc among small boats on the harbour:

> Boats are sailing majestically over the bay, while those anchored off ride proudly on the water. A mighty roar is heard ... and you literally see the wind bending the trees on the mountainsides and tearing up the waves in its strength ... and not a breath of wind fans your face, but the noise is warning enough. The sails in every boat are taken in with the utmost rapidity and every exertion is made to reach the land as quickly as possible.

The characteristically gusty Wellington conditions, a natural and frequent occurrence in a windy harbour surrounded by high steep hills, was to have a profound influence on the development of sailing there and elsewhere in New Zealand.

New Zealand's first organised regatta occurred on Wellington Harbour in January 1841 when, just two months after that equinoctial squall, a two-part celebration took place on shore and on the water to recognise the first anniversary of the landing of the New Zealand Company's first arrivals in Port Nicholson.

The 1841 Anniversary Regatta consisted of sailing and rowing match races, although what was described as 'stormy weather' delayed the sailing events planned for the Saturday until the Monday holiday. This occurrence was the beginning of a long tradition for Anniversary weekend, both for the regatta itself and for the effects of

▲ The New Zealand Company artist Charles Heaphy painted this view of Wellington's inner harbour in 1841, more as an advertisement intended to attract emigrants to the town founded the previous year. For this reason it portrays the place with gently sloping hills surrounding a placid harbour with numerous sailing ships and small craft reflected in its surface.

Wellington's weather on its programme!

The occasion of this first Wellington regatta also reveals a tradition imported from Britain in its organisation, however. The 'Selects' – otherwise defined as the capitalists of the new settlement – arranged a 'subscription' ball for the Friday evening and a rowing match race for the Saturday, while the 'Populars' – otherwise defined as the workers – organised a whaleboat race and a sailing match race for the holiday Monday.

Such distinctions of social class easily survived transplantation to New Zealand, because, during the three-month-long voyage out to the new country, captains and cabin passengers kept it alive by insisting on the observation on board of the old standards they were sailing away from. But in the community at large it generally took both those who imposed and those who suffered it much less than three months to realise how different things were going to be, in the long run, in their new colony.

Recreational sailing, even in small boats, continued to reflect this imported differentiation for a decade or two into the twentieth century – but it lasted only as long as it depended on expensive and complicated boat-building techniques. Most owners of racing yachts were men who could afford to indulge in it as a luxury sport, commissioning professional designer-builders to produce new boats to beat those of their similarly endowed competitors.

For more than a hundred years, all immigrants came to New Zealand by sea, many on three-month-long voyages in sailing ships. After such an introduction to the feel of a boat's lifting to the wind, it was natural for some of them to see New Zealand's sheltered coastal waters as a place for recreation. It was also natural for those who did to become competitive and want to sail faster, and then faster still.

In 1892, the 50th Wellington Anniversary Regatta saw the first sailing races run under the rules of the newly formed but short-lived New Zealand Yachting Association. Six years earlier, in the United States, a canoe sailor by the name of Paul Butler had begun his remarkable competitive career. He invented the sliding seat, hollow spars, reefing gears, clutch cleats, the self-draining cockpit, and watertight bulkheads, all of which were devised to compensate for his very light body weight. But canoe sailing was long considered a sport beyond the pale of true yachting, and his original and innovative ideas were to take a long time to reach and influence the New Zealand sailing scene.

▲ The Dragon class provides excellent one-design racing for its three-man crews, including at international level, but it is all a relatively sedate affair, as this picture illustrates. Admittedly it is light weather, but a quick comparison with any fast light boat of Kiwi origin makes clear the Dragon is not rigged and fitted out for athletic crewing.

▼ Taken at the Anniversary weekend regatta in Wellington in 1908, this view of the 'second class yacht race' shows gaff-rigged boats well reefed down in strong winds. A flotilla of naval ships lies at anchor between the keelers and Oriental Bay in the background.

◀ The Patiki *Shingana*, being sailed to windward in rough water and a strong breeze, requires all her four-man crew, including the skipper, out on the rail just to keep the boat reasonably upright. It would have been the lively 'out of the cockpit' sort of crewing seen here in a 1909 picture which had the yachting press of the day describing such unseamanlike behaviour as 'acrobatic'. Both the masthead pennant and the trees in the background reveal how hard it is blowing.

◀ Boats designed and built by the Logan Brothers of Auckland had a profound influence on early developments in small-boat sailing and racing. The 24-foot Patiki *Ngaroma*, built in 1904, has, as this picture shows, something of the look of a planing hull, especially in its forward arrangements. Long before the First World War, the Patiki class planed in strong winds and flat water. In this picture, the lift of her bow and the wave at her sidestays give her the appearance of doing so, even if her wake seems quite sedate.

Plane sailing

Until the 1890s, all recreational sailing, in New Zealand and elsewhere, was done in what we would now describe as 'heavy displacement' vessels, of essentially the same sort as were used for commerce on the seas of the world. The story of the phenomenon which became known as planing, and of light-displacement racing yacht design in New Zealand, begins just before the turn of the century, with the class of boat known as the Patikis.

In 1898, the Logan Brothers of Auckland were asked by the newly formed Parnell Sailing Club to design for them an economical centreboarder suitable for younger sailors. (Twenty years later, a similar request gave rise to the P, Z, and X-classes.) In response, they produced an 18 ft 6 in clinker-built boat that the club called a 'Patiki', from the Māori word used for various kinds of flat fish.

The design was described as a 'restricted half-rater' in the imported keelboat yachting language of the time, but it was much more like a modern dinghy than anything that had come before it in New Zealand. The Patiki was light, with very short overhangs and relatively small sail area. It was also very fast. Fleet racing in the class soon attracted interest for what the newspapers of the day called 'a very fast turn of speed' and the 'acrobatic performances' of their three-man crews.

There can be no question that such boats *planed* when well handled in a strong breeze, but it should come as no surprise to find no use of the term in describing their performance at that time. The word *plane* derives from an event which had not yet occurred. The powered flight of the Wright Brothers in the US and of Richard Pearse in New Zealand was still five years away.

Though the word is said to come from the seventeenth-century French word *planer*, denoting the way a bird soars with its wings spread out in a wide flat plane, its connection with powered flight came a few years after the Wright brothers achieved it in 1903, when the supporting surface of the newly invented flying machine's wings became known as a 'plane'. Soon the machine itself was described as an 'aeroplane' or 'monoplane' or 'biplane', often shortened to 'plane'. By the beginning of the First World War, planes capable of taking off and landing on the water were being called 'hydro-aeroplanes' and later 'sea-planes'.

Around 1907, the term was applied to engine-driven boats designed with a plane surface on their underside, so shaped as to make them capable of moving more quickly by lifting partly above the surface of the water and skimming across it, thus reducing the drag effect of water along the boat's underside.

Such boats were said to be *planing* when they achieved that state, and many were built, light and strong, and with powerful engines, to take advantage of their greater speed for naval purposes during the First World War. Amongst the leading builders of such boats in Britain were two companies, Thorneycroft and Saunders Roe. Both were to have a connection with yachting. Tom Thorneycroft became a leading helmsman in the dinghy class known as International 14s after the war, and Uffa Fox, a leading English designer and helmsman in the class, had worked for Saunders Roe.

Since the late 1920s, the conventional wisdom in the world-wide sailing community has had it that *sustained* planing, as distinct from occasional bursts of speed on suitable wave formations in gusts (which, since the advent of pure planing, has been considered to be only 'surfing'), was achieved by one of Uffa Fox's International 14 designs in 1927. For the more than 60 years since then, essentially through his numerous books and magazine articles, Mr Fox's International 14s, notably *Aerial* and *Avenger* in 1927 and 1928, have been deemed to be the first sailing boats to be capable of planing in a sustained fashion, as against those simply able to surf on occasions.

▲ For a while in the 1940s, Tasman Empire Airways Ltd., the forerunner of Air New Zealand, used the Evans Bay Yacht and Motor Boat Club's buildings and jetty as their Wellington shore base, and flying boats were a familiar sight on the bay. This Sunderland, *Aotearoa*, is just about to touch the water, carrying Australian representatives to New Zealand's centennial celebrations in 1940, and its curved and stepped undersides are plainly visible. Those shapes, and their 'unsticking' take-off purpose, have a direct parallel in the 'planing' hull shapes and language borrowed from early aircraft and powered sea craft by recreational sailors just after the turn of the twentieth century.

▼ Still being sailed in somewhat gentlemanly fashion, these two International 14s are just a little later in time than Uffa Fox's *Aerial* and *Avenger* but they are demonstrating the planing capability for which Uffa claimed precedence in 1927/28.

▲ A grey, southerly day in Evans Bay gives a chill air to this picture of a 470 half out of the water as it planes through a wave while heeling slightly to windward. The crew are concentrating on keeping it going fast and may well be thinking about crouching forward to assist gravity as the boat slides down the wave face.

But a careful examination of New Zealand small-boat sailing history indicates very much otherwise. It is clear from such research that consistent planing by sailing dinghies was first achieved in New Zealand, and that it was achieved many years prior to 1927.

The rig and sail configuration of a boat are vital elements in achieving high performance and high-speed sailing, but even more vital is hull form and lightness – to which must be added vigorous and well-co-ordinated crewing. This interactive realisation came very early to the designers, builders, and helmsmen of small boats in New Zealand. As has been said already, in at least one class sustained planing of the sort which meets the definition was achieved right at the turn of the century – several years before the Wright brothers invented both their heavier-than-air machine and the word used to describe its form and behaviour.

Even if the well-recorded small-boat events of the last years of the war and the first few years of the 1920s were not considered by some to be sufficient to establish the case, the story of the turn-of-the-century Patikis would be convincing on its own.

There is of course a fundamental difference between the way an aeroplane *flies* in the air and the way a powered or sailing craft *planes* over the water. The essence of the difference is that the aeroplane flies because it rises into the air by means of the difference in air pressure between the upper and lower surfaces of its wings due to their shape, while the sailing craft planes because its speed through the water due to its lightness and shape is such that it is lifted out partly on to the surface of the sea, reducing the area of its hull touching the water and thus the amount of friction between the two.

This reduction reduces drag, just as it does in powered boats, and allows the sailing craft to sail faster — faster indeed than its theoretical maximum hull speed.

In Ross Garrett's book *The Symmetry of Sailing* he puts it, a little more scientifically, thus:

> The basic difference between a yacht sailing in the displacement mode and one that is planing is that in the latter case the weight of the hull is offset not just by buoyancy but also partly by dynamic lift forces. A boat which is stationary or moving without planing displaces a weight of water equal to its own weight. This, of course, is the famous law that Archimedes was so happy about ... When a hull is planing we have at our disposal two upward forces, buoyancy and dynamic lift, the sum of which must be equal to its weight if the boat is in equilibrium. Dynamic lift has its origins in the way the water flow is shaped under the hull. One can think of the hull as acting like a stubby airplane wing of very low aspect ratio ... The planing hull is only half a wing, however: there is no upper surface in the water so dynamic lift comes only from increased pressure on the underside. Because of this and because of the low aspect ratio a planing hull is a somewhat inefficient lifting surface.

But whatever logic and sequence lay behind the shift from the air to the sea, the term *plane* successfully migrated from its aerial beginnings to adapt to a new watery life almost 100 years ago, and has thrived there ever since, simply but not only because it elegantly fits and describes the lively phenomenon observed there.

In much the same way, Mr Marconi's strikingly tall, stayed radio masts on land, necessary to transmit and receive radio signals, and quickly very numerous in the landscape in the early days of radio, soon gave rise to their maritime equivalent. In the early twentieth century, the term 'marconi' became an adjective instead of a surname and was used to describe the new, tall, single-spar mast which, as sparmaking and rigging technology advanced, and, most importantly, in order to increase speed by reducing weight and improving sail shape, replaced the traditional but clumsier and heavier two-spar gaff rig in many racing boats.

▲ In the open sea at Napier, which suggests that the picture was taken some time after the 1931 earthquake that destroyed the inner harbour there, the Patiki *Kahurangi* is clearly planing, in a wind strength which has not even raised white caps on the waves, and with six men aboard. *Kahurangi* was taken to Wellington to demonstrate her capabilities, and she did so, but the local sailors thought the Patiki too fragile for the conditions often found on the harbour, and never took it up as a class.

The Patikis of Auckland, designed for the Waitemata Harbour, did not stay there. Although the round-hulled Patiki had been intended to be built by amateurs and crewed by newcomers to sailing, professional builders and helmsmen dominated in the class. Arguments about particular boats that didn't comply with measurement rules added to the ill-feeling caused amongst younger enthusiasts by this domination by skilled and experienced yachtsmen.

Soon most Patikis were sailing elsewhere, some at Rotorua and more in the old harbour at Napier, where they thrived as a class and planed in the flat water in strong winds. (The Ahuriri Lagoon was destroyed in the 1931 Hawkes Bay earthquake. Its seabed was uplifted by some one to two metres and, no longer capable of taking commercial shipping, was eventually filled in to become a lucrative industrial site.)

▲ There are eight Patikis at this jetty in Napier. Such numbers of very similar boats, by their weight and shape all clearly capable of planing, must have made for exciting fleet-racing. Though the date of this picture is unknown, it is very early, judging by the garb of the sailors. *Illinoie* is being heeled over in the shallows, presumably to allow work to be carried out on her underside, and her lightness is elegantly shown by the way she floats high on the water.

◀ Though it is flat calm in this picture, it was the fresh breezes and sheltered waters of Napier's inner harbour that provided a natural second home for the Patikis. Sitting high and still on the mirror-like water, their lightness and generous spread of sail is well illustrated here. Without question, the Patikis were remarkable late nineteenth-century precursors to the fast light boats which Kiwi sailors have gone on to design, build, and sail in large numbers right up to the present.

▶ The mullety *Tamariki*, here racing downwind in a moderate breeze on Auckland harbour, represents the class which formed one of the design strands joining the late nineteenth-century Patikis and the early twentieth-century centreboarders.

◀ Running down-wind on opposite gybes, these 18-footers display their huge areas of sail. The heaviest boat, with Miss Jantzen on its mainsail, has trapezes fitted, the handles of which are visible just below the spinnaker boom.

Meanwhile, in Australia, a centreboard boat of similar size to the Patiki was being developed. What has long been known, at least in the southern hemisphere, as the Aussie 18-footer had its origins in Brisbane, Australia, where Toby Wherat built what is regarded as the prototype in 1930. With a crew of six and a huge spread of sail, these boats were said to have achieved speeds of 26 knots in the 1930s, but their large sail area and heavy crew loads demanded such strength and weight that planing was not possible – surfing perhaps on occasions, but not consistent planing and, to put it bluntly, the speeds attained were the result of brute boat and rig strength and not at all due to lightness.

It should be mentioned that the skills of the crew and helmsmen were of a very high order indeed and much admired by those who read about and saw them in action.

International competition in centreboarders did not begin for New Zealanders with the 18-footers however. In 1938, at the Royal Hobart Regatta, two Kiwi 14-footers, *Vamp* and *Impudence,* handsomely beat the Australian 14-footers. *Vamp* won the 14 ft Dinghy Championship of Australia and *Impudence* won all three regatta races for the class. Clive Highet, nephew of Harry Highet, the creator of the P-class, and owner of *Impudence*, explained the outcome of the trip to Tasmania:

> The success of the New Zealand boats in Australia was due, I think, to the radical difference between the Australian and New Zealand boats. The Australian 14 footers ... were what is known as 'displacement' boats. In New Zealand the practice is to try to combine in the 14 footers the two types – the displacement and planing boats. *Vamp* is a good example of the type of boat I mean. Having the advantage of the displacement principles, she is suitable for working to windward and having the principles of the planing boat also, is equally successful going off the wind to leeward. *Impudence* is much the same also. She is able to plane successfully, both on a lead or off the wind ... I think, as a result of the success of *Vamp* and *Impudence*, that the designs of Australian 14 footers will undergo radical alterations in the future.

From these published notes it is clear, had the Australians and others only realised the significance of them, that the cat was well and truly out of the bag a year before the Second World War. Developments in planing hulls and the associated attitudes to sailing techniques which went with them were to become the underlying driving force behind increases in speed in low-cost small boats.

After-sail service

So much, for now, for hull design. What about the sails?

In an article in the October 1972 issue of *Sea Spray*, Roy Whittenbury of Ratsey & Lapthorn Ltd, long time sailmakers in the UK, gave a succinct summary of the English viewpoint of the early development and uses of sailcloth, saying;

> The basis of a good sail is good cloth. This elementary fact tended to be forgotten in the old days, when they relied on traditional flax and cotton from the English Mill. It had been woven in the same way for hundreds of years, at first by hand, then by water power and latterly by steam and electricity ... English cotton sailcloth, woven from the best Egyptian staple cotton was the best available and, made into sails, used by top yachtsmen all over the world ...

Whittenbury then went on to describe advances in sailcloth manufacture, in particular the introduction in the 1950s of the polyester fibre cloth which became known as Terylene in England and as Dacron in the USA. The superior qualities of the latter fabric proved crucial to the American win in the 1964 America's Cup challenge by England.

In the days of cotton cloth, sail care used to occupy much time and effort. Care is still necessary, of course, but because of the development of new materials, the nature of the care is very different these days. The process as it then applied, and had done so for many decades, was well described in 1948:

> Sails should never be left flapping on the mast. Sailmakers tell us that this is one sure way of ruining the shape of the sail. After use, sails should be spread out on a lawn or hung up from the corners, flat, and in a place where the wind won't cause them to flutter. Small boat sails are easily taken care of in a dry warm basement or an attic and they should be hung up just as soon as possible after you get ashore. Good racing sails should not be used after sundown, as the dew will readily fix them up in a hurry.

In a 1949 *Sea Spray*, Leo Bouzaid gave advice on the breaking-in of new sails:

> Choose a fine, sunny day, when the breeze is light. Bend your sails on spare, at a good hand taut. 'Hand taut' may not be sufficient for some ropes – i.e., a three-quarter-inch rope would not need as much pull as a one-and-a-half-inch rope. It is advisable to pull ropes out until the wrinkles in the canvas, near the rope edge, disappear, or pull to measurements given. When the sail is on, get under weigh and have several hours sailing,

▲ The brand new mainsail on *Demon*, one of the Idle Alongs built at Worser Bay in 1930, looks rather wrinkled and baggy here. No doubt its owner was adhering to the rule which said not to stretch it too soon.

but NOT on the wind. Never set a new sail in hard breeze, as this causes you to luff or but half-fill the sail. Never set a new sail in damp, foggy weather, and never hoist the sail without battens in their respective pockets. Never leave your reefs tied in longer than necessary.

Time and new materials have changed all that, of course.

I'd rather be sailing

For anyone who has raced in Wellington for any length of time, there will have been occasions when races have been cancelled due to the weather, in conditions where no one has even left the hard. For them, more than for most, the once widely observed bumper sticker which read 'I'D RATHER BE SAILING' rings all too true. The feeling is strongest when the prospect of lively competition on the water is denied at the last minute, because it is just too windy. All the business of boat and personal preparation has raised expectations to a high pitch, and the cancellation comes as a severe let-down, even when it brings a secret twinge of relief at the resultant avoidance of high-risk sailing.

The truth of the sentiment colours the recording of yachting history, because amongst those who would rather be sailing are the press-ganged administrators and reporters of the sport. Records and information dating from the early days in particular tends to be scanty and widely dispersed, which makes it hard to research.

Club minutes and race records are often lost or scattered, contest conference minutes and race results have suffered a similar fate, and the newspapers and sailing magazines no longer cover as many sailing events as they did in earlier days. That is not to deny the massive contribution made to sailing by those who have put their time and energy into running clubs and associations, taking on the task of Reporting Steward, and keeping the race records and minute books – but the stock of early contributions is by no means complete or easy to find.

Not much has been written about the experience of racing in small boats from the competitor's point of view. Races have often been described by yachting reporters, of course, but even the best of them write from outside the contest. In big-boat racing,

▲ Deep-keeled, narrow boats with substantial wooden spars and hefty rigging were the classic solution to the need for recreational craft to stand up to the rigours of heavy-weather sailing, much as in big sailing ships. This unidentified keeler, well reefed down and with her lee rail already buried in green water, is making her way out of Clyde Quay boat harbour at high tide on a very windy day indeed.

many such accounts have been put on paper, but it is rare that the story is told from within a centreboarder. One such account of a small-boat race was published in *Sea Spray* magazine in 1949. Although it is written about T-class dinghies, it is revealing about many of the things then going on in small-boat competition of all sorts.

In the late 1940s, the standard of competition between those racing New Zealand's classic P, Z, I, and X-class boats was reaching its peak, and the subsequent period of innovation and interweaving of design and construction ideas from other classes had only just begun. In 'The Race is to the Swift' Peter Smith writes with considerable insight and understanding, with little of the old fashioned sort of language one used to find in sailing stories, while revealing much of the new knowledge that had become necessary in order to prepare and compete well. With the occasional change in the language used, and with the technical terms updated, it could well have been written in the 1990s.

Anyone who has competed in small boats, especially those who did so in those early post-war years, will recognise the authenticity of Peter Smith's account. Those who have not experienced such competition will find in it something to explain what those people are doing in those boats that apparently just glide to and fro out on the water. The location, as becomes clear in the account, is Auckland's Waitemata harbour.

▲ This 1922 picture of the T-class *Valet* looks at first glance to have been taken on a non-racing occasion, especially when the relaxed stance and felt hat of the helmsman are noticed. But there is another boat sailing the same course as *Valet*, its spinnaker just visible, and there may well be a race in progress.

> Saturday morning. From the bedroom window the gum-trees in the park are swaying rhythmically. There's wind, and the clear sky betokens a good day. The nine o'clock weather report confirms this with its 'moderate to fresh winds'. The sails are taken down from the rack where they have been airing, and are stowed one by one into their bags.
>
> Down at the Bay the forward hand has the cover off my fourteen. Given a coat of polish after the last outing, her hull gleams in the bright sun and the varnish on coamings and spars is a bright reward for the long hours of winter work.
>
> *Alert* has done a few seasons now, but she still gains her places during the season, sometimes without need of her four or five-minute handicap. Clinker-built, she is an unrestricted round-bilged T class, and her powerful bow sections and flat run aft betray her sail-carrying ability. On her 30 ft. mast she carries the maximum 250 sq. ft. of working sail.

With a beam of 6 ft. 6 in., she carries this area comfortably enough, except in the heaviest of weather, with her four-man crew lying well out to windward and the main wet up to the second reef.

The rest of the crew arrive, carrying on a good-natured but derogatory conversation with the owner of our rival further along the strip. The big jib is clipped onto the forestay, and we stretch the main along the boom. The wire halyard is shackled onto the headboard and the slides slipped onto the track. We check the leech cord and slide the battens into place. The mainsheet is rove through the double purchase block on the horse and coiled down on the floors.

The breeze is fresh now and white caps appear on the outer harbour. With an eye on the fluttering masthead pennant we carry the big and small spinnakers over to the lawns and wool them into compact rolls, ready for rapid hoisting. Some of the 18s racing earlier than us are already in the water, and the bay is lively with small craft. Bright sun creams the arcing sails, and outside the breakwater the jib on a tall keeler crackles for an instant as she shoots into the wind.

Spare sails and extras are stowed, sheets and halyards are freed, and we have a sandwich before we put *Alert* in the water. Already I feel the uneasy tension that mounts before a race. As we roll the trailer down the ramp the mainsheet hand rushes to the stern with a wild cry and hastily screws in the bungs. We sweat the halyards taut and coil down. With the forward hand holding her head into the wind I ship the rudder. The plate is partly lowered. As her head pays off the main fills and she heels briskly. We luff for an instant as the plate goes down to its full depth, then haul hard on the wind. Out go the crew as she takes the full force of the breeze past the headland.

The forward hand shudders as the first flurry of spray is whipped back over the bows. 'Why did I ever leave home?' he moans, as we punch into the short chop outside the gap in the breakwater. Our course is up-harbour. We can just lay the starting line. In spite of the sun, the wind-driven spray cuts, and the mainsheet hand and I am glad of the protection we gain at the expense of the other two, their oiled life-jackets running with water. The spare man has the jib as the forward hand checks the 'kites'. Already his hands are cramped with straining at the bar-taut sheet.

Starting down-wind, the 26-foot mullet-boats revel in the fresh conditions. Their crews rush to break out extras, while we buck through the broken water of their wakes. With time to spare we idle behind the starting-line, a cautious eye on other boats. Five minutes before our flags go up the Ys crowd the weather end of the line, then stream away as the gun barks. We watch these square-bilge fourteen-footers carefully to see what they make of the weather, then pay off and start the nerve-racking jostle for position on the line.

It will be a beat to the first mark moored off Watchman Island. We crowd into the lee of the clubhouse from which the races are started. The lull in the wind warns us not to be caught out here, and we dodge back a little as we overhaul the line. Coming up again on port tack we have to pay off around the stern of *Valiant* on the other tack. Two flags are down and we check the watch. Twelve boats are jockeying for position now, and we are all alert as they slither and jostle, tack and run. Close to the line and the third flag is down. We are in a bad spot with the others crowding us out and across the line. I take the risk of a late start, gybe and run back as the seconds tick past. Sails slat and the mainsheet block slams across as we round up in front of three boats edging up for the final leg to the line.

The second to last flag is down. Our way carries us into the weather position of these three and we surge up on the rest of the fleet. Sheets are eased. With seconds to go, we gather more way, boats on each side hauling on the wind with us. I lose the mainsheet's call on the watch of '... four, three, ...' The puff of smoke floats out from the clubhouse and the gun jolts us into activity. There are three boats to windward of us, and we are a few valuable seconds late.

We settle down to work her up to the first mark. The crews are lying well out, and there is little movement except for the skipper's handling of the tiller. With an eye out for boats on the starboard tack to leeward of us, I can catch sight of *Awatere*'s white plate knifing through the water, burying her lee decks. *Menai* is in the lead up to windward, and has blanketed *Talisman*. To windward of us but falling back a little is the gaff-rigged *Makura*. Suited to lighter conditions she is staggering a little and her pump is already in action.

Cliff trims the mainsheet in a bit closer; the crew edges a little bit further forward and we thrill as she punches the rising waves. *Menai* puts about to cover *Talisman*, which had endeavoured to break away. We carry on a few minutes, one eye on the red-flagged buoy

▲ *Frenzy*, R 120, winner of the Leander Trophy for Graham Mander in 1959, 1963, and 1965, appears elegantly balanced and under absolute control as she planes across Lyttelton harbour, but her mast broke just after this photograph was taken. Nevertheless, it nicely captures the fast light boat image the class demonstrated as its performance capabilities were continuously enhanced by enthusiasts in the revolutionary decade in which this boat was dominant.

just visible fine on the weather bow, one eye on *Pursuit*, which is romping through down to leeward.

The crew is ready as I signal, and a second later on the order they let fly. We are off again on the other tack. Most of the others follow suit soon after, heading off on a short board to give us room to lay the mark. *Menai* is first round the mark. Her spinnaker boom shoots out as she squares away for the Chelsea mark. As the wooled extra breaks loose we can see she is carrying her small spinnaker from the lower hoist. It is a reach, so we decide for the small one also, and it is clipped on in readiness.

Fourth to the mark, we have the spinnaker hoisted as the buoy comes abeam, and the boom is run out as the sheets are eased. The swing and roll from the swell ceases as the 'kite' takes hold, and the crew pile out on the weather quarter. The boom is well forward, and she is buried to the lee coamings in the puffs.

This is a thrilling point of sailing. We delight in the powerful, steady surge forward, the bow wave spurting from abaft the chainplates on the weather side, the clean rush of green water from the stern. Now and again *Alert* seems to take charge; the tiller freezes and she lifts bodily. The familiar rush of the water disappears as she planes effortlessly, smoothly.

Makura, which nipped round the mark just ahead of us, has flown a big spinnaker and is having trouble. They are forced to bear away several times as it threatens to 'sky', and we are up to windward of her. A few minutes later and their spinnaker sheets let fly. The boom whips off the mast in the confusion, dragging the cloth under the boat.

Menai maintains her lead round the next mark, gybing her extra and carrying it closer for the lead back to a buoy east of the starting line. Her crew is working hard now to keep her down, and I wonder whether we should carry ours.

Close on the heels of *Talisman*, we prepare for the gybe. The spinnaker is taken in to the mast, the boom is changed by the forward hand, the main boom swings across and the lee backstay slides on its runner. On the starboard tack, the extra goes out once more, but the sheet is foul of the jib. We heel dangerously. The sail bellies between the forestay and the mast and I square away as the bow digs in the water.

Pursuit chases us while we shake out the tangle and sheet her home again. It is hard work on this long leg across the harbour. The strain is beginning to tell. The crew is silent as sheets are eased, then inched in again. *Alert* is a little too heavy on the helm now and I wish I had the leader up. *Pursuit* has the legs of us this time. Carrying her sail well she gradually works level.

Talisman hangs onto *Menai* about 100 yards ahead of us, while astern *Makura* has fallen right back. There are five in a bunch close astern, and the crack *Estralita*, after making a bad start, is working through. The buoy ahead seems a long way off as the fleet strings out. I hope desperately that we will be able to hold our position until the next mark. *Estralita*, spinnaker changed for a leader, seems to be making better weather of it than the rest and is slowly creeping up. *Matariki*, another scratch boat, is also improving her position.

Behind the breakwater the wind is a little easier and we carry our spinnaker down as far as we dare. The big silk sail thrashes as the sheet is let fly and then the boom is aft and the sail is a heap on the deck as we round the mark. *Pursuit* has the inside position and leads us for the second slog up to the Herne Bay mark.

Estralita works her way up on the beat to the windward mark, surging with a flurry of foam across our stern as we cross tacks for the last time before rounding the mark. We hold our own with *Pursuit* and the three boats scramble for the inside position at the buoy. *Menai* and *Talisman* have their small spinnakers up again for the long run to the Inner Shoal Bay mark. The forward hand starts to clip ours on again until I call for the big one. I hope she will carry it. With its 250 square feet of silk it brings our total area of sail up to 500 square feet!

Still in fourth place, I luff up a little under *Pursuit*, which luffs to cover us. Meanwhile, our big spinnaker has snaked up to the masthead. I take the mainsheet to free Cliff for the spinnaker sheets. The fourth man runs out the preventer, as Trevor swings the boom forward. In the wild sway off the wind it is hard to slip the jaws in place. With the gusts forcing the main boom into the water at times, I wonder if it is foolhardy to set this kite, but even while I do so the boom is swung out, and Cliff tugs at the sheet, concentrating on keeping her steady.

Watching *Pursuit* out of the corner of my eye, I hardly see the tiny triangle of cloth break the first two ties. Then as the wind fills it the big sail blossoms out into a hard bellying arc. The sheet is hard in, and *Alert* steadies, drops forward into a trough until the bowsprit submerges in a feather of spray, then rises and leaps forward. The tiller is steady, and the roll is gone. I can take my hand off the tiller and she will maintain her endless, onward rushing drive.

The spinnaker boom is hauled around a little, water squeezing from the rope at it takes the full strain of the sail. We ease the sheet out and out until the sail rises up and up, pulling her out of the water. We pile aft and sit tight. I know from the feel of her that we can carry this extra safely. We already are pulling away. Now it seems as if the whole boat was a living thing, a perfection of man. There is a unity and understanding between crew and yacht, the whole delicate balance of wood and sail and mind.

The box pump takes out the water that has sluiced aboard on the beat, and we are ready to hand the spinnaker at the next mark, the leader replacing it. The big kite is hastily stowed, and sheets are trimmed for the last lead. After breaking away from *Pursuit* we have had a clear run down and are lying third, with *Estralita* a dangerous fourth.

We lose valuable seconds at the bottom mark where the spinnaker boom has fouled the jib sheets, and we fall away from the mark. *Menai* has opened out a lead from *Talisman*, who is lying to windward from us. The crew is alert, now, to every move and we swing out to hold her down in the gusts. The water is flying back over the bow in sun-shot showers. The deck gleams with wet, and the sun is striking the waves ahead of us, waves that fold back in hissing curves as the forefoot lifts and cuts forward, biting into the steep seas.

Ahead of us the bright afternoon light streams through sails wet half way up the mast. It is a stiff beat dead to windward to the finishing line, and the staunch little fourteens slog tack for tack up the sparkling bay. Try as we may, *Estralita* hauls up on us, with *Pursuit* close astern.

We reckon on the number of tacks required to make the buoy. I give the order and we move swiftly to spin her about. On the starboard tack again we head directly for *Estralita* converging on the port tack. We swing out to windward and point her an inch or two higher. Cliff has his eyes glued on the luff.

Estralita, with her tough and experienced skipper squatting in the stern, doesn't give us an inch until the last moment, when he eases a fraction to send her surging past our stern in a flurry of foam, so close it seems she must brush our boom. We carry on minute by minute.

Estralita is about and is following across to get clearance for the final leg to the mark.

We watch the mark moving against the shore, estimating how far we must carry on. I weigh up the distance once more, then call. The jib slats madly for a moment as the tiller goes down and the water sweeps away in a wide curve from the transom. In comes the main, and two hands haul the jib taut.

With luck the incoming tide will push us far enough up to carry us across. *Estralita* is about again and is right alongside. The gun crashes out and we hardly notice that *Menai* is across. There is nothing for it now but to carry on until we hit the line.

The buoy seems an alarming distance up to windward, and *Estralita* is to weather of us and nearly equal. We hold our course minute after minute, terribly conscious of the trim cream boat that eats out to windward of us. The buoy is close now. I can see the shadow it casts on the waves, the flurry of broken water that spills away from it. It is touch and go and I wonder if I allowed enough on the last board …

Yards away, and we head straight for the buoy. *Estralita* picks up a puff which carries her over. It hits us and as she buries her decks I run her into the wind. Our way carries us past the buoy and we ease sheets. *Estralita* runs back past us as we sit in. 'Nice going!' 'Thanks!'

We gybe her for the last time and ease sheets for the run home. Cigarettes come out from mysterious places. Over six miles of racing, this weather makes for sore hands and tired arms. We wipe the salt spray from eyes and lips and settle down for the trip back. We have got a fourth place without handicap. On corrected times we should have a place, perhaps even a first. Yes, there's life in the old girl yet.

One hundred years of development in competitive small-boat racing in boats which planed has of course seen a parallel development in the way such races are written about, though similar descriptive phrases occur in both. Not from an individual entrant's point of view, but nevertheless lively and revealing of the sort of racing now going on, this extract from the Canterbury R-class Squadron Internet Web page at www.themarina.co.nz gives a good idea of the activity during races 3, 4, and 5 at the Leander Trophy, the class national championship series, in 1999:

▲ Stephen Hogg's bus company-sponsored R-class/12-foot skiff *Stagecoach* exemplifies the state of fast, light boat development as it planes past the Worser Bay Boating Club. With two on trapezes, and about one third of the hull touching the water, it would be hard to drive a boat of this size any quicker.

The start of race three was as usual a hotly contended affair. You try manoeuvering on a start line with 25-odd other boats and a two-meter long prod. The top part of the fleet got away to a blinder in the patchy and shifty conditions. Stress was high in the top ten, with placings changing constantly. This race was all about picking the shifts and making the most of every puff, something that Alex Vallings and Andrew Meiklejohn in *C-Tech* were able to do well, taking out their second consecutive race for the regatta. Second was *Design Source* and third *Stagecoach* ... Race four, sailed in a building breeze, was an all North Island affair, Auckland's hold on the top four only broken by *Stagecoach* in third ... Once again, the racing was hot in the building shifting breeze ... Race five saw the breeze building further, with some of the boats not even making it to the start line. The start was hell, with most boats capsizing at some stage. The remaining boats were able to send it to the max. in the 25 plus knots providing some challenging racing. *The Guru* (Tim Bartlet) eventually took this race out, a feat in itself considering some didn't even make it to the start line in the challenging conditions ...

These modern R-class boats, in their construction and appearance, as well as in their rigs and sails, look very little like the small boats which started it all, but they and the vigorous way in which they are sailed owe much to the innovators of 100 years before and to the ideas men of their own R-class of the 1950s.

Boats, yachts, dinghies, and centreboarders

There is a difference between the uses of the word 'boat' and the word 'yacht' in sailing circles — at least in those circles where the difference matters, which is amongst those who call their clubs 'boat' or 'boating' clubs and not yacht clubs. The difference is a significant one and has mostly to do with size. It not only indicates the smaller size of sailing craft catered for by the clubs which use the term 'boat' in their title, which is very often the case, but also the *sort* of club it is. Members of beachfront yacht clubs, to revert to the generic term for a moment, are frequently limited to small sailing craft that are capable of being manhandled into and out of the water by their crew of one or two or three, and then able to be stored in a shed or taken home by road. Most of them refer to their craft as boats, not yachts. ('Yacht' usually denotes larger vessels, with keels rather than centreboards, and the club name may also include the term 'cruising' to indicate the activities and interests of its members.)

Small boats may also be referred to as 'centreboarders', because of the vertical sliding or pivoted timber board or metal plate they are fitted with to stop them simply sliding sideways when sailing up or across the wind, or as 'dinghies', because that term has for a very long time now been used to describe what the OED calls 'small pleasure boats'.

This book is mostly about small boats, their designers, and the enthusiasts who raced them, and tells the story of the influence they have had on the development of sailing and boat-design skills in New Zealand.

◀ Most of these boats taking part in the Akarana Winter Series on Auckland harbour are being sailed and crewed in fast light boat fashion. Some of their hull-forms reveal dinghy design influences, and many of their crewmembers are perched along the weather rail adding maximum weight to the righting moment.

◀ The UK Maxi-yacht *Rothmans* is shown here taking part in the 1989 Fastnet Race. Ten of her crew are dangling their legs down the windward topsides, and the shape of her hull, revealed by the wave formation captured by the camera, is clearly evolved from fast, light boat thinking. That's a New Zealand Maxi obscured to leeward, being sailed in similar fashion.

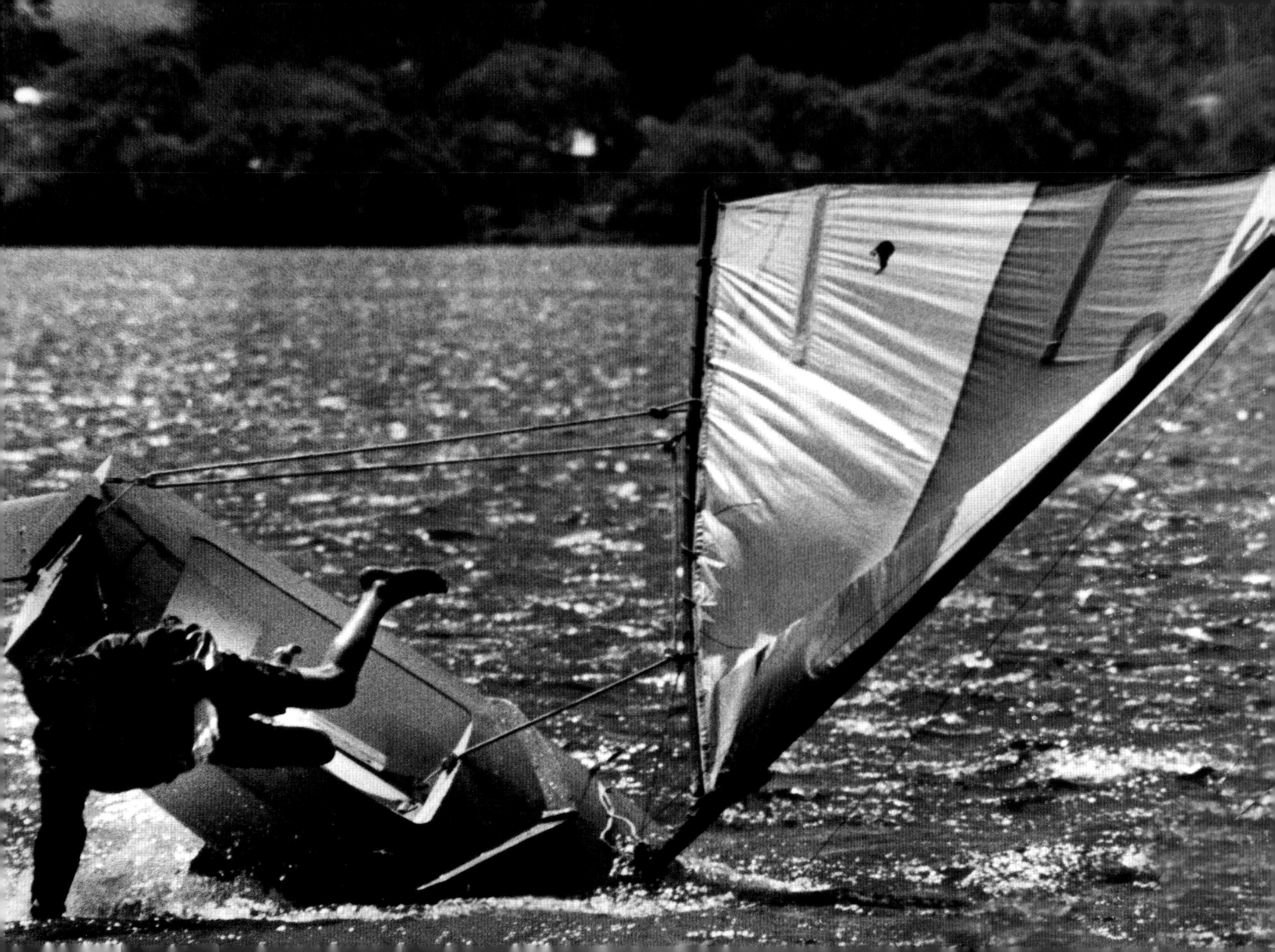

Chapter 2
The advent of P, Z, I, & X

Even before the First World War had ended, the lines had been drawn for one of the boats which were to dominate competitive centreboard sailing in New Zealand for some 40 years. By the summer of 1920/21, three of the four 'stepping stone' classes, P, Z, and X, were fleet racing in various parts of the country, though the vital con-nection between them had not yet been recognised.

The first three boats were northern designs, two in Auckland and one in Tauranga. But the lines of the Idle Along, the centerboarder that filled out the series, were set out on the floor of a tiny house at the water's edge in Wellington in 1927, though the significance of its place in it was not realised at the time.

It was another three years before the first boats were built to this 1927 design. This seems to have been largely due to the Depression, but also to the popularity in Wellington of one of the other already established classes, which was supported by local clubs, and built and sailed there in some numbers.

For each of these classes, though less so for the X-class, the concept behind their designs had, as all complex concepts do, several influences bearing on it, in addition to the intentions of its authors, designers, and early builders. The radical departure from the nineteenth-century master and servant relationships, together with

> The phenomenon which led to this sudden separation of boat and sailor is known in the sport as 'pigrooting'. P-class boats are renowned for it. This one displays to the camera its bending boom, eased right out to the side-stay; its too-loose kicker; its tiny cockpit and seat; and the hard-down centreplate, which no doubt contributed to the situation.

▼ The very essence of this sunny action shot lies in its depiction of lightness. Carried with ease down to the water's edge at lunchtime by just two bare-footed men in shorts and tee shirts, the boat is fully rigged, its rudder pivoted ready for launching in the shallows. There is no sense of strain in the boat carriers and the whole scene is small-boat lightness epitomised – which is no doubt why the picture was taken.

the increased leisure time afforded by the eight-hour working day, created new freedoms. These profound social changes were seen in attitudes to recreational sailing, just as they were in many other aspects of life in the new colony.

Yachting was a rich man's sport right from its beginnings in Europe in the seventeenth century, if only because the cost and upkeep of yachts of the sort and size then indulged in was inordinately high, to the point where it was just as much the sport of kings as was the traditionally connected one of horse racing.

So, the concept of a smaller yacht, outwardly a response a the need for boats capable of being sailed by young men, carried with it smaller outgoings and fewer crew. It was those aspects that appealed to both young and old. But in the pursuit of simplicity and low cost of construction, as well as of ease of handling to and from the water, the concept also contained the essential idea of *lightness*, which brought about greater speed on the water.

Then and now, the advantages of lightness have to do with boat handling ashore as well as boat performance at sea (and are especially important to those who have to do both jobs themselves). Very early on in the folklore of centreboard boat construction in New Zealand, the claim that 'two men lifted it off the mould' took hold and became translated into the belief that the same could be said of a boat when handled into and out of the water at the beach or launching ramp, and up and down from the beachfront clubhouse storage shed.

Many of the long-held traditions of seamanship inherited from the navy and merchant ships were amongst the mind-sets of those immigrants familiar with the way the sport of yachting was undertaken back in Europe: keeping inboard and sailing upright, reducing sail in order to do just that, steering a straight course, and making things very strong, and by implication heavy, in order to withstand whatever weather might be met on long voyages.

In the aftermath of the devastation of the First World War, many of those surviving social customs brought to the Antipodes were finally seen as inappropriate here, and in this regard small-boat sailing attitudes changed radically also.

There had of course been occasions before that war when the competitive crews, if not yet the skipper, of generously canvassed and well-sailed small yachts had risked falling overboard by sitting well out on the side of their boat, feet off the cockpit floor, and hanging on to the sheets as they urged their boat on in strong winds, but they were the exception.

By contrast, the very first time a Z-class was sailed in such conditions, by young men who were at least a generation away from the old traditions of seamanship, it would have been both natural and necessary to do just that. And the thrill of the outcome, planing, as well as the result, winning, would have encouraged others to do the same once they realised why they were being beaten.

The Zeddies sailing off Takapuna in 1921 would therefore have been planing. This was at least six years before International 14s such as *Aerial* and *Avenger* first achieved what their UK creator Uffa Fox defined as sustained planing.

Emphasising the primacy of this antipodean achievement is not simply to claim precedence in the matter, though it is indeed that, but, more importantly for the story of New Zealand's fast light boats, to make clear the part such attitudes to boat handling played in the development of those boats.

The early but undated photograph opposite shows an unidentified, open-cockpit, gaff-rigged small yacht off Wellington's Point Jerningham one sunny day in a northwesterly of at least 40 knots. The mainsail is reefed right down to the point where the gaff jaws are at the gooseneck, no headsail is set, and the lee rail is under the water. But the crew are all sitting inboard and upright, one with his feet against the lee coaming, no one's backside is anywhere near the weather rail, and no one is wearing a lifejacket.

By contrast, one of the earliest photographs to be found of an X-class (opposite, top) shows a Southland boat making its way up Evans Bay in a gale during the Sanders Cup contest in 1924. The photo illustrates the athleticism required of the crew in the newly developed boats. The story that this book tells can be seen in the difference in sailing styles and techniques between these two pictures.

▶ A one-design class conceived by Glad Bailey, son of the famous Chas Bailey, the X-class had its first national contest for the Sanders Cup in 1921. The fourth such championship series was held in Wellington, and the first race was postponed from 11 am to 2.30 pm owing to a gale force southerly. When the race started five boats representing Auckland, Hawke's Bay, Southland, Wellington, and Canterbury took part, but after one round it was called off because the wind increased and there were not enough rescue boats. The picture shows *Murihiku*, the Southland boat, well reefed down and making its way up Evans Bay into the gale. No life jackets were worn (they were developed in the 1930s), and a strange assortment of hats makes a lively silhouette.

▶ The sunlit sea surface well to windward in this early Wellington Harbour scene is spume covered, and the wind is blowing at least 40 knots. Though the solidly-rigged, round-bilge, open-cockpit boat is well reefed down, with its mainsail rolled round the boom to the point where the gaff jaws are just above the gooseneck, and has no headsail set, the crew are simply sitting upright along the weather coamings. Faster, lighter boats came along and obliged the crew to sit out on the gunwale and lean their bodies out further still.

▲ No spinnaker has been set and one of the three-man crew of *Viper* is sitting inboard and to leeward, perhaps bailing, in this 1921 view of X 17 on a two-sail reach. The X-class clinker planking was not always watertight.

◀ There is a sequence of photographs which shows that this apparently out of control M-class survived the incident shown here and did not capsize. The act of sustained planing sometimes ends in disaster, especially when the spinnaker skies as it is doing on reefed-down M 16.

Another, and equally vivid, illustration of this sea change is provided by the Henry Winkelman photograph of the X-class *Viper* two-sail reaching on Auckland harbour in 1921. The wind here is relatively light, and one crew member is sitting inboard, but the other two are up on the weather deck, one of them with his backside well over the rail. Judged in modern terms, both crew should be out there, holding the boat flat and working their body weight with the waves to make it plane, while the helmsman should sit to leeward to maintain balance as necessary – and the pressure of competition in near-identical boats would have had them doing so before long.

This fundamental change in the antipodean sailor's psyche, which was in evidence in the Patikis at the turn of the century, and in the new cheap boats as early as 1921, lies at the very heart of the fast light boat story. The overwhelming desire to go faster was self-reinforcing, since the boats' designers, builders, and sailors were often the same people in earlier days, and are frequently still so today.

That boats under sail respond to the wills and minds of their helmsman and crew, as well as to their hands, is no new concept. It has surely been of the essence of sailing since the very first, but adding vigour and athleticism to the process is a product of that remarkable period of innovation in New Zealand just after the First World War.

Very rapidly, within just two or three seasons in the early 1920s, there were small fleets of inexpensive and almost identical boats racing at several New Zealand clubs. All of them were capable of planing, all of them were liable to capsize if sailed beyond their limits, and all but one of them were capable of being righted, emptied out, and sailed on to finish the race once the new skills had been mastered. Only the most senior of them, the X-class, lacked that capability.

The idea of national contests, in which the representatives of provinces and ports competed for trophies with strong patriotic and sentimental connections, spread this new attitude throughout New Zealand with great rapidity. Word of mouth and news items in the daily and magazine press could not have achieved it on their own – competition was the critical element in its spread. The concept of safe, quick, small boats capable of being built by amateurs, stored on land, and handled on the beach and on the water by two or three young men, spread out from their home clubs like wildfire.

That this set of events occurred at all is remarkable, but that it seems to have come about by chance is at first sight incomprehensible. It was not by chance, however, as closer examination reveals, though the interconnection between the several developments took some years to come to the notice of class enthusiasts and yachting administrators alike.

▲ This series of pictures is remarkable not only for its poor image quality (the newsprint source explains that) but also for its great significance in the history of New Zealand yachting. It records the 1920 exhibition off Onerahi Wharf of the first P-class with its designer, Harry Highet, at the helm. A demonstration capsize and re-righting was included, as the right-hand picture shows.

The P-class

On New Year's Day 1920, at a regatta on Whangarei harbour, a returned serviceman demonstrated the seaworthiness of the 7 ft boat he had designed for the young son of a yachting friend by capsizing and righting it in front of the spectators.

The boat was the prototype of the P-class (a design that has subsequently become truly ubiquitous throughout New Zealand), and the demonstrator was a Wellingtonian called Harry Highet.

Harry Highet later took one of his tiny, safe boats with him when he moved to Tauranga (safe, because it had watertight bulkheads and was therefore 'unsinkable'). A Tauranga local, Percy Carter, built two for his sons and promoted the class there. (Several years later, in 1936, Carter crewed for one of his sons when they won the first Moffat Cup.)

▲ Bill Hayman is in his P-class *Houdini Jnr*, representing Wellington in the first national contest for the Tanner Cup at Evans Bay in 1945. He has his sail eased and is thus experiencing much less weather helm than is Bill Ross, the nearby Auckland skipper.

▼ These five seven-footers demonstrate the blunt-bowed seaworthiness of the first of the stepping-stone classes in strong winds in Lyttelton Harbour. In such conditions, a large part of the art of winning consists of sailing in a way which keeps as much water out of the cockpit as possible and manually bailing out what does get in without adversely affecting the performance of the boat.

    The Ps, originally known as the Tauranga class, spread quickly throughout New Zealand. Their national contest eventually became one with two parts: one was an interprovincial series for the Tanner Cup, presented by George Tanner of Wellington, conducted between boats whose skippers had won their local representative trials, and the other was an interclub series for the Tauranga Cup.

    Bill Hayman of the Evans Bay Yacht & Motor Boat Club – until very recently a competitor in the Wellington R-class fleet – won the first Tanner Cup contest in 1945 sailing *Houdini Jnr*. Graham Mander of Canterbury was also one of the contestants.

    In 1947, *Sea Spray* magazine, in a revealing article about the usefulness of the class, appropriately titled 'The Cradle of Yachting', said:

> The boats are very safe for learning. They have four watertight bulkheads, with a very small cockpit holding little water. Under the supervision of club officials and competent yachtsmen, the boys are taught to capsize their craft, right them, and proceed in their racing with little delay. This gives the boys confidence in both themselves and their craft. It must be gratifying to the sponsors of this class to see the progress that has been made, the fine type of boy it has developed, and the skill with which they handle their craft in all kinds of weather.

Therein lies much of what brought about, and still brings about, though not with the same dominance in the field, most sailors' early familiarity with how sailing boats work and what their limits are.

    Blunt-bowed, almost as though they had been made a few inches shorter by cutting off the point of the very first of them in order to make it only seven feet long, and cat-rigged (that is, with only one sail set on a mast stepped very close to the bow), the 'seven footer' is by no means an elegant craft, though the best of them can be quite impressive in appearance with their high standard of finish and equipment.

    At the end of the twentieth century, some seventy years after the boat's debut at the regatta in Tauranga, both the Tanner Cup and the Tauranga Cup are still contested for by P-class boats. Young men and women are still graduating from sailing Ps and going on to dominate national and international yachting at the highest level – David Barnes, Russell

Coutts, Chris Dickson, Leslie Egnot, and the Dodsons amongst them.

The Z-class

It is said to have been a group of Takapuna Boating Club yachtsmen who commissioned the design of a new centreboarder. It was to have what they described as 'low first cost, ease of construction and an ever watchful eye on speed and performance under Auckland harbour weather conditions'.

RB Brown drew the lines of the 12 ft 6 in two-man boat and built the first of them. The new design became widely known as the Zeddie, though in the early years it was just as often known as the 'Taka' – an abbreviation of the name of its originating club.

Cat-rigged, plus a spinnaker, the Z-class could (at the risk of offending the ghosts of the designers of both) be described as a narrow Idle Along without a jib.

The word spinnaker is said by the OED to come from the word 'spanker', used to describe one of the sails set on the mizzen mast of sailing ships. A modern version of the sail was certainly in common use in New Zealand in the early 1920s, but it was invariably set to windward of the forestay because it was considered bad seamanship to have the sheet carried around it and to leeward – as can be seen in the photographs of the Zeddies of the time.

The Zeddie had a similarly shaped hard-chined hull and was the same length as the I-class, discounting the 2-inch trim added to the bow of the I-class boats. It was

▶ This picture of the Zeddie *Tatariki* three-up with sheets eased on a reach was taken in 1924. While not demonstrating the planing capability of the class, it shows well the partly-raised centerplate and the out-of-the-cockpit stance of two of the crew which, given a quick sheeting-in of the mainsail and a twitch of the tiller as a puff arrived, readily led to planing once the art had been mastered.

▼ The boat is just beginning to plane, as Zeddies have been able to do on a reach from the beginning. With the spinnaker set to windward of the forestay, as was the custom then, and with the crew not yet hiking, it cannot be on too tight a reach or they would be in trouble. The boat is the Paremata representative in the Cornwell Cup, sailing at Tauranga, and the conditions are such that the race committee appear to have allowed life jackets to be carried and not insisted that they be worn, which they would require in strong winds.

designed to be framed and built in much the same way for exactly the same reasons. The Zeddie suffered somewhat in the way of windward performance when compared with the Idle Along, but its two-man crew could, with the application of skill and vigour, easily match the more senior three- and four-man-crewed stepping stones off the wind.

As was to be the case with the later Idle Along class, the Takapuna Z-class proved to be outstandingly popular with younger sailors once they had reached the age limit for the P-class. It quickly spread nationwide and soon became the acknowledged intermediate-stage centreboarder for those under the age of 19.

The Z-class national contest differed from others in that it was based on representation of ports rather than of provinces, on the crews swapping boats race by race to even out the minor differences between the home-built boats, and the winners being the first crew to win three races. The trophy competed for was named in honour of John Travers Cornwell VC, a young First World War Royal Navy hero.

At the end of more than 60 years of pre-eminence and fame, in sailing circles at least, as an intermediate class, the final representative contest in Z-class boats for the Cornwell Cup took place in 1973.

▲ Though *Idle Along* is generally considered to have been the first of the class to be built, it had sail number 12. *Rongomai*, built at the same time and allocated sail number 11, is shown here running down wind on Wellington Harbour, three-up in a moderate northerly.

▼ In a picture taken in 1930, the same year the first Idle Along was built in Petone, the brand-new Worser Bay Idle Alongs *Kiwi* and *Demon* rest on a stony piece of sandy beach on the eastern shore of the entrance to Wellington Harbour. During the Depression of the 1930s, young Worser Bay sailors used to camp near here, and live off fish caught nearby and occasional gifts of food from club supporters.

The I-class

In 1927, a year after he had become the founding commodore of Wellington's Worser Bay Boating Club, Alf Harvey drew the lines of a beamy, hard-chined, three-man, 12 ft 8 in centreboarder on the floor of his tiny house opposite the beach at the bay. The boat was designed with brisk Wellington conditions in mind (hence the wide beam).

The newly-formed Worser Bay club had several of the new two-man Z-class centreboarders for intermediate sailors in its racing fleet, some of which had been built by senior club members for the younger ones to sail. For that reason, the committee was unenthusiastic about encouraging the construction of the Commodore's proposed three-man boat, although they already had reservations about the suitability of the Zeddie for Wellington Harbour conditions, given the club's location near its wind- and sea-swept entrance.

Having moved his home north across the harbour to Petone, Alf Harvey joined the Heretaunga Boating Club based on the beach there. In 1930, with others, Harvey built the first two boats to his design, *Idle Along* (which gave its name to the class) and *Rongomai*.

By the end of the 1930/31 summer, Worser Bay club members had overcome their lack of interest in the new class and built two of the boats, *Kiwi* and *Demon*. In the following few years many more were built there. The 'butterbox', as it was called by some of its detractors, had arrived.

In his book *Little Ships*, Ronald Carter describes the form of the I-class on its arrival in the early 1930s:

> Less than ten years ago, Mr. Alf Harvey, of Wellington, conducted a series of experiments in an effort to evolve a suitable small class racer, and the results of his efforts are seen today in the ever-increasing fleet of Idle Along craft, which proved themselves in their fast and weatherly qualities. The boats are of a restricted type, and measure 12.8 feet overall, and have a beam of approximately 6 feet. They are built on the square chine principle, with a good rise in floor forward of amidships, which flattens out to a broad tuck stern ...
>
> The original model was gunter rigged, but it was found that without any alteration to the existing sail plan, the boats perform better with a Bermudian rig. By doing away

▲ This carefully posed picture of *Idle Along* on its big-wheeled beach trolley was taken outside 20 Aurora Terrace, Petone, in September 1930. The boat was built in a shed behind the house, and its designer-builder is standing behind it, flanked by family and helpers.

▼ Alf Harvey sailed *Idle Along* for several years, often in inter-club races for the class. Here he is, leading the fleet, shortly after a heavy weather start, big numbers and a big dragonfly on his reefed-down mainsail.

with the spar which carries the head of the sail, and is of necessity somewhat heavy, and eliminating the 'sagging to leeward' tendency which this stick caused to the upper portion of the mainsail, it had been proved that the lighter Bermudian mast is preferable. The sail area comprising mainsail, jib, and leading jib, totals 130 square feet, 90 of which goes into the mainsail. Redeeming features of the Idle Along boats are the watertight compartments fore and aft which have sufficient buoyancy to allow a capsized craft to be righted and bailed out; simpleness of design for the benefit of the amateur builder, and the moderately low cost of construction. Having been thoroughly tested in many ways, the plans of the original yacht Idle Along were laid before the Wellington Provincial Yacht and Motorboat Association for approval, with the object in view of having one more class for New Zealand championship competition.

A one-race harbour championship for a trophy known as the Reid Shield was established by the Heretaunga Boating Club. In the 1933/34 season, the annual race was held at Worser Bay in a very strong northwesterly which had prevented almost all other small-boat activity on the harbour.

Some 26 Idle Alongs took part in the race, and though only six finished, the reputation of the class as one which could cope with Wellington's winds was well and truly established – particularly when dramatic photographs appeared in local newspapers, showing the boats competing under reduced sail in rough water shortly after the start.

The first interprovincial Idle Along national contest was for the Moffat Cup, named in memory of Jack Moffat, a much-admired local yachting administrator and sometime chairman of the Wellington Provincial Yachting Association. It was held in Wellington in 1936 and resulted in a win for the Bay of Plenty representatives, sailing the original *Idle Along* which had been lent to them by the designer.

A year later, the first of the class in Auckland was professionally built for Len Hodgkinson, who met with verbal abuse out on the water off Northcote from those who preferred to sail the Zeddies that were by then well established on the North Shore.

The I-class prospered for another 30 years. Its maximum numbers were at one time quoted as some 2000 by its enthusiasts, but the claim is hard to confirm because class registration was province by province and not centrally administered. The final national contest for the Moffat Cup was held at New Plymouth in 1969, and was won by the Taranaki representative. Though the Idle Along was an important national class for only 33 years, yet because of its widespread fleets and fiercely contested national championships, it was a significant player in the story of New Zealand small-boat development over that period.

▶ This planing Hawke's Bay Moffat Cup representative has just arrived at the wing mark and is bearing away in preparation for the hazardous business of gybing around it in heavy weather. The obscured boat is unreefed but three-up, the one to leeward, two-up but reefed, has the forward hand out on a trapeze. The hard-chined planing form of the Idle Along is well illustrated here.

▲ This Winkleman view shows the X-class *Rona* engaged in sustained planing on Waitemata Harbour. Recorded in the photographer's collection as having been taken in December 1922, it is this photograph in particular which establishes that planing was achieved in the Antipodes well before 1927.

The X-class

Absences and shortages during and after the First World War brought about a decline in yachting. The committee of Auckland's North Shore Sailing Club, many of whose senior members were overseas or otherwise unavailable, saw part of the solution to be a centreboard class smaller, less expensive, and more evenly matched than the 16 and 18-footers then sailing on the harbour.

At the end of the war, the North Shore Sailing Club commodore, Bill Wilkinson, commissioned the designer Glad Bailey to draw up and build a suitable sailing dinghy. The outcome of that commission, the 14 ft, one-design, clinker-built *Desert Gold*, became the prototype for the senior centreboard class soon to be raced at clubs in many parts of New Zealand. Frank Cloke and Joe Patrick bought the boat and sailed it with such success that others were quickly built to the same lines.

Because of the wide variety of boats then racing, handicapping dominated most keeler classes sailing here. But it was the enthusiasm of the famous Lord Jellicoe, New Zealand's newly appointed Governor-General, for one-design racing amongst evenly matched boats which gave the Xies (the diminutive by which X-class boats were known) their boost of popularity and turned them into a New Zealand-wide class.

▲ Though no identification letters or numbers show, this is *Iron Duke*, the X-class originally owned by Lord Jellicoe, sailing with eased sheets on a sunny afternoon on Wellington Harbour. Perhaps the eased sheets and lack of sail numbers reveal new sails being tried out for the first time.

His *Iron Duke*, sailed much of the time by the man who had commanded the British flagship of that name, was one of the new 14-footers which took part in a race in Auckland in January 1921, in what was called 'one of the prettiest ever held on the harbour ... all in their bright paint and clean canvas, coming to the line together'.

In March that year, two boats, *Iron Duke*, having won a series of trial races in Auckland and representing that province, and *Heather*, having done the same down south representing Otago, sailed a five race series on the Waitemata harbour. This was the first contest for the Sanders Cup, named after a posthumous New Zealand winner of the Victoria Cross and won on this first occasion by the Otago crew.

The final step in the establishment of the Xie as a national class came with the performance of the Auckland boat *Rona*. This boat won the 1923 contest in such a convincing fashion that her lines were adopted as the basis of a one-design class, which, in honour of their newly famous national champion and of their long-renowned Governor-

◀ The letter on the sail indicates the boat is the Wellington Sanders Cup representative, and it is probably the *Peggy*, which took part in the 1924 contest in Wellington. This view may well be of the last race in the series, held in a fresh northerly. Bright sunshine makes the boat stand out sharply against the northern harbour hills, and the crew's white sweaters again show the absence of life jackets.

General enthusiast, became known as Rona-Jellicoe boats, with the letter X on their sails, to compete on behalf of their provinces for the Cup.

By 1936, when the I-class held its first national contest, all four boats, P, Z, I, and X, all capable of amateur construction and none demanding wealth and status of their builders and crew, were in place as sequential classes offering a clear and unique progression from novice to expert for young New Zealand sailors. Four years later in 1940, despite the war just begun, all four classes combined to hold their national championships and conferences as part of Wellington's 100th anniversary celebrations. From then on, their four-part coordination was firmly established for the first time – albeit with the occasional debate between classes about venues and dates as the seasons went by.

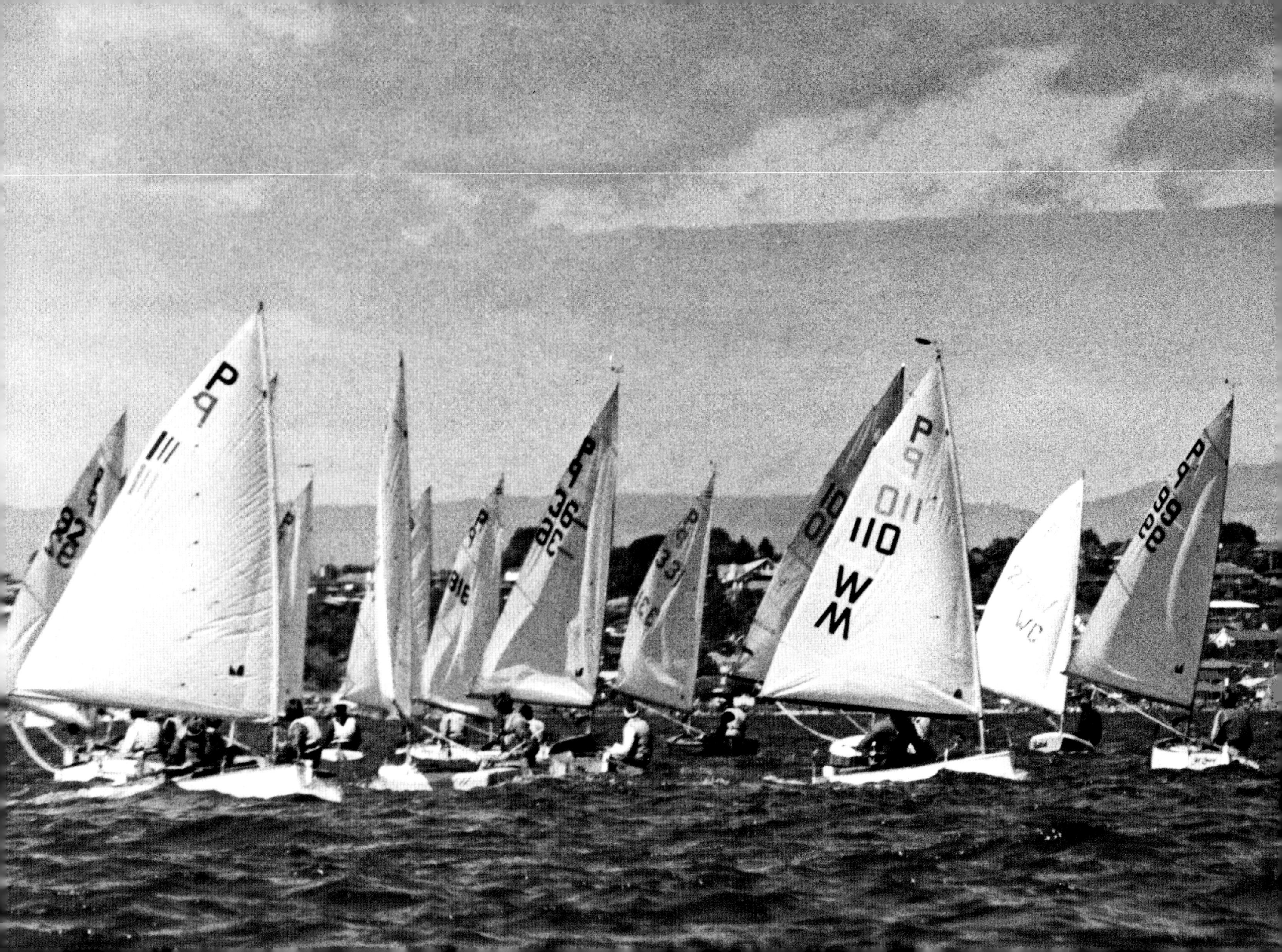
P
111
P
110
WM

Chapter 3
Stepping on the stones

If, in the period after the First World War, a New Zealander of great foresight had set out to put in place a national small-boat competition with a framework of classes that was designed to produce sailors of international race-winning standard, the arrangement which came into being largely by chance would have handsomely fitted the bill.

The competitive expectations of young and typically impecunious sailors were brilliantly catered for by the lucky sequence of nationwide age-group classes of small centreboard boats that were designed and brought into being during the years between the wars. The attitudes to sailing that were bred by competition in inexpensive boats of controlled design and construction became embedded in the psyche of many of the New Zealanders who raced over the next fifty years. This was the heyday of the stepping-stone series, when the one-design P-class, Z-class, and I-class, and the restricted X-class dominated small-boat sailing in New Zealand.

The first three of these classes required boats to be built so as to conform to a strict design. It was a system that was clearly established to suit the needs of amateur boatbuilders. For a small fee, the class administrators made available to prospective builders a set of standardised, comprehensive drawings and specifications. Newly built boats were checked by official measurers to ensure that they measured up.

> The Tanner Cup contest over, the Wanganui-Manawatu P-class representative jostles with some 25 others in this view of the pre-start manoeuvres in the interclub contest which follows it, the Tauranga Cup. By this long-standing, annual national competition process, many of New Zealand's competitive sailors have become experienced in evenly-matched, big-fleet starts very early in their careers.

▲ When the contest was held at Lyttelton in 1926, the Canterbury boat *Betty* won the Sanders Cup for the first of the three occasions on which she did so. The famous Xie is shown here with a rather well-dressed George Andrews at the tiller, apparently sheltering from a wave just striking the boat. The remainder of the crew look to be already wet. They have the rather more appropriate casual look about them which is usually associated with Kiwi small-boat sailors.

Within small tolerances, the boats were required to be built and kept in accordance with the strict requirements of the 'one design' approved and controlled by the class administrators – hence the term. But those tolerances were the subject of much contention over the years, as skilled builders used them to make small differences in hull shape they believed would make their boat go faster. The term 'one design' also referred to sail area and shape, as well as to spars and other 'attached' elements.

In the one-design classes these were all strictly controlled. In restricted classes, in contrast, hulls and sails in particular were allowed to be freely arranged within certain prescribed limits.

For the X-class, the original intention was to limit construction to 'one design'. But within a few years, during which time faster new boats easily out-sailed older ones, the class rules were changed to allow more freedom in hull form and sail area within certain restrictions – and the X-class thus became a restricted class.

The national conferences that were held in conjunction with national contests became the venue for vigorous debates over a whole range of issues which beset each of the classes. The problem for P, Z, and I-class administrators was that relatively small tolerances in hull form, and equally tight tolerances in spar and sail arrangements, had to be met by builders who were, for the most part, amateurs – and some of them were extremely keen to make the most of the inevitable loopholes in the class rules and to pursue innovations that would give them greater speed.

As the years passed, the limitations on design and construction that were imposed by the rules in those classes caused friction between the advocates of the 'one design' and 'restricted' boats and those free spirits who were determined to innovate and experiment in every aspect of boat design. The adherents of the two schools of thought eventually came to terms with each other and also with developments in the wider world, and began to borrow one from the other, but as the years went by all but one of the stepping-stone classes were superseded. The first and smallest of the stepping-stone boats, the P-class, is the only one to survive to the present day in more or less its original format.

As it happens, we have by far the most intact record of the design development of the one-design class that was the last to come into being, the Idle Along, as well as more complete information on I-class administration and contests. From the outset the originators of the

Idle Along put the control of the class into the hands of one of the provincial yachting associations, and the minute books of its contests remain largely intact and complete. Because of the paucity of detailed information on the other classes, largely due to the greater informality of their national administration framework, the more complete story of the I-class will serve to illuminate the kind of things that happened with the other classes, but of which rather less detailed record now remains. But first, a discussion of more general matters.

Age-group sailing in small boats

Not every New Zealander who takes up sailing goes on to take part in competition, racing with others in successive seasons over several years. The joy of sailing, the simple pleasure that is given by the surge of energy as a boat moves forward in response to the wind, is for many sufficient in itself. But for those who had a mind to (or whose parents and mentors did) there was from the early 1920s onwards in New Zealand a system of age-group stepping stones. The four interconnecting classes undoubtedly came about as a happenstance and not by planning, and the connections between them were always a loose fit. Nonetheless, they created a competitive pathway which young sailors could progress along, developing their sailing skills not only as they became more experienced but also as they grew bigger and stronger, and therefore better able to handle a larger boat.

▲ Complete with a big-boat sounding name, a famous-maker sail, an expensive universal-jointed tiller extension, a Windex pennant on the foredeck, cunningham luff adjustment, black mast band, colour-identified ropes, class number on the topsides, racing lifejacket, wetsuit, wetboots, and long blond hair tied back in a pony tail, this young woman epitomises the modern competitive P-class sailor. Only the big-boat sounding name is atypical. Seven-footers more often than not have fun-names influenced by the in-language current amongst their young skippers.

▲ Almost completely hidden in the midst of these 50 or so P-class boats can be seen the 'clothes pegs' sail symbol of a single Phase II, New Zealand's precurser to the international Laser II. But this midday beach-scene photograph is all about the lunchtime break between races in the interclub Tauranga Cup series, with all the boats sitting on their beach trollies, their sails flapping gently in the soft offshore breeze.

Class racing in New Zealand was done in fleets of boats that were capable of being built by amateurs, of being carried into the water by the crew, and most importantly, that were capable of planing. Every year, the young sailors took part in selection trials to find the most able skipper and crew to represent the local port, province, or club in the national championships. From these formative experiences many young men – and they were almost exclusively young men, not young women, until well after the Second World War – developed sailing skills of a high order. By the 1950s, the best of them were to find their abilities unequalled anywhere in the world.

The country-wide stepping-stone effect began with the introduction of national championships contested by representatives of provinces, ports, or clubs, according to the various class rules, with a maximum age of 16 years for the P-class and 19 years for the Z-class. The stepping stones were established with a minimum of inter-class rationalisation to provide fairness within each class. But the age restrictions in Ps and Zs, and the absence of an age restriction for Is and Xs, along with an assumption that the 14-footer was the most senior class, meant that individual class administrations had put in place a sequence which made sense on a *national* scale. There was thus a progression of relatively high-performance centreboard classes, all capable of planing, arranged in steps from small to large. Each of them could be built and sailed by enthusiasts of modest means.

Each stepping-stone class had its own way of selecting those who were to take part in its national championship and of deciding the winner of the series.

For the P-class, there were two complementary selection processes. The first, and more grand, was a series of provincial trial races, run more or less on the same basis as the national championship. In the early years, in order to take part in the local trials it was necessary to be considered good enough by one's club, but later on they became an open-entry series. This arrangement meant that the national championship fleet contesting the Tanner Cup was limited in number, though it was generally made up of high-quality young sailors. Competing in the Tanner Cup, therefore, did not give the contestants an experience of big-fleet competition. In contrast, selection for the other P-class national championship, the Tauranga Cup, was by club-by-club representation. The result of this arrangement was that the fleet competing for the inter-club Tauranga Cup was very much bigger, over 100 boats in recent years, though much less even in quality.

In consequence, these complementary national events sailed in demanding small boats have, since their inception in 1945, led to the identification and fostering of the very best of young New Zealand sailing talent. Though they have been much modified by time and many influences over the years, the stepping-stone classes have profoundly influenced the way New Zealanders, young and old, men and women, have built, rigged, and sailed their boats. They have also played a major part in creating the country's international reputation.

There were sundry other classes of small boats being sailed in various parts of the country at the time, each with their enthusiastic local adherents. But it was the processes of competition in this sequence of nationwide restricted and one-design classes that first influenced small-boat development, and then big-boat sailing methods, over the ensuing 30 or so years. These processes included new approaches and attitudes to design, construction, rig, sails, boat handling, and competition. Though the mode of competition differed from class to class according to the traditions that quickly built up amongst their adherents, it led to the early introduction of high standards in every facet of small-boat development.

In some classes, and in some places, the standards were so high that it was said it was harder to win the representative trials than it was to win the national contest itself. This may be more a measure of the unevenness of standards around the country than anything else. But there can be no question about the importance to the widespread development of sailing ability in New Zealand of the long history of well-run national competitions in small fleets of nearly identical high-performance boats, held between representative crews selected in equally competitive local trials.

How significant was the New Zealand stepping-stone system? Compare it with the situation in Australia. As late as 1950, our nearest and fiercest yachting rival still had no small-boat class which was raced throughout the whole country, which meant that Australia lacked a truly national championship competition. The stepping-stone classes certainly gave New Zealand sailors an edge over the competition when the time came to compete overseas.

Contests and regattas

In the early days of national contests, boats were freighted to and fro by rail and ship. Out-of-town crews and conference delegates were often billeted in the homes of local sailors or their friends. This system continued well into the 1950s, until car ownership became more common. From then on, contestants tended to drive to contests, towing their boat on a trailer, and often stayed in hotels or motels.

In that early period of private transportation of small boats, when national contests and big regattas were still largely gatherings of the stepping-stone sailors, contests consisted of small fleets of nearly identical boats sailed by representative crews that had been selected in local trials. Trucks and trailers were often used in combination to carry boats and their crews from one end of the country to the other. The proliferation of classes and the lightness of boats in recent times has led to a similar proliferation of transport methods, some using trailers, some using roof-racks, and some combining the two, with spars projecting fore and aft to the maximum allowed.

To begin with, the courses for national contests simply consisted of the course usually sailed by the club hosting the event, and the starting and finishing procedures and directions were also those of the host club. Local regattas, where boats from several nearby clubs would take part, followed the same pattern.

▶ *Windhover II* travelled to and from Auckland by rail in a crate in the summer of 1953–54. The three-man crew shown here are, judging by their attire, working on the crate at the Moffat Cup venue at Point Chevalier and not in their home port of Wellington. By the following summer, do-it-yourself road trailering of small light boats was much more common.

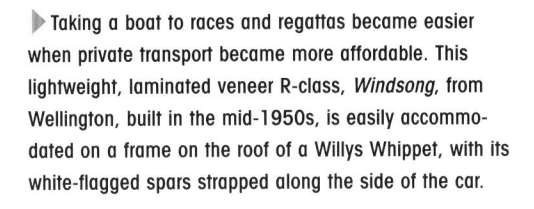

▶ Taking a boat to races and regattas became easier when private transport became more affordable. This lightweight, laminated veneer R-class, *Windsong*, from Wellington, built in the mid-1950s, is easily accommodated on a frame on the roof of a Willys Whippet, with its white-flagged spars strapped along the side of the car.

▲ This very sophisticated mobile sailing school package arrives at the Westhaven launching ramp complete with coach/patrol boat, and a ready-to-sail seven footer can be quickly set up on a beach trolley alongside the road trailer.

▶ This enclosed trailer unit belongs to a sailing school and has room for at least four P-class boats, six masts, and as many booms. The seven-footers fit side by side, densely packed on end, one behind the other, and the rear tailgate serves as a ramp for the beach trolleys packed in with them.

▲ For the 1955 Moffat Cup contest at Lake Brunner, on the West Coast of the South Island (not a common venue for national contests), the Wellington Boat *Windhover III* was towed there on a somewhat massive road trailer. This picture shows the assembly being repackaged on the railway station platform, following the completion of the championship series.

Local knowledge obviously gave an advantage to the home contestants, though over the years the advantage was at least spread around, since each class had rules which ensured the contest moved from venue to venue over time. But perhaps the most significant effect of such championships was to educate young sailors in the differences to be found between one harbour and another – strong winds and light, tides and currents, smooth water shallows, and deep water ports with big seas rolling in from the ocean.

As early as the 1930s, sailors familiar with developments overseas, whether as competitors or, more frequently, as avid readers of imported magazines, began to encourage club racing committees (and later the class administrators and budding national organisations) to better regulate races under their control.

On-the-wind starts and finishes, with five flags or discs lowered at one-minute intervals to show when the start was due, and alternating windward-leeward and triangular laps of a course set true to the wind direction, gradually became the norm. Alf Harvey, the designer and builder of the first Idle Along, was a man who had access to the latest yachting magazines. He was one of those early advocates of better regulated races, both at Worser Bay Boating Club and later at the Heretaunga club.

If, over the years, New Zealand's national yachting contests had served no other purpose than to remind Aucklanders that the sport thrives beyond their province and its harbour and gulf, they would have been a profound influence on its development. If the feeling amongst Aucklanders that New Zealand ends at the Bombay Hills is prevalent in any sport, it certainly is in sailing. This attitude has all too often been inflamed by the language used and the attitudes expressed in the pages of *Sea Spray*, the country's longest-running sailing magazine.

Parochialism has always been present in the sport. Even when *Sea Spray* was produced in Wellington, which was the case until the end of 1950, Auckland was seen to be the centre of sailing interest. After 1950, when its offices moved to Auckland, the magazine became, at least to those who participated in sailing elsewhere in New Zealand, even more interested in northern sailing activity at the expense of what was going on elsewhere. To give just one example: in a contributed article to *Sea Spray* in December 1949, Ronald Carter, the author of *Little Ships*, a classic history of sailing in New Zealand up to 1945, wrote about sailing in what he called 'A Hundred Years of Yachting'. The article was in fact a potted history of 100 years of Auckland Anniversary Regattas, celebrating the 100th of them, to be held a month later.

The article itself is interesting and lively, though almost all the events in the first few regattas were for boats powered by oars rather than sails. But it neglects to mention that the first regatta celebrating the anniversary of the founding of Auckland took place ten years *after* the first one held in Wellington, and that by 1850 sailing regattas were an established part of Wellington's anniversary celebrations. The absence of such a reference is not of great significance in itself, but it is an example of the attitude that has long been prevalent in the sport and in the magazine – and in New Zealand society at large.

▲ The Wellington Idle Along *Windhover*, the first of three with the same name and sail number (I 111) first saw the light of day when it was eased through the door of the basement in which it was built in 1949. Not quite a push fit, but not much room to spare.

Backyard construction

The designers of the P, Z, and I-classes were, at different times and in different parts of the country, responding to a perceived need for simplicity of construction, so that amateur boat-builders with limited skills could build them, and thus revitalise the sport with young men.

In each case, the hull was made up out of regularly placed transverse frames, fixed to a curved wooden keel set up on a temporary support. The whole arrangement provided simple 'hard chine' shapes capable of being clad with thin planks of wood enclosing the sides, underside, and deck.

In each case also, the frames were so arranged that their interior struts provided a support system not only for the deck and the outside of the hull but also for thin interior timber linings which formed watertight compartments. These built-in buoyancy tanks ensured that the boats remained sufficiently free of water to enable them to be righted and sailed away following a capsize.

Kauri was the timber much used in the early years of the stepping-stone classes, chosen for its classic qualities of durability, strength, and ease of working. For as long as its relative heaviness was not perceived as a disadvantage, it remained the preferred material for quality boats; indeed, it was sometimes specified in the class rules.

But the pursuit of speed and success in competitions through lightness inevitably led to the use of other timbers. Native species were invariably required by class rules, and kahikatea (white pine) and kaikawaka (southern beech) replaced heavier timbers as time went by.

The use of lighter native species for the stepping-stone classes was still the vogue right into the mid 1950s. Nonetheless, by then the availability of waterproof plywood had already revolutionised small-boat construction in the new classes then burgeoning.

Non-ferrous fastenings, nails, and screws were the assembly methods originally used, along with copper rivets for joining the components of frame members. These techniques were slowly replaced by gluing and screwing as time went by and as reliable waterproof adhesives became available.

The P-class successfully made the change to plywood construction in 1956. Though the Z-class was converted to ply in 1958 and the Idle Along in 1960, these changes failed to save them from extinction as viable national classes. Later still the P-class changed from ply to fibreglass, without any serious harm to its viability – though the high cost of a fully competitive boat and rig nowadays must be of serious concern to those interested in the future of the class.

For the X-class, the construction expertise necessary in order to assemble its round-sectioned hull was much more of the order of skill to be expected of professional boat-builders. The Xie hull was formed out of closely-spaced transverse ribs of small-section timber, bent to shape and attached to a bent keel set on a shaped temporary base. The compound curves this system allowed were planked with narrow strips of timber lapped one over the other, much as bevel-backed weather boards are on a house, and attached with copper rivets to the ribs.

Despite this relative complexity, many X-class boats were nevertheless amateur-built, and many amateurs won in competition. But complex construction took its toll as time went by and the newer classes appeared, and though fibreglass was introduced in 1957, it failed to save the class.

▶ In the upper picture, the classic small shed in the backyard scene is shown. The clinker-built dinghy is being repaired, upside down on carpenters' stools. Even in such a tiny boat the ribs and keel are of quite substantial dimensions. Below, in more modern fashion, a boat several times the size of the dinghy is being built with slender battens spanning widely spaced frames, again upside down.

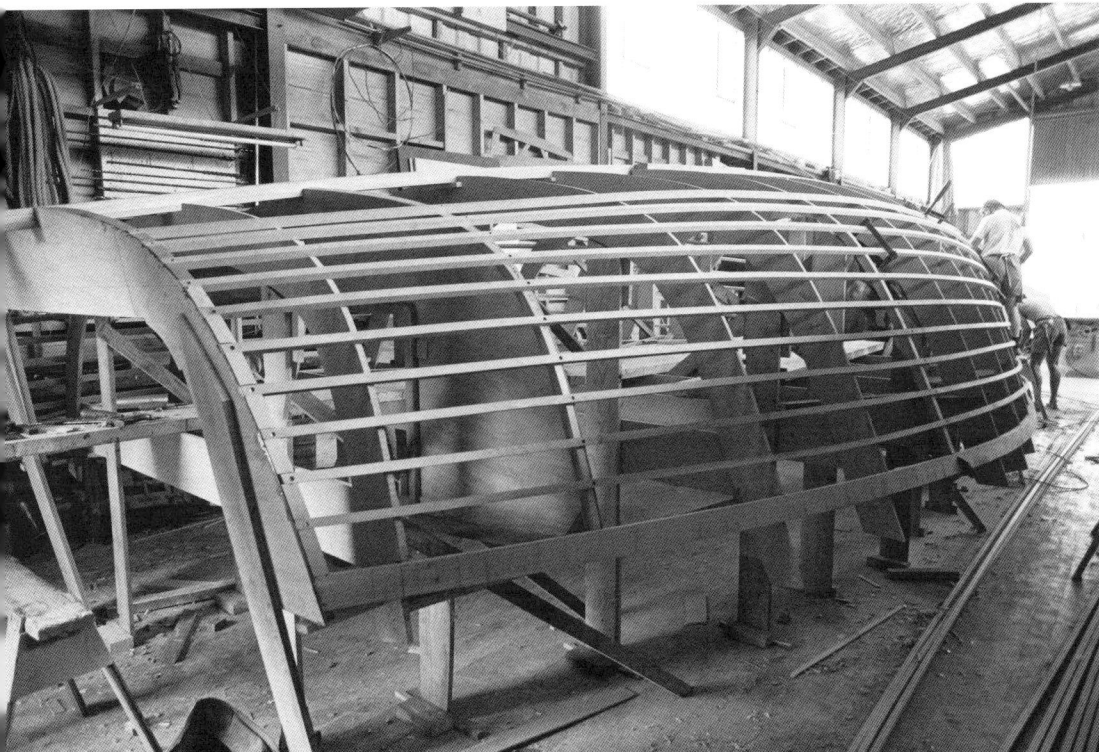

For the P and Z-classes, the single-handed crewing of the one and the two-handed crewing of the other found their natural equivalents in the coming revolution. But the original three-man crew for the I-class and the four-man crew for the Xies eventually caused problems: the third and fourth men became harder to find in changing times, as more and more sailors found it possible to build or buy and sail their own boats.

The advent of aluminium and stainless steel gradually changed the way yachts were rigged and fitted out. At first, stainless steel and aluminium were non-specific and unreliable (especially so in the case of aluminium), but marine-quality grades later became available, and were used in the small-boat classes. Masts and booms made of aluminium, fitted together with stainless steel and with slender but strong stainless-steel attachments of all sorts, replaced the more cumbersome oregon spars and their equally cumbersome fittings.

Stainless-steel rigging, in both stranded- and solid-wire forms, was long viewed with suspicion by some small-boat and big-boat sailors. Eventually, it replaced stranded galvanised steel rigging, especially when clever and strong end-fittings were devised for attachment to spars and to chainplates.

The new materials invariably cost more than the old, but their higher strength-to-weight ratios meant that less weight could be readily converted into more speed. In the long run this ensured that they were adopted.

Cotton sails required careful stretching, washing, and maintenance. Quite early on they were superseded by sails

▲ Amidst all the complex lightweight technology evident across the stern of this eighteen-footer, two feather-light plastic funnels hang slack on the shockcords which keep them from falling out of the holes they fit into. Pulled tight once the boat is afloat, they cheaply and neatly close the two large drainage openings, ready to be released when cockpit water has to be got rid of. Reminiscent of the landsman New Zealander's 'Number eight wire' equivalent, they are quicker-acting than the venturi bailers visible each side of the centrecase.

▶ This close-up of the deck gear and controls of an R-class shows something of the complex technology and inventiveness these boats have incorporated over the years. A cat's-cradle of ropes, wires and struts leads almost every control system out to the two trapezing crewmembers.

made of a kind of tightly-woven material called japara.

The Idle Along specifications allowed japara to be used almost from the beginning of the class in 1930. Japara was in turn superseded by Terylene, Dacron, and much later, by Kevlar for some.

Sheets and ropes of all sorts, the boat's running rigging, were originally sisal or hemp in most cases. Hemp and sisal ropes were stretchy and very water-absorbent, which made them heavy when wet. The ubiquitous pitch-smelling 'marlin' was used for small-scale tasks, such as tying the stays to the chainplates. These materials subsequently gave way to the much stronger, much less stretchy nylon, to Terylene, and eventually to the polypropylene ropes that are now almost universal.

The stepping-stone designers and sailors also borrowed go-fast fittings, like hiking straps and kickers, from the designers and builders of the more inventive classes, such as the R-class of Canterbury.

In order to keep the cockpit dry (and make the boat lighter and more stable), self-draining devices were also introduced. At first, they were simply flap-controlled outlets through the stern. Later, metal tubes were fitted through the hull which used the Venturi effect to remove water when the boat was running downwind. As the design of the fitting was improved, it

Helmer Pedersen's well-clad FD crew demonstrates here not only the classic trapeze arrangement of wire, tee hand grip, choice of connecting ring height, and wide double-strap open-loop harness but also a refinement consisting of a further suspension loop arranged to support the head and neck of the trapeze hand.

With lightweight, transverse timber frames at one-foot centres, the seven-foot long P-class looks deceptively simple to build in these 1951 construction diagrams. The 7/8" tolerance allowance referred to in the accompanying specification, though intended to provide for the vagaries of amateur construction, has long been the means by which more sophisticated builders pursue quicker hull shapes within their limits. Complexity comes with the rig, sails, and performance characteristics of this demanding little boat.

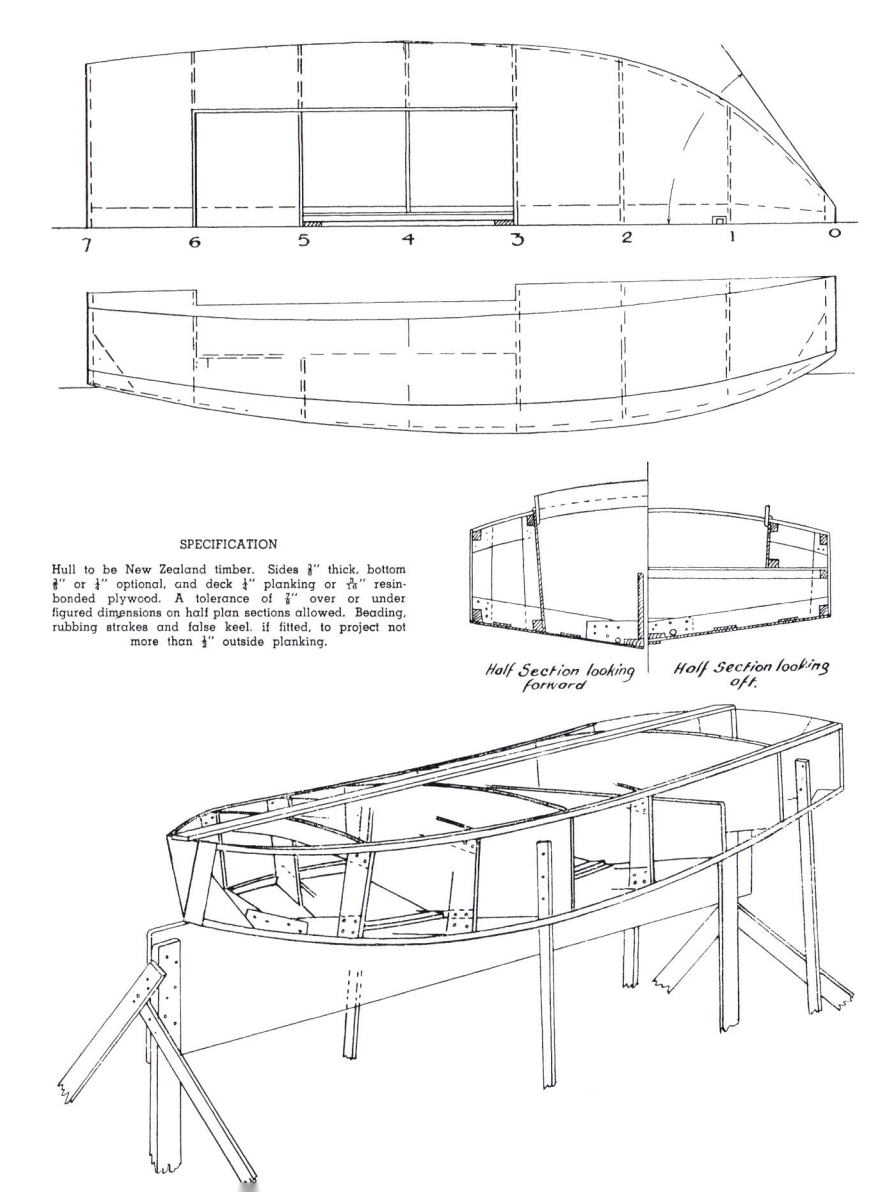

became possible to use the venturis to drain the cockpit when sailing on the wind as well.

The arrival of the trapeze in the three larger stepping-stone classes was a highly visible innovation. The trapeze revolutionised the way boats were sailed. Before the trapeze, the maximum extension of crew weight was limited by the crew's ability to lean out for long periods from a sitting position on the side of the boat. There were impressive demonstrations of trapeze technique (and its effect on speed) in the more adventurous classes, which soon had the conventional ones bringing its use within their class rules.

P-class – the seven-footers

Apart from its boxy look, toy-like size, and tiny cockpit, all emphasised by the life-jacketed and be-capped adult hunched there sailing it, the boat that Harry Highet had demonstrated in front of a wharf full of onlookers at the Onerahi Regatta in January 1920 was by-and-large unremarkable. Few of the onlookers could have realised that it was to become of great significance in the history of New Zealand yachting.

Blunt-bowed, gaff-rigged, and without a single batten to hold out the rolling-in leech of its single sail, the prototype boat barely had room in its cockpit for the tall man sailing it. He must have had to lie almost flat on the deck to miss being hit on the head as he tacked or gybed. Even though there was nothing to hold down the long boom above him, the gooseneck was

SPECIFICATION

Hull to be New Zealand timber. Sides $\frac{3}{8}$" thick, bottom $\frac{3}{8}$" or $\frac{1}{4}$" optional, and deck $\frac{1}{4}$" planking or $\frac{3}{16}$" resin-bonded plywood. A tolerance of $\frac{7}{8}$" over or under figured dimensions on half plan sections allowed. Beading, rubbing strakes and false keel, if fitted, to project not more than $\frac{1}{2}$" outside planking.

Half Section looking forward

Half Section looking aft.

▲ *Staccato* has won more than one P-class national contest. Her deck and cockpit arrangements have long been of interest, which probably explains why they were photographed. The mainsheet system, together with its lazy block and side-deck jamb cleats, the traveller slide controls, the double-sided cunningham control lines, and the adjustable shock-cord-lifted hiking straps, are all clearly shown in this carefully arranged, indoors picture.

◀ This photo of the Tauranga Regatta in December 1926 was taken from Coronation Pier. The race is between the first ten P-class boats built in Tauranga. They are identified by a letter on their sail, taken from the first letter of the boats name, rather than the numbering system used today.

right down at deck level and must have made going about more than a little difficult.

But there was one spectator who did see the boat's significance. By the time he wrote about it in 1924, there were eight of them fleet-racing in Tauranga. WW Waddilove said of Harry Highet's invention:

> I believe that this midget class is the greatest step for catching the boy that has ever been made. The design and building instructions are set out so that any boy who can saw a straight line and drive a nail can build it. It is the cheapest practical sailing boat, all things considered, ever designed, and the safest that can be built.

In the 79 years between Harry Highet's first very public demonstration and the celebratory championships held at Tauranga in 1999, the cost of a P-class has risen from a few pounds in 1920 to some $10,000, according to television reports of the 1999 contests. There have been many changes in the interim, of course, and an examination of those changes reveals much of the story with which this book is concerned.

The beginnings of sophistication in rig and technique can be seen in the eight-boat fleet at Tauranga in 1924. In all of them, it seems, sail shapes have been well set up (just compare them with Harry's in 1920), and body weight for the leading boats is well forward as they reach on port tack. Much more was to come along to improve performance and add to the demands placed on young skippers.

In due course, hiking straps were added. These, in combination with tiller extensions, allowed full extension of the upper body out beyond the gunwale. Kickers, sometimes called vangs, were added to keep the boom down and contribute to the control of sail shape. 'Cunningham' ropes were added at the foot of the luff, to control the position of fullness in the sail. Eventually, in order to win, the boat demanded great concentration, athleticism, and skill from its helmsman.

Skill and attention to detail were required by builders of the boat. Tiny differences in its shape (within the class construction tolerances, of course!) and maximum reduction in its weight proved to be important factors in achieving greater boatspeed and race-winning performance.

As occurred in the other stepping-stone classes, the gaff rig was replaced by a single-spar marconi mast, and designs by CG Denniston for plywood construction were adopted in 1956. By 1975 there were said to be some 2000 P-class boats in New Zealand, which was co-incidentally the same total figure that had been claimed for the Idle Along class at its peak in the early 1950s. By 1975 also, the P-class had an alloy mast, and moulds for fibreglass hull construction were under consideration. (Some hesitation about the fibreglass hull was expressed by Harry Highet when he was consulted about the change in materials.)

But those changes simply reflect the basic developments to be found in small-boat construction over the long lifetime of the class. There were many other changes as well, whose introduction turned the boat into a complex and demanding miniature sailing test-bed in which many New Zealand yachtsmen learned and honed their skills before going on to other classes and bigger boats.

▶ This picture of a very tall Harry Highet and a very diminutive Jon Gilpin was taken at Tauranga in 1951. Gilpin is still the only person to win the Tanner Cup/Tauranga Cup double three times – in 1951, 1952 and 1953.

▲ This mass of sails has been created by seven-footer skippers crowding at the committee-boat end of a start line, presumably one set with a bias towards that end. The sailor in P 35 seems to have decided that better wind conditions can be found towards the pin end, at least enough to make up for the disadvantage of starting out there. A race official can be seen on the foredeck of the committee boat, no doubt keeping an eye out for premature starters and ready to pass on the sail numbers of transgressors to his fellow officials.

Each class went about its competition arrangements differently. In the seven-footer P-class, a two-part national contest had been developed by 1945. Until then, there had been an annual inter-club competition for the Tauranga Cup involving representatives from the yacht clubs at which the boats were sailed, a number that grew year by year.

The original national competition had been an inter-provincial one, but petrol rationing during the Second World War made it too difficult to transport boats around the countryside and the contest lapsed, as it had for the other stepping-stone classes. When the national contest resumed in Wellington in 1945, competition between young yachtsmen representing their province was reintroduced, and the cup donated that year by Wellington's George Tanner became the annual trophy presented to the national provincial champion. It is still raced for today.

This two-part contest, in tiny boats sailed by youngsters who had to be no older than 16 on the first day of January in the year it took place, may seem to those unfamiliar with the P-class to be of minor significance in the story of New Zealand's fast light boats. But because it gave so many of New Zealand's young sailors their first taste of racing, the P-class competition is at the heart of that story.

The Zeddies

The essence of the attraction of the Zeddie, right from the outset in 1921, was not only that it could be readily built, rigged, manhandled, and sailed by relatively unskilled young men, which was the undoubted intention of its designers and those who commissioned them. It was also that it planed, though this characteristic may just have been due to chance.

The early boats were built of kauri and had a relatively heavy oregon timber mast, gaff, and boom rig, with a hard-chine hull form and easy curves fore and aft – all born of the need to keep construction simple. But because of these features, when a Zeddie was sailed on a reach with spinnaker set in moderate winds, it quickly lifted out and planed. This experience must have thrilled the first few youngsters to sail the new boat, just as it has many since.

Twenty-four years later, class numbers had grown to such an extent that there were 94 Zeddies racing in two divisions in the 1945 Auckland Anniversary Regatta.

In 1949, the *Scandal* dispute enlivened the Cornwell Cup contest and demonstrated some of the difficulties inherent in one-design classes (and the complex business of keeping them so). A Canterbury boat, *Scandal*, was one of 19 taking part in the swap-boat contest. It won four of the races, each time being sailed by a different crew, as was the custom in the class. As a result, it was considered by some to have thus been a rule-cheater in some way. The debate raged at the contest and for some time afterwards.

Just as he was to do for the Idle Alongs two years later, John Spencer adapted the Zeddie to plywood construction in 1958, though the class still retained the wooden, two-spar gunter rig until aluminium spars were introduced in 1961.

Ten years after the change, and only five years before the end of the Zeddies as a national class, yachting reporters in Wellington were waxing enthusiastic about what were seen as 'large fleets of ply Zeddies' racing locally; commenting that it was hard to believe that some leading yachtsmen had been predicting the early demise of the class. 'The keenness of the boys who stuck with a boat they enjoyed sailing combined with solid club support in Wellington have turned the tide.'

▲ Looking much as do other Zeddies in photographs of those times, *Scandal* lifts her bow a little as she is sailed one-up with eased sheets, the centreplate partly raised, with the Canterbury identification letter on the sail. The straight-up gaff shows the meaning of 'gunter rig' as distinguished from the simple and more old-fashioned 'gaff rig', where the gaff is rigged out at an angle to the mast and the sail shaped accordingly.

▲ When national contests in the PZIX classes became established, the wearing and swapping of representative ribbons (some misspelled!) became an important part of the annual occasion. Keeping and including the collection in a framed picture of your boat was also customary. This example is from Bob Williamson's participation in the 1947 Cornwell Cup at Tauranga in his Zeddie *Slipaway*. The boat, seen here planing on Tauranga harbour, was painted in an unusual fashion, yellow on one side and green on the other, at least in part to confuse the competition!

Not for long it hadn't — the tide was too strong and the incoming wave of small-boat designs was much too powerful.

In this class too, even though hull construction, rig, and sails all developed and were accepted in the minds of the class's adherents, the changes could not stop the trend towards boats born out of the new materials and forms of the post-war decades.

Amendments to the class rules of what had become known as the Takapuna One Design class suggested in 1972 were not proceeded with. The next year, in 1973, the Cornwell Cup contest at Lake Reserve in the Wairarapa was the last one ever held under the old class and competition rules. A year later, almost as a wake for the old days and old boats, the Takapuna Boating Club, the original stronghold of the Zeddie, held an open single-handed series for several of the classes whose arrival had spelled the end of the Cornwell Cup: OK Dinghies, Finns, and Contenders. The revolution had well and truly begun.

I-class – the 'butterboxes'

The Idle Along was the frequent butt of two unflattering nicknames. This was partly because of its shape — hard-chined and squarish, and wide for its length — and partly because of the kahikitea that was soon adopted as its favourite construction timber, but also because it arrived late on the centreboarder scene, and thus had to put up with derogatory remarks from supporters of its class neighbours who were anxious about the effect the interloper might have on their numbers.

The first and most widespread nickname was 'butterbox', after the 'white pine' of which many Idle Alongs were built — an odourless timber that had for many years been used commercially to make bulk butter containers. The second name was 'aircraft carrier', simply because of the I-class proportions, squarish shape, and wide flat decks. But the unkindly nicknames seem to have done the class no great harm.

By the time Alf Harvey put on paper the drawings and specifications for the first Idle Along, there had been some ten years of club and contest experience in the other three classes for him to draw on, in addition to his first-hand knowledge of the capabilities required of small boats in Wellington's notoriously windy conditions.

Alf Harvey had built and sailed a Zeddie, *Shirley*, named after the first of his four daughters, in the years between 1927, when he laid out the lines of the Idle Along, and 1930, when he and others built the first two. He would have been well aware of the constraints involved when he set out the specifications for materials, construction, rig, and sails, so as to allow for the vagaries of amateur construction, and yet achieve close enough end results to ensure that the competition on the water would be between sailors rather than builders.

In the 1920s, before he became a full-time sail-maker, Alf had worked as a window dresser for Whitcombe and Tombs, the bookshop on Wellington's fashionable Lambton Quay. This may seem an unusual occupation from which to develop small-boat designing skills, but it meant that he had early access to overseas yachting publications and the ideas that were expressed in them – and was perhaps even aware of Uffa Fox's views on planing dinghies.

As with the design of the P-class and Zeddies, Alf Harvey had no serious intention of creating a boat for national competition. (This was in sharp contrast to the origins of the X-class, where designing a boat for serious, widespread competition seems to have been in mind from the outset.) It is inconceivable that he could have foreseen the rapid and widespread growth of the Idle Along fleet when he built the first of them, although he may have had an inkling of it by 1932, when he gave its drawings and specifications, already much in demand, to the Wellington Provincial Yachting Association to distribute and administer.

The first national interprovincial contest in the I-class took place in 1936 at the Heretaunga Boating Club, on the northern shore of Wellington Harbour. Only four provinces were represented, though more had been invited, and the Bay of Plenty crew won in the original *Idle Along*, which had been lent to them by Alf Harvey.

▶ Too late to save them from virtual extinction as a national class enjoying an annual competition, the Idle Alongs eventually adopted the trapeze for its forward hand. This boat is rising up onto the plane in quite moderate conditions, its crew out on the wire holding the spinnaker sheet and its skipper ever watchful of the mainsail, the jib, and the proximity of the spinnaker boom to the forestay.

▲ In a very strong northerly in 1934, Wellington's very new Idle Along fleet gathered at Worser Bay to compete for the Reid Shield. Alf Harvey sailed his *Idle Along* (I 2 in this picture from the beach) to third place. Everyone is reefed down, and many have their headsails set from the stemhead in order to reduce loads on the bowsprit.

In the first six years of its existence the class had achieved a remarkable reputation amongst local sailors. One notable event was a widely reported 26-boat race at the Worser Bay Boating Club in 1934, on a day when other sailing on the harbour, keelers included, was cancelled. The original *Idle Along* took part, sailed by its designer and builder, in wind strengths which had all competitors using reduced sail. Only six boats finished, the others having returned to the beach, but that the class was out on the water and held an inter-club race in such conditions was an impressive performance, and much enhanced its popularity.

By the time of the first national contest, there were some 40 boats registered with the Wellington Yachting Association. But already there was debate about boats not meeting the measurement requirements. Though the Idle Along had been designed for amateur construction, they were not easy to get right, especially in their much-curved forward sections. As a result of this, each club where members were building and racing the class found it necessary to appoint measurers and to report their findings to the Wellington Provincial Yachting Association, where the class was administered.

National contests also became the occasion of national conferences attended by provincial delegates. At these conferences the procedures for the control and administration of the class were established and amended – with much strident debate soon becoming the norm.

Race control, in terms of the number of races to be held, the starting arrangements, courses, points systems, protest procedures, and the racing rules, all developed over the years alongside the class control processes. These developments eloquently illustrate the way sailing and racing fast light boats profoundly influenced New Zealand yachting in general. As time went by, the procedures became more and more in line with international standards and those racing under them thus more familiar with them. Once New Zealanders began taking part in international competition, this experience proved invaluable.

In the innocent days of pre-war small-boat sailing, local boats were available to be borrowed by those who were unable to bring their own. A newspaper article published just prior to this first contest expressed concern that sailors from other classes might obtain Idle Alongs simply so they could participate in provincial trials, and thus possibly win representation in a class not generally considered to be their own. Similar concerns were to be raised much later, and with much rancour on occasions.

That first 1936 Idle Along championship was decided over five races on a simple points system, as were those for the class over the ensuing three years. But the watershed season for Idle Alongs and for all four stepping-stone classes was the summer of 1939–40. This was not only because the war had just begun, and it was for some sailors the last championship they would take part in for the foreseeable future (and perhaps forever), but also because it had been agreed by *all* the class administrators to hold their 1940 championships on Wellington Harbour as part of Wellington Province's centennial celebrations.

The Sanders, Moffat, Cornwell, and Tauranga Cups were all competed for in conjunction with Wellington's traditional Anniversary Regatta in late January, though they were held at different times and on different parts of the harbour. The definitive rules for the Moffat Cup contest were adopted by its conference of delegates at these championships.

Sixteen provincial districts were identified in the rules, and it was set down that the winning province had the right to hold the next contest on its home waters – though this right could be foregone (as was to be the case several times over the ensuing years) with the agreement of the Wellington Association as Controlling Body for the class.

Plans and specifications for the class were not to be changed without agreement by a majority of the delegates at the conference, and all crew members were required to be financial members of the club to which they belonged.

Construction tolerances were set down, but though either sliding gunter or Bermuda masts were permitted, no hollow spars were allowed. It was specifically stated that spinnaker sheets were allowed to be carried to leeward of the forestay rather than to windward of it, after years of this practice being forbidden, due to the belief that it was unseamanlike. (Yet another small step had been taken in the process of making small boats sail faster!) By these 1940 Rules, what became known as the Highet points system, based on the formula $200/N+1$ (where N = the placing), was adopted for the contest series, as were the racing rules of England's Royal Yachting Association.

At this contest, too, it was ruled that the date of the I-class national championships was to be arranged to fit in with other national contests. (Co-ordinating with the dates for the P-class championship, with which class the Idle Along seems to have been linked since its beginnings, was not specifically mentioned.)

▲ Bob Williamson's Idle Along *Ricochet* won the Moffat Cup for Wellington in 1957 and 1958. She is seen here planing across Evans Bay, three-up in a brisk northerly, and heading straight for Mount Victoria in the distance. The class rules always allowed a choice of two or three in the crew. Deciding how many to have was frequently difficult, especially in Wellington's gusty conditions, and making the right choice was often vital to winning.

▲ Handwritten in white ink on dark green paper, this 1932 specification accompanied the one sheet of drawings as the authorised documents setting out the requirements for boats to be accepted as true Idle Alongs by the Wellington Provincial Yacht and Motor Boat Association. The hull was required to be 'all New Zealand timber'. Over the years, this specification was updated and amended, and the plans revised, most significantly at the time of the Centennial Contest in 1940 and when John Spencer drew the plywood version in the 1960s.

From 1940 onwards (with the exception of the war years), the PZIX-classes were the subject of often fiercely contested representative age-group trials in early summer, with contestants sailing relatively low-cost and nearly identical boats on their home waters. The national championships, equally fiercely contested, were held early in the New Year at locations all around the country. All in all, it was an almost perfect specification for the production of top-class boats, gear, skippers, and crews. And that is of course just what happened.

For more than 30 years, until the demise of the Moffat Cup in 1969, the Idle Along attracted its share of innovators. Despite the restrictions on design changes, numerous adjustments were achieved more or less within the required tolerances. The people responsible for the innovations were invariably the builders, both amateur and professional, and the young (or not so young) skippers and their crews. Many of the top Idle Along sailors went on to achieve recognition in competitive sailing in other classes, and at all levels of competition.

In 1946 the first Idle Along class national championship to be held in Auckland was won by Hugh England from Canterbury in *Nada*. As planned, the P-class Tanner and Tauranga Cup contests were held there at the same time.

In the years immediately after the war, the stepping-stone classes were co-ordinated and promoted around the country's various sailing centres in order to more firmly establish their fleets and their reputation as the class to go for to get fair, inexpensive, and well-run competition.

Ten provinces were represented in the 1947 contest at Lyttelton. It was agreed at that contest that Otago should be the venue in 1948, to celebrate its centenary year, and Auckland won the contest on Otago Harbour. Peter Mander became class national champion in a race-off with the Auckland entry on the Waitemata Harbour at Westhaven in 1949.

Revised class rules were adopted in 1947, confirming, amongst other things, the introduction of five-flag starts on a line at right angles to the wind, and the Highet points system over a five-race series, with the right of challenge for any boat having beaten the points leader on three occasions after five races. Added to the class rules was the requirement that 'under no circumstances is Nylon material to be used in sails for the contest'.

The 1948 conference minutes were the first to mention arrangements for measuring templates, though they were not the first to record debate over measurement matters and construction tolerances. These aspects of the restricted-design class were to become the source of much dissension over the years as builders, who were almost always owner-skippers as well, sought performance advantage within the rules.

These templates were used at the contest in Auckland in 1949. No one other than the measurers and the representatives of the boat being measured were allowed to be present while the measuring was being carried out. This gives an indication of the difficulties that had been experienced on previous occasions when owners and delegates were present. At this contest also, floating judges were appointed for the first time – two of them, on separate boats; radio broadcasts of the races were arranged; all races were to start on the wind; and skippers, having signed for them, were provided with course charts for the series. Small-boat racing at the top level in New Zealand had become a sophisticated business for competitors and administrators alike.

▲ Oiled fabric jackets with kapok-filled buoyancy panels front and back were the approved form of life jackets for decades in New Zealand. Two of the crew of this Idle Along are wearing the approved type, the effective lifespan of which was about one season, the third has on a home-made jacket of darker material.

▲ This view of an Idle Along class representative trial race in Evans Bay, Wellington, in 1949 reveals the wind strength, not only by the reefed-down mainsails on all the boats, but also by the wet bottom areas of all their sails.

▶ Idle Along I 6 is the ex-Canterbury boat *Myth*, and I 111 is *Windhover* from Wellington. They are competing in the class championship race at the Paremata Easter Regatta in the year *Myth*, sailed by Clem Gestro won the Moffat Cup for Wellington.

— 65 —

The Evans Bay Yacht & Motor Boat Club built a surveyor-accurate plastered concrete slab with which to measure by offsets the hull forms of Idle Alongs prior to the representative trials. Here Hugh Poole's Loraine *is undergoing measurement watched by a number of interested club members.*

Barney Scully and Grahame Anderson at the EBYMBC jetty in 1950, modelling standard centreboarder clothing and conditions – tousled hair and sodden rugby jerseys.

Much of the history of the class and of its lively annual contest conferences is illuminated by the heated pre-race debates which took place at the 1951 contest. Such debates frequently took place in each of the stepping-stone classes. They were an essential element in the process by which small-boat development, race management techniques, and competitive attitudes, having been well established during the 1920s and 1930s (and having lain dormant for five seasons from 1940 to 1945), were developed and honed in the decade following the Second World War, largely in isolation from the rest of the world.

Reports of the Idle Along conferences for the period, and often the newspaper reports as well, were full of the debates, which were often heated and occasionally damaging to the advancement of the class in the eyes of many, but mostly vigorous and well informed. They reveal much about the New Zealand attitude to the ideas that were being put forward and the advances being made. In the PZIX-classes, design innovation was subservient to the principles of even competition amongst skippers and crews in boats that were as close to equal as they could be (given their generally amateur construction).

The Lyttelton championship in 1951 was the first contest at which the lead delegates were described as 'managers', a further sign of maturity in representative sailing matters. Graham Mander's Canterbury entry *Whisper* was rejected at Lyttelton, because of the boat's unusual construction: it had been built to dimensions which appeared to take maximum advantage of the permitted tolerances. As a result, he had to sail a borrowed boat at the contest. The *Whisper* controversy coloured the whole event, and its ramifications greatly influenced Idle Along builders for years afterwards. Deliberately using tolerances to achieve what seemed to be greater speed, and deliberately arranging construction to achieve greater lightness, were by no means confined to the builders of the Canterbury boat, however.

The contest at the Heretaunga Boating Club in 1952 featured sophisticated and well set-out alternating windward-leeward and triangular courses, with a flagged launch to stand by as an indicator of the location of the weather mark; but the problem of *Whisper* and its shape and construction had to be dealt with before racing could get under way. After meticulous measurement, six boats, including the Canterbury entry *Whisper*, were rejected by the conference and six alternatives were found. Then it was discovered that the measuring templates themselves were incorrect, and to everyone's relief it was decided to accept all those boats previously rejected.

Unsuccessful attempts were made to impose a minimum weight limit in 1954, but the main bone of contention at this contest was the fully-battened Auckland mainsail. It prompted serious concern at the conference, and there was a formal proposal that 4 ft be the maximum permissible batten length in future.

At Lake Brunner in 1955, in circumstances reminiscent of those at the 1952 contest, every boat but one failed to pass measurement. The templates were again found to be faulty, so all the rejected boats were reinstated. The matter of sail-batten lengths was resolved by adopting a revised mainsail plan setting out the location limits for a maximum of six battens, as well as their maximum widths and lengths, and in addition outlawing sails made of 'silk (Japara excepted) Nylon and related synthetics'.

Permitted materials had been set out in the original plans and specifications for the class. The hull had to be constructed of New Zealand timbers, spars were allowed to be of oregon, and sail material was optional, including japara, though silk was forbidden.

In response to the possibility of strangers to the class entering and winning provincial trials and perhaps the national contest, a ninety-day provincial residential rule was introduced in 1956. That year, the NZYF set out the definitions for what it called 'Established' and 'National' classes, in order to cope with the number of new classes appearing throughout the country. It also recognised the need for the recognition of Class Associations in yachting administration.

Solid-drawn stainless-steel rigging arrived at the 1958 contest, with the conference allowing its use despite expressions of concern about its tensile strength. Restrictions on sail materials were also removed in 1958. Nylon and Terylene sails were used on several boats in 1959 – with some considerable discussion about the need to enforce the IYRU requirement for boat identification on spinnakers. It was reported at that conference that only 12 planked boats had been built in 1958.

In 1960, John Spencer was instructed to draw up plans for plywood construction, following a proposal made at the 1958 contest. This had been prompted by concern at the decline in popularity of Idle Alongs, coupled with a belief that greater ease of construction would boost the class. A minimum hull weight for plywood boats was imposed, and the new

▲ Arguments at national contests over the measurement of boats led to the use of moulds into which boats were placed and checked. At the Moffat Cup for Idle Alongs at Lake Brunner in 1955, following just such an argument, Hugh Poole, the Wellington team's manager, was hung in effigy in the measuring shed for his part in it.

November 30

JOHN SPENCER
DEEMING ROAD,
R.D. 1, RUSSELL,
BAY OF ISLANDS, N.Z.

Dear Barney,
What a pleasant surprise to recieve your letter and pic's of Why Not. It would have been your (younger?) brother I found when I visited. I remember him showing me pieces (chisel, bedsaw, or such like) you had made first in Rimu but replaced after obtaining some boatbuilding timber (Kauri perhaps). Remember Jim Synnott from those days and he's not been unheard of since — R Class particularly.

I should have guessed since that Why Not was designed by Wm F Crosby. The Snipe parentage was obvious had I known in 1945 what a Snipe was. I had picked her to very likely have been a U.S. design or your own inspired by their sort of dinghy.

In those days I lived near the top of Mt Victoria and was one of the Balena Bay Boys — Bill Yates, David Catchpole, Graham Anderson, Bill McQueen, Phil Drucker and myself. After I left Wellington end of 1946 you

◀ John Spencer wrote to Barney Scully in 1990, recalling the origins of his interest in sailing and in plywood. This is a page from his letter.

drawings included advice on how best to build the boats in the new materials. Though it was given consideration, a proposal to allow hollow masts stepped on deck was rejected on the advice of John Spencer, who said mast stresses were such that solid spars were desirable and that better support was obtained from the continued use of a mast box.

The Olympic points system, over a five-race series rather than the seven favoured internationally, was proposed for the Moffat Cup in 1960, some six years before it was ratified by the International Yacht Racing Union. However, the drop-race clause, by which competitors were allowed to omit their worst performance from their points tally, was rejected after much debate, because it was seen to provide an excuse for bad sailing. The old-fashioned 200/N+1 Highet points system continued to be used until the end.

◀ Built to an English design by Ken and Barney Scully at Shelly Bay in Wellington, the plywood centreboarder *Why Not* was noticed by John Spencer and inspired him to use the material as the basis for his early designs of small boats and later designs of big boats. *Why Not* is shown here being rigged on the beach at Shelly Bay, on the eastern side of Evans Bay.

At the 1962 contest in Wellington, the Auckland delegates' proposal that hollow masts stepped on deck be allowed was again rejected, as was their suggestion that the contest become inter-port. The latter proposal was an attempt to sustain interest in the class and increase the numbers taking part in its national contests, for which provincial representative entries had fallen to nine. This idea was accepted the following year when only eight boats arrived.

At a time when 25 boats took part in the first one-of-a-kind regatta in Auckland, only six provincial entries were received for the 1964 Moffat Cup. It was resolved to hand over control of the contest from the WPYMBA to the NZYF, and to adopt the Auckland inter-port proposal rejected in 1963. At the 1965 conference, hollow spars were at last permitted, though the use of aluminium was refused, as it was again in 1967.

The Auckland delegates, perhaps more aware of what was happening in yachting all around them, led in many of the proposals to adapt the class and make it more attractive to sailors. They were also no doubt encouraged to do so by the example of the well-organised Auckland P-class clubs, which had commercially-made kitsets available. (OK Dinghy kitsets were to come on to the market in 1968.) At the 1965 conference, the Auckland delegates were asked to look into designing a new rig and sail plan in order to further this adaptation idea.

The Aucklanders duly brought along their experimental mainsail to the contest in 1966 and it was demonstrated at the conclusion of the championships, but nothing appears to have come of it. That such radical changes were necessary was made clear to supporters of the traditional classes when Rothmans added the Olympic Dragon and the OK Dinghy to their list of sponsored classes – at that time consisting of the Finn and Flying Dutchman – and the era of advertising came into full swing, passing by the stepping-stone classes as it did so.

At the 1967 contest in Timaru, nine boats took part and it may have seemed that all was well, but only six went to Rotorua to compete for the Cup in 1968, and of those six the Auckland entry arrived very late. Taranaki, who were the winners in Rotorua, asked for the 1969 contest to be held at their home port of New Plymouth.

Taranaki won again in 1969 on their home waters, but it was the end of competition for the Moffat Cup. Though nothing was formally recorded in the 1969 minutes, they were the last record of proceedings for the contest. There was no ceremony, no forewarning – just silence, then and afterwards.

Later that year the WPYMBA, in recognising and trying to understand the trends, optimistically described the Z-class as 'the largest crewed yacht class in New Zealand and the fastest growing', and said sadly that 'unless at least eight entries were received, the next I-class national contest would be abandoned and this would certainly mean the end of the Moffat Cup'. Though it was the end of the Moffat Cup, it did not signal the end of the Idle Along. Much as in the manner of the Z-class, and in an atmosphere of nostalgia which has a renewed appreciation of the 'real' materials of which they are made, the Idle Along has seen a modest revival in recent times. There is now an Idle Along Association for owners and class enthusiasts, and in January 1998 ten boats competed in a five-race series on Auckland Harbour for a new trophy, named after their designer, and presented to the winner by two of his daughters.

The Xies

Fourteen feet long, plus a bowsprit, the four-man X-class was clinker built. It had narrow strip planking lapped and riveted to bent ribs that were shaped to form a compound-curved hull form of much greater technical complexity than those of the other stepping stones.

The boat had a pivoting steel centreplate, an open cockpit (without the watertight compartments built into the P, Z, and I-class boats), and rather narrow side decks. These differences made the most senior of the stepping stones a much more demanding boat. It was not only demanding to build, but also to sail and to keep free of water and upright in heavy weather – in many ways, though old fashioned ones, it was an ideal culmination in training for what was to come in small-boat development.

Despite this complexity, or, given the Kiwi attitude to such challenges, perhaps because of it, many X-class boats were built by sailors. Though they could certainly not be described as professional boatbuilders, they had in many cases built their own P-class and Z-class boats, and were by no means amateurs at the task.

Often crew members took part in the construction, fitting out, and rigging phases of the boat they intended to race together. By these means other skills were brought to the boatshed, adding to those of the owner-skipper.

▲ Of these six Xies running downwind in close proximity, X 2 & X 3 have begun to move ahead, taking advantage of a breeze from the right-hand side of the course which has not yet reached the other four. Every boat is gaff rigged, every mainsail is made of narrow cloths, and every spinnaker is set to windward of the forestay. The fact that every main boom is tilted up at an angle well above the horizontal, which means that not one boat has been fitted with a kicker, confirms it is an early photograph.

▼ Tacking downwind and making up for the greater distance sailed by sailing quicker on the reaches, where conditions are more favourable for planing, only became fashionable when boats themselves were built light enough to plane readily. So the boat way out to port in this Wellington harbour picture might just be about to gybe and sail across in front of X 2 & X 10 on a plane and beat them to the bottom mark. X 2, being sailed directly downwind to the mark, is *Betty*, winner of the Sanders Cup three years in a row in the late 1920s when she was sailed by George Andrews of Canterbury.

The X-class was originally established as a one-design boat, based on the hull form of the early 1920s Bailey-built classic *Rona*, with very little in the way of tolerances allowed. But in 1936, it was decided to revert to restricted-class status, after George Andrews' *Betty* from Canterbury had outclassed even the legendary *Rona*. Though creating its own problems for class administrators, the greater freedom for designers became a significant element in the success of the X-class over the ensuing 35 years, since it avoided much of the heat and noise of contest-measurement debate which preoccupied one-design classes at almost every national contest over the years.

As early as 1921, as Wheatley and Reid put it in their 1946 *History of the Sanders Cup*:

> No longer were the boats mere training ships for the younger generation of yachtsmen. Old hands left their big keel boats and got out their sweaters and old pants from bottom shelves to meet the challenge of the lively 14-footers. Men's work this, and a serious business.

Seven years later, all five provincial representatives competing in the 1928 Sanders Cup at Stewart Island sailed boats which had been professionally built. This expensive trend added greatly to the popularity of the alternative, the Idle Alongs, when they arrived on the scene in Wellington in 1930, because their simple, hard-chined construction meant they were easier for amateurs to build.

Once the I-class had arrived, there were never as many X-class boats sailing as there were Idle Alongs. For senior centreboard sailors who were not skilled boat-builders and who could not afford professional construction, the complexities of the clinker-built X-class hull were daunting to say the least, with its steam-bent ribs and long, narrow, shaped planks, as well as the riveting together of them all. The Idle Along flourished because it met the sailors' needs, and they could build it themselves.

But many X-class boats were nevertheless built by amateurs. Having a professionally-built boat was not a necessary requirement for success at the national championships – sailing skills, and hull and rig arrangements mattered much more.

A metal X-class mould was produced for the Sanders Cup contest in 1933. (It took almost another 20 years before one was built for the I-class.) The mould was an accurate

▲ Late in the history of the X-class, when fibreglass hulls were standard, Hugh Poole, sailing *Charade*, won the Sanders Cup for Wellington on several occasions. Here he is on Auckland Harbour, sitting inboard across the stern with his crew out on their trapezes, all three men concentrating on sailing the boat up to its maximum reaching performance.

measurement device, used to overcome arguments about whether boats did or did not lie within the tolerances laid down by the class rules.

Six provinces contested the first Sanders Cup series after the Second World War, with Auckland's *Davina* winning five races. By 1949, the reputation of the class as the most important in New Zealand centreboard yachting had weakened to the extent that a correspondent to *Sea Spray* that year was prompted to write:

> It is frequently stated that the Sanders Cup is the blue riband of New Zealand yachting. This may have been so once, but I venture to suggest that either the winner of the Cornwell Cup or the winner of the Moffat Cup must produce form that more entitle him to hold the 'blue riband' if there is such a thing. The class of boats used in both the latter contests put a premium on skill. The present restrictions allow for so little variation in hull form that performance is largely governed by the skill of the skipper and crew in sailing practice and race preparation. This is borne out by the fact that several quite old boats are still in national class.

The significance of this comparison was not lost on small-boat sailors. The more easily built and more evenly matched Idle Alongs and Zeddies thrived as a result, and their builders and crews quickly learned about high-quality competition and what it demanded of them.

The 1956 Sanders Cup was the last one to be contested for by the traditional wooden clinker-built X-class fourteen-footers. In 1956, a design competition was held for a replacement in fibreglass. Graham Mander's design won, and boats from the resulting mould contested the cup from

▼ This Canterbury representative Xie is one of the fibreglass hulls designed by Graham Mander. She is making something of a fuss on a reach under spinnaker, her bow very high, on a bright sunny day.

The Javelin class eventually took over the mantle once proudly worn by the X-class as the self-proclaimed 'blue riband' of New Zealand small-boat sailing. This one is being sailed flat and fast to windward by its two-man crew in windy conditions. Bright sunshine is making the sea sparkle and showing up the full-length battens on the tall, narrow mainsail.

The Xie *Charade*, three-times winner of the Sanders Cup, has been refurbished to showcase perfection by its builder-skipper Hugh Poole. The boat now displays every detail of finish, fittings and rig of the era in which it competed.

1957 until 1970. But the fibreglass boats never really found favour, at least in part because their commercially produced one-off mould prohibited amateur construction. This constraint, which had not been the intention of the competition, led to much argument, and at the 1970 contest it was clear that the fibreglass boats were about to disappear from the competition.

A year after the demise of the I-class in 1969, owners of X-class boats voted to make competition for the Sanders Cup open to all 14 ft NZYF-recognised national dinghy classes. It was obvious to supporters of the X-class that the John Spencer-designed Javelin, by then spreading into several sailing centres, would be the only other serious contender for the cup on its 50th anniversary in 1971.

In the event, only three provinces were represented at the first 'open' Sanders Cup contest, held in strong winds off the Heretaunga Boating Club in 1971. All three entries were sailing John Spencer's 1958-designed plywood Javelins.

Within a year of the demise of the Idle Along as a National Class, the X-class had ended its 49-year run. From then on, the Javelins contested the Sanders Cup, though they also continued to compete each year in a separate contest for their own national trophy.

In a way which echoes the mood of the Z and I-class 'revivalists', there is at least one Xie still in pristine condition. The fibreglass *Charade*, in which Hugh Poole won the Sanders Cup four seasons in a row between 1967 and 1970, has been fully and elegantly refurbished by its skipper with the intention of its being displayed in Auckland's Maritime Museum.

With the virtual demise of all the stepping-stone classes but the P-class, the way was open for the rise to prominence, and eventual domination of the small-boat scene, by the already burgeoning range of new, fast, light centreboard classes.

New Zealand designers, builders, riggers, sailmakers, and competitors were to find in them an outlet for their talents, which had been frustrated during the latter years of the long reign of the traditional classes. The serial arrangements of the traditional classes had developed their skills to international levels, but those skills now surpassed the demands of the boats which had served the purpose for some 50 years.

▲ The Zeddies in this photograph handsomely demonstrate the planing capability and attitude of the class. They are part of the modern resurgence of interest in the class. Some of these new boats took part in what, for a few years, their supporters called a 'World Championship', but the national sailing organisation put an end to that, saying there was no proper basis or authority for such a title.

▲ With the same sail number as the original, *Slipaway Revival* planes in the open sea off Plimmerton. The Zeddie's newness is given away by the shape and set of her sails in this lively photograph. The class was capable of planing from the beginning, more than 70 years before this picture was taken.

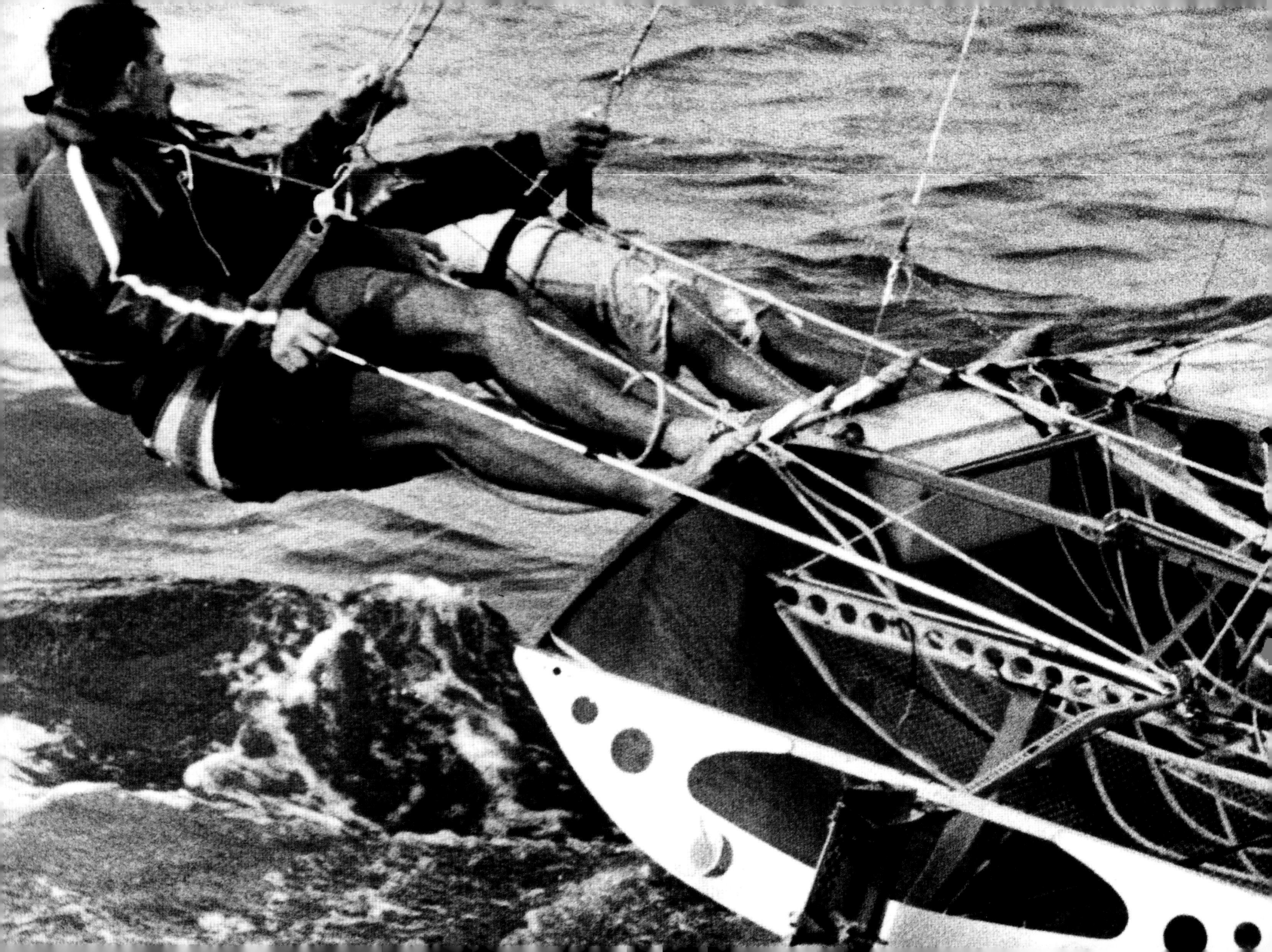

Chapter 4
Technology transfer

That things were changing, and that the sport of sailing was booming, was most impressively demonstrated on the occasion of the Auckland Anniversary Regatta in January 1950, the summer before the beginning of that remarkable decade of diversification, 1951–61.

Sea Spray, rather carried away by it all, and as firmly focused as ever on the Auckland scene, called it 'The Regatta of the Century', and described it as 'the greatest yachting event ever to take place in Auckland's or New Zealand's history'. Some 1300 boats took part in the 80 races held over the two days of the regatta. The sport of sailing was beginning to show the results of the application of new techniques, new materials, and new enthusiasm, following the wartime and post-war shortages of all but the last of those things.

The changes that came about in the 1950s in the world of New Zealand sailing eventually turned into a revolution. In the early years the process of revolutionary change took place alongside the steady evolution of the established classes. During the first phase of this process, small-boat sailors had more and more classes from which to choose, but inevitably as time went on there were fewer and fewer boats registered in each of the traditional classes. Nevertheless, as we have already seen, the stepping-stone classes learned from and adopted ideas that had been developed by the newer classes, while at the same time teaching some of them the competitive and race administration techniques they had evolved in their various contest systems. Inevitably, though, the new classes took their toll on PZIX, leading to a steep

> Drilled-out struts and slender bracing keep *Smirnoff's* thin-shelled hull in shape, and formed blocks of foam keep it afloat should a capsize occur. The cockpit is a maze of ropes all let off to the trapezing extensions of the sailing machine.

▲ This Flying Dutchman appears to have burst upwards out of a wave, but the appearance is deceptive. Her New Zealand crew have just sailed through a crest and are about to experience the thump of the next wave as the bow comes down again. Keeping the boat moving fast through the water, and keeping it upright with the sails properly trimmed, is made even more difficult when the sea surface is as rough as this.

▼ This unfinished eighteen-footer hull provides an excellent illustration of the way lightness is pursued. The narrow, lightweight timber strip planking has yet to be trimmed off at the stern, and the deck has yet to be fitted to the hull. This view reveals the elegant simplicity achieved in the designer/builder determination to reduce weight. Every shape and junction is arranged to provide maximum strength with a minimum of material.

decline in numbers and the eventual demise of the stepping-stone system. Today, only the P-class remains, and though it is still the first step for many young sailors, what follows it is a very different path.

In December 1966, an article was published in *Sea Spray*, looking back on the 21 years since it was first published in 1945. It was already describing the changes as 'radical', but there were another two decades of revolution yet to happen:

> In five years after the war some radical changes were already being felt – in 10 years they had become well established – in 21 years, yachting in New Zealand has been almost completely changed in character, and probably to a far greater extent than any other country. As well as new blood and new ideas, a higher standard of living and closer international ties have all contributed. In many ways the changes have been more like a revolution than evolution.

The technological aspects of that revolution are the subject of this chapter, while the impact of new classes introduced from overseas and developed at home will be described in the one that follows.

Losing weight

Building your own boat, rigging it, fitting it out with spars and sails and gear, much of which has been home-made, making it plane and go well to windward, and then doing all those things better than your local and national competitors, has been an ethos widespread amongst New Zealand small-boat sailors since the opportunity to do all those things for themselves first became available to them in the early 1920s.

Avoiding the complexity and near-professional building skills required of clinker-built boats such as the X-class was for many sailors, especially the young and non-affluent, a major factor in choosing which class to compete in. As we have already seen, the Zeddie and the Idle Along were popular because of the attractive combination of being comparatively simple to build and being assuredly able to plane.

Once the boat is built, though, the benefits conferred by simpler construction vanish. Then, all factors beyond hull construction become much more equal across the classes.

Lightness of construction thus became a primary aim in all New Zealand centreboard classes, largely because it makes sustained planing more likely, and sustained planing makes winning races much more likely.

During the Second World War a new material had been developed that was both strong and light: waterproof plywood. It took some years for quality marine-grade plywood to become generally available in New Zealand, because of post-war import restrictions. But when it did appear in quantity, it proved easy for the amateur boatbuilder to work with, and it was adopted by the stepping-stone classes one by one.

In April 1951, *Sea Spray* reviewed a book from Rudder Publishing in the US, *20 Plywood Boats and How to Build Them*, and commented positively on the new material:

> The publishers do not suggest that plywood is the answer to all boat building problems, but do suggest that properly designed craft in a wide variety of styles can be durably made of plywood.

For New Zealand sailors, in big boats and small, and rather sooner than for recreational sailors in other countries, these were prophetic words indeed.

Significant though it seemed at the time, the availability of marine ply was just the first of many innovations that affected small-boat construction. After plywood, another new construction material followed that was to profoundly influence the way New Zealanders built and sailed small boats: moulded fibreglass. Its use led to the production of many nearly identical hulls off a common form, which conferred a uniformity on the final product that wooden boats lacked. The material was first referred to in New Zealand sailing publications in a 1949 article in *Sea Spray*, in which the headline expression used was the Americanism 'Plastic Hulled Sailboats'. It is evident from the language used that the moulding technique, which had been developed during the Second World War, was new to the country.

▶ Aircraft-like in its drilled-out and spidery delicacy, the framework of this International Moth is built like that for exactly the same reasons, the pursuit of lightness, strength, and speed. Not an ounce of unnecessary weight is carried. Even the corners of the timbers will have been arrissed off to save weight.

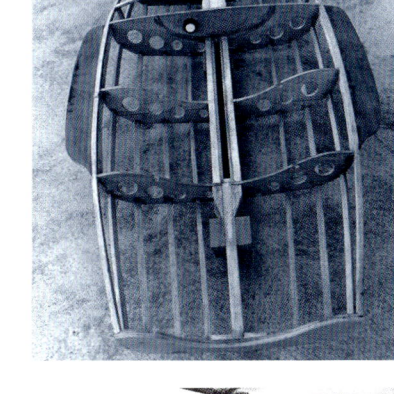

▶ Looking like a mockup of exquisitely symmetrical industrial design, a space ship perhaps, this International Moth hull rests on somebody's driveway as though it were about to take off. The feather-light boat is actually facing away from the camera.
The elegant wing-like metallic attachment in the foreground is the tiller extension/tiller/rudder assembly. The longitudinal slot is the centrecase and the bridge across it is the traveller. The fittings near their forward edges of the linking extensions are sail- and sheet-control cleats. The Moth class provides an outlet for innovative and skilled sailors to put their ideas into effect.

▶ The 14 ft single-handed international Laser class is a unique case of a standard-production fibreglass boat built by the hundreds of thousands and sailed all over the world. Precision moulding of the two halves 'hull and deck' and the standardisation of sails, spars, foils, and fittings ensures that every boat is as identical with the others as can be achieved. Even dark-colour pigment is considered to add to the weight of the fibreglass mouldings, and for this reason the most sought-after colours seem to be white and cream. The most even-handed one-design competition in the world is obtained by such construction methods. Not originally intended for use as a full-on competition boat, the Bruce Kirby-designed 14 foot single-hander has a reputation for inflicting a leg complaint known as 'Laser-knee' on those who campaign them for too long.

▲ Fibreglass construction of a high order not only ensures standardised boats, and therefore standardised competition in which the skills of the sailor make the difference, but in the Laser it also ensures the reliability of the generous built-in buoyancy so that, when capsizes occur, the boat floats high in the water and is readily righted. The Laser's shallow, self-draining cockpit means keeping the water out is almost a thing of the past. In the end though, it is often the stamina of the sailor which determines just how many capsizes can be survived! Strength counts too!

▼ The Tornado catamaran is one of the quickest in the New Zealand small-boat scene, and its standing as an Olympic class, especially as one in which New Zealanders have won both gold and silver Olympic medals in recent times, means that national representation is keenly fought for. This BNZ-sponsored boat, lifting its windward hull in quite light conditions, is sailing on Evans Bay, one of the windiest parts of Wellington Harbour.

> These hulls, fashioned over wooden molds, are made of fibreglass and resin. The fibreglass is applied in cloth and mat form. Four layers of cloth and mat are interspersed with applications of the resin, which is brushed and sprayed to form each hull shell ... It is placed in an oven heated to about 300 deg. and pressure is applied. After about two hours the 'cooking' process is completed. What takes place is a chemical (molecular) change in the resin, not involving the fibreglass, which acts only as a reinforcing agent. The shell is actually 'plastic'. An interesting fact is that it is translucent. In war service this material was called 'light armour'. It has very high strength. The surface hardness is said to be greater than that of aluminium and it can be hit with a sledge-hammer without signs of visible damage ... The result is a hull that is impervious to bugs and decay.

A promotional tone is evident in the article!

The top-of-the-page picture to *Sea Spray's* October 1967 article about foam sandwich construction, above a headline which described the method as 'Light and strong, simple to build ...' was an advance on the longstanding claim that 'the boat could be lifted by two men'. It showed Don Lidgard and Tony Bouzaid lifting the 12-footer *Query* with three fingers, and was a dramatic illustration of the weight-saving capabilities of polythene foam core.

The 1966 end-of-year issue of *Sea Spray* – as it happens, the very issue in which the advantages of foam sandwich construction were discussed – had this to say about the changes in materials which had occurred since the end of the Second World War:

> One of the most important factors in increased speed in all types of boat is weight – getting rid of it or putting it in the right place – and new building materials and techniques introduced since the war have contributed more to the revolution than anything else.
>
> Foremost of these is the introduction of good quality, marine grade plywood ... Allied to the use of ply was the introduction of resin glues and later of fibreglass and dynel sheathing, used in great quantities by N.Z. amateurs while professionals overseas were still thinking about it.
>
> Another method used by our amateur builders when there were few firms anywhere in the world doing it, was cold moulding. The basic technique has now spread to bigger and bigger boats where it is considered a logical development of the old 3-ply diagonal planking used on keelers at the beginning of the century.
>
> Other new methods include fibreglass reinforced plastic boats, which, after a shaky start, now appear in greater numbers every season ...

If there were to be only one illustration of the pursuit of lightness in small boats which pervaded the decade of the fifties, it would have to be the picture of Dave Marks' experimental clinker-built *Pathetic*, apparently designed to no particular class requirements but certainly designed for speed, being held overhead two-handed on someone's driveway. The September 1951 issue of *Sea Spray* which carried the illustration made no comment on the significance of the demonstration, but accompanying views of the boat show the designer's intense concern for lightness – to the point of absolute delicacy in the case of some major structural elements – evident in all aspects of *Pathetic*'s construction.

Another indication of the demand for weight reduction in small boats occurred in the same issue of the magazine as that which carries *Pathetic*'s impressive 'two-hands' demonstration. An advertisement for boat fittings in what is called a 'Tempered Light Metal', claimed to be lighter, stronger, and cheaper than brass, illustrates sister clips, jib hanks, cleats, snap shackles, and pulleys all made in the new material – presumably aluminium, but not identified as such.

In the July 1969 issue of *Sea Spray*, David Pardon, talking about both big and small boats, began his article about the next strong, light material, carbon fibre, with a succinct résumé:

> Fifty years ago racing craft had one thing in common: they were all built of wood. Design theory and construction techniques outstripped all progress in the materials field and only in the comparatively recent history of racing have science and industry combined to produce the rapid changes in fashion from clinker to steel, to aluminium, to fibreglass and now to combinations of foam and fibreglass, plywood and concrete.
>
> But what comes next? Is the progression from wood to metals and from metals to plastics likely to reverse? Is it back to aluminium's successor and to synthesised products of the timber industry? Or is there an alternative?…
>
> Generally speaking, a carbon-fibre reinforced plastic is approximately four times as strong as steel and a fraction of the weight. Its outstanding advantages over fibreglass are its greater tensile strength and, even more importantl, its rigidity, or 'stiffness' …
>
> Certainly for the yacht designer it seems to offer exciting possibilities and it will be interesting to see who takes the first step.

David Pardon wrote a similar article for the June 1970 issue of the magazine, this time about balsa-core construction, suggesting the material might best be used in early applications in New Zealand for deck and cabin elements on bigger boats.

▶ Sister clips, jib hanks, cleats, snap shackles, and simple pulleys are shown in this 1951 advertisement from *Sea Spray*. The metal from which they were made is described as 'Norwegian Rustless'. Though the word aluminium is not used, it must have been that alloy to be as strong and light as is claimed.

▼ Without apparent effort, Dave Marks holds aloft the hull of *Pathetic*, taking one stage further the claims to lightness often made for small boats in the days when Kiwi sailors mostly built their own.

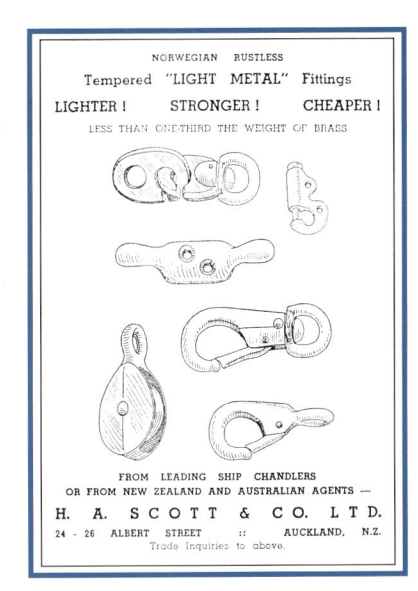

▼ This P-class has a reef in, its barefoot young helmsman is wearing a full-head-support life jacket, and his wind indicator is a piece of light cloth tied to the forestay. Seas coming aboard are a constant problem in such conditions, upwind and down. The vee-shaped coamings just foreward of the mast cannot keep all of the water out of the cockpit. Though the P-class is small, the weight of water it can hold profoundly affects performance. Bailing that water out again is absolutely necessary if boatspeed is to be maximised. The classic hiking posture shown here will have to be interrupted now and then in order to do so.

The twenty years of development between 1950 and 1970 had seen considerable advances and much complexity in material choices for boatbuilding, and New Zealanders took great advantage of them all in building faster and lighter boats, both small and not so small.

Keeping dry

There is no point in building a boat light if it cannot be *kept* light when sailing in conditions when water comes aboard. So ways of getting the water out again are of great importance if boat speed is to be maintained.

In P-class boats, the competitive sailor has always had to learn efficient ways to bail out the water from its tiny cockpit while not affecting performance. Dealing with this has long been a particularly important part of the skill of sailing P-class boats in heavy weather.

Bailing the water coming aboard is important in all such boats, of course. But using hand-held bailers on the outside end of a stick or piece of cord attached to the boat, which has long been the technique used in P-class and Zeddies, has been superseded by much more sophisticated methods. For years, Xies and Idle Alongs used hand-operated plunger pumps of metal or wood attached to the aft end of the centrecase or set up to leeward on each tack. Crew numbers were such that one of them could be spared from full-time boat handling to be a 'bailer boy', working the pump.

The April 1951 issue of *Sea Spray*, in a delightful passage redolent of the Kiwi 'Number 8 wire' view of life, said:

> There are some who claim that a little bilge water helps a boat through a short sea, but most agreed that it was a good thing to be able to get a boat quickly dry when required. The bailer, (by which is meant a bucket or similar) be it fancy in shape and fitted with a handle, is still an antiquated device. You cannot bail effectively and still stack out to best advantage. When there is no handle at all, as is often the case, you just can't afford to bail when the going is tough. The bailer is reduced to a purely off-the-wind weapon, while the privileged are enjoying a quiet smoke ... Your pump needs to be designed to fit into that part of the boat where the water collects ... and discharge down the center case. Reliability is important; that generally means good valves. A piece of little brother's schoolbag will do, but it should be pliable, well fitted, and the valve ports should be as large as you can make them if you want to shift the water quickly and easily. A large spout helps, too ... Lastly, a plea for the much-maligned pump-hand. By adding an extra two inches to the length of

the pump you can have a simple gland of cotton waste. If this is done, the pump hand will not be compelled to receive half the discharge over himself ... Four rubber stops, familiar sights on the under side of toilet seats, complete the job. They not only allow the water to flow easily into the pump, but also protect your paintwork and planking from damage.

Later, across-the-boat lever-action pumps mounted low on the cockpit floor did the job more efficiently and enabled the pumping crew-member to remain further outboard as he dealt with the water. Later still, flap-controlled ducts leading from the aft end of the cockpit through to the stern, and then Venturi-action self-bailers – the latter borrowed, along with several other innovations, from Canterbury's R-class – made it possible to remove the water efficiently with little direct involvement from the crew.

Though the ducts only worked when sailing downwind, the venturis did so upwind as well, especially once their design had been improved to the point where the effect could be obtained at relatively low speeds. In due course, they became part of the standard equipment in most small boats.

Surface improvements

The significance of hull finish on those parts of the boat in contact with the water was perhaps one of the less considered facets of speed improvement in the earlier years of the centreboard classes, though smoothness was recognised as important. Waxed paintwork – that is, a wax finish applied to carefully painted or varnished surfaces, no doubt spray-painted in the early calm morning hours when it could be afforded or arranged to be done inexpensively on a mates-rates basis, was still the norm well into the 1950s.

In due course, the advantages of a more scientific understanding of laminar and molecular flow along such surfaces became known and the practice of using 'wet and dry' sandpaper of something like 400-cut coarseness took hold. Nowadays, this sort of 'cut' surface finish is much used by those who pursue every conceivable speed-making technique.

As late as the mid-1960s, however, the technique was still only in the process of being accepted. Gordon Shepherd, the sales manager of the New Zealand branch of International Paints, said (with some care not to be dogmatic) in *Sea Spray* in November 1967:

▼ The Javelin *Topaz* has been laid on her side fully rigged, and this may have been done to get access to her sails and spars before launching. But it also reveals the hull bottom finish, which appears to be the graphite paint system that is believed to assist water flow along its surface. There are the almost inevitable scratches and patches in places. It may be that the crew have some burnishing of the graphite in mind to improve its condition and effectiveness.

It is generally agreed that first class results can be obtained by rubbing down an apparently smooth painted surface with abrasive paper of about 400 grade. This process produces a finish to the surface which is acceptable for most racing conditions. But now the doubt arises as to whether this surface can be improved or deteriorated by using *finer* abrasives to get an even finer surface or, ultimately, a polish.

One of the most satisfactory ways of testing the surface in relation to laminar flow conditions, is to flick a drop of water on to it; if the surface is such that the water spreads out under its own weight to a large patch, this is an indication that the surface will move very easily through the water.

…Over the years, enthusiastic yacht racing helmsmen have applied wax, silicone, graphite or something of this nature to the bottoms of their boats — but the number of successful helmsmen who use such preparations is very small indeed and if the results had been of any benefit, it is likely that the practice of using such materials would have continued and increased. All the evidence points the other way — so try the water droplet test and prove the point to yourself.

Gear changes

Patriotic Englishmen say the kicking strap – known as the boom vang to some – is a mechanism attributed to their own inventive designer-sailor, Uffa Fox. There are others, particularly New Zealanders it seems, who say otherwise. It is generally agreed that the mechanism began its life in dinghies. The 'strap' part reflects its relatively small-scale origins, of course. In bigger boats the boom vang has to be a much stronger and more complex arrangement (and on 'keelers' these days they are often hydraulic). But the original kicking-strap was a simple, pulley-enhanced, light but strong wire or rope system that was usually found sufficient for the task.

Those patriots who attribute the kicker to Uffa also say that it came into use in the early 1950s, when lighter aluminium booms replaced the heavy wooden ones which had better resisted the upward lift of the sail when sheets were eased on a reach or run. Those who used them early in New Zealand say that they were fitted on wooden booms well before the advent of alloy spars.

Whatever its origins, its purpose is to make the boat go faster by better presentation of the sails to the wind. It first came into use in small boats when it was realised that the round-the-course speed advantage their ability to plane gave them was further enhanced if the eased mainsail was held down as they did so. Not too far down, though, since allowing the

▼ There are various ways of applying sufficient force to the boom to enable the crew to keep it down when the mainsheet is eased. This P-class setup uses a pivot and pulleys to provide sufficient leverage for the task. The control lines from the pulleys can be seen led out to jamb cleats at the cockpit corners so the young skipper can adjust them while hiking. The cunningham controls used to adjust luff tension are led there for the same reason. Hiking straps can also be seen, kept tight with shock cord so that feet can slip under them without having to find them loose on the cockpit floor.

boom end to drag in the water could lead to disaster if the drag effect became strong enough to overcome the skipper's corrections and capsize the boat.

One of the mysteries of early pre-kicker times is raised by quoting from Peter Norlin's April 1973 *Sea Spray* article, which he ends by saying, 'To delve more profoundly into kicking strap study, the serious student might try disconnecting the tackle when running downwind in a squall ... but remember to duck when you do!' Well, there are many New Zealanders still about who learned the art of downwind sailing in strong winds entirely deprived of the control to be got from such a fitting and who survived strong squalls while doing so.

Hugh Poole, who did his early centreboard sailing out of the Heretaunga Boating Club in Wellington and was one of the more inventive small-boat sailors, tried out a triangular steel kicker on his Idle Along *Elaine* in the 1949–50 season. But there simply wasn't enough distance between the gooseneck and the deck for any efficient vertical dimension to the metalwork, and in any case, under even moderate load the fitting put dangerous stresses on the boat's long and slender wooden boom. Even the most sophisticated late-era I-class boats never had such gear, as photographs show.

Wind-direction indicators more sophisticated than the traditional fluttering masthead class or racing pennant almost certainly came from small-boat sailing – but there seem to be no indications of attribution to Uffa Fox. Nowadays, they are available from ship-chandlers and the like, where the trade-name Windex has passed into the

◀ On certain points of sailing, boats will sail quicker if the boom is held down with a kicker. This is very well understood by sailors. But for really small boats such as this Starling class, sailed by youngsters too old or too big for the P-class, the mechanism poses real problems. This sailor is having difficulty keeping clear of the kicker as he gybes the boat. If caught in his clothing, it could easily lead to a capsize if the boom fails to clear his back and the sail remains filled on the same side of the boat as the crew.

▼ On big boats such as this Whitbread competitor, boom vangs have to be strong hydraulic struts capable of resisting very heavy loads. Downhill rides in strong winds and big seas such as this test them severely.

◀ Registration number 2246 on the sail of this Flying Fifteen shows it to be a very recent example of the class. Nevertheless, its owner has chosen to use an old-fashioned feather for its masthead pennant, rather than a manufactured, plastic wind indicator. Though the class has a cast-iron keel of considerable weight, the hull form and the vigorous crewing technique employed by its crew clearly has this boat planing. No doubt his home-made pennant is helping the skipper to judge the best course and sail settings to achieve this impressive downwind response from the boat.

▼ The brand name Windex has come to be the generic term for a wind-direction indicator. The black plastic pivoting arrow with a red tail is nowadays the most readily available and most commonly used instrument. Available in several sizes, the smallest is fitted to boats such as this Starling. The indicator's arrowhead, triangular tail, and vertical stem are just visible through the spray. Its low-down position half way between the forestay and the mast enables the sailor to keep an eye on the wind direction without lifting his head to look at the masthead, the usual location for such fittings on bigger boats.

sailing vocabulary as a generic term for the mechanism, in sizes and degrees of complexity appropriate to the size of the boat. For most of the first two decades after the Second World War they were, for small boats at least, home-made from available materials both natural and man-made.

In the late 1940s, wind-indicator pennants were still thought of as pieces of cloth, sometimes triangular, sometimes rectangular, flapping at the masthead from some sort of pivoting device. Even well into the 1950s, it was common practice in small boats for their builders or crew members, many of whom took part in the building process and so understood what their boats could stand under the stresses of competition, to manufacture their own out of a length of brazing rod (stiffer and stronger than Number 8 mild steel wire!), copper strip, washers, and a feather.

It was preferably not a seagull feather, though, because of their considerable and unalterable sideways curvature. The whole assembly was balanced with a tiny weight and let into a push-fit hole drilled into the top of the timber mast. Inexpensive and capable of being made at home several at a time, to cope with the inevitable damage and losses from capsizes (especially in shallow water!), such pennants added greatly to the quality and extent of incoming information about wind direction, and thus to boatspeed – their ultimate purpose.

Tiller extensions were an inevitable outcome of the vigorous sailing techniques developed to keep small boats planing and flat when sailing upwind. It was soon realised that, not only in single-handed boats but also in those with two or more in the crew, it was no longer acceptable for the skipper to linger inboard, crouched on the edge of the cockpit and keeping relatively dry in the lee of the crew just in front.

To begin with, a rope extension, used in combination with a well-placed foot on the tiller to provide the return force when weather helm eased off, half-did the job, but somewhere in the mid-1950s in New Zealand the extension became a swivelling rod with a grip or handle on its outer

▲ Tiller extensions become a major spar when the helmsman becomes a trapeze hand, as in the case of this Farr 3.7. Going about without mishap takes on new meaning when such a fitting has not only to be kept out of the way but also kept ready to hand on the other tack. Athleticism is called for, as well as considerable sleight of hand!

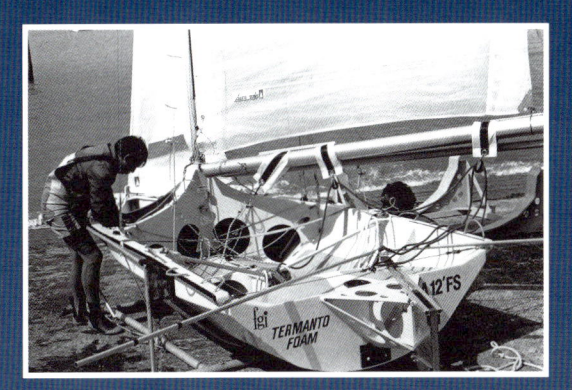

▲ In the foreground of this picture of the twelve-footer *Termanto Foam*, standing out as fine straight lines against a maze of apparently disorganised ropes of various sizes, the lightweight, plastic-tube tiller extensions are almost as long as the boom, a length made necessary by the fact that the helmsman also stacks out on a trapeze.

▲ The port and starboard trapezes on this Flying Dutchman are linked across the boat by a wire, presumably to keep the leeward one from flopping about and disturbing the set of the mainsail. Just another strand in the cat's cradle.

end and led in due course to the sophisticated arrangements seen today on all sorts of boats, big and small – but it unquestionably came from the small boats.

As has already been noted, trapezes were used in the multi-crew traditional classes in the Moffat and Sanders Cups in 1955 – well before their demise. But just a year before, in the summer of 1953–54, there was a heated argument amongst 18-footer enthusiasts about their origins, during which it was said that they had been introduced in New Zealand following the Second World War.

However, in December 1954, *Sea Spray* published an impressive 1937–38 season photograph of the M-class *Manaia* well reefed down in a blow and with no less than three of her five crew out on trapezes, accompanied by an article headed 'New Zealand First?' It may not have been done first on *Manaia*, but it seems to have been done in New Zealand well before its use in the International 14s in the UK on an occasion in the 1950s that has been well-publicised by Uffa Fox. *Manaia* looks to be hard on the wind in the photograph, and well heeled also, but she must have made an even more impressive sight on a reach with three on the wire.

One of the little-recorded outcomes of this change from the small-boat crew's habitual position sitting on the side deck, though one frequently mentioned in the early stages of

▼ This sail, spar, and rigging plan for the M-class boats *Manaia* and *Mercedes* was drawn by one of their designers, the Logan Brothers of Stanley Bay, in 1935. No trapeze wires are evident in the drawing but *Manaia* was definitely fitted with, and used, them in the 1930s.

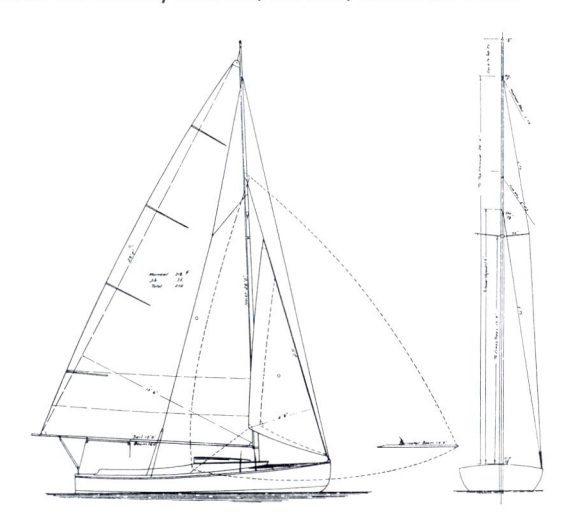

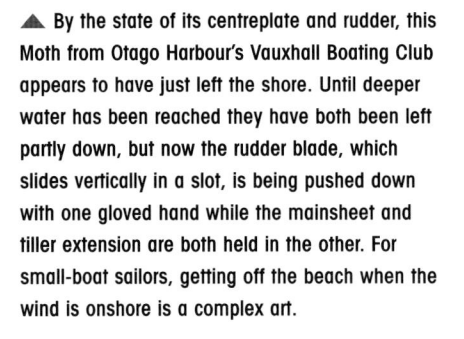

▲ By the state of its centreplate and rudder, this Moth from Otago Harbour's Vauxhall Boating Club appears to have just left the shore. Until deeper water has been reached they have both been left partly down, but now the rudder blade, which slides vertically in a slot, is being pushed down with one gloved hand while the mainsheet and tiller extension are both held in the other. For small-boat sailors, getting off the beach when the wind is onshore is a complex art.

◀ The ultimate demands in small-boat athleticism must surely come with the single-handed Contender, whose skipper sails the boat from out on a trapeze. One hand looks after the mainsheet and the cunningham control while the other holds the tiller extension in a most delicate fashion, the whole exercise one of great agility and balance. Sustained planing here is a truly great achievement.

races on cold windy days, was that it gave the skipper the same exposure to the seas as everyone else and no longer shielded the afterguard with the upwind crew-member's body, much to the delight of the latter.

The most efficient shape and profile for centreplates and rudders became matters of interest once high-performance sailing theorists found time to look into the possibilities for those building and racing small boats whose class rules allowed some latitude in their construction.

Plates and foils

Jack Brooke, in a *Sea Spray* contribution in August 1951, discussed these possibilities at some length. Much of what he had to say concerning the most efficient aspect ratio and profile nicely presages modern thought, especially the idea of something approaching an aerofoil section, with its maximum thickness somewhere 'slightly ahead of the centreline' of the centreplate. It was to be many years before the NACA sections, nowadays *de rigueur* for what are these days called foils, came into the sphere of small-boat design, but Jack Brooke's advice on profile, and the importance of a sharp trailing edge, is not far from the mark, though he advocated a near-symmetrical section.

Attitude and athleticism

There are a number of ways in which speed can be increased, especially if speed around the course is the aim and not just speed itself. Boatspeed is of course a vital factor in getting to the finishing line first, but the ability to do so in the midst of all the vagaries of a race is a much more complex business.

Overlaying all of them is the business of attitude. The continuous, concentrated, and vigorous interaction between boat and crew, and wind and sea needs to be applied from well before the start gun all the way to the end of the race, and beyond it if post-race analysis is included, as it ought to be.

This lively interactive attitude has been more widely evident for longer amongst New Zealanders than in most other places, simply because the sorts of boats they have been sailing for so long demanded it of them if winning was the aim.

A *Sea Spray* article in the autumn of 1947, under the heading 'Was It Lawful To Rock The Boat?', posed a question which seems to record the birth in New Zealand of a problem which, along with other 'kinetic' boat-handling techniques, still exercises the minds of rule-makers more than 50 years later.

During an interclub series in Auckland in which many well-known yachtsmen took part, the drifting conditions of the first race led to questions being asked about the legitimacy of rocking the boat, and thus artificially propelling its sail through the still air as though a light wind was blowing, in order to make progress through the water. An unnamed competitor had been seen to be doing this in order to avoid being set back by the adverse tide. Many asked whether this action could be termed a 'fair means of propulsion'. No consensus was reached at the time, and the question, though ostensibly now covered by the rules, still raises debate during competition when the technique is employed continuously and with great vigour by some competitors.

Boats sail to windward more efficiently, and thus more quickly, when not heeling too much. The positioning of crew weight is critical to achieving this desirable condition in strong winds. For some time in what one might call New Zealand's planing classes, this still meant both helmsman and crew sitting near or over the outside edge of the deck and

▲ Sailing downwind, the centre of effort of the sail is most efficiently employed if it is kept directly over the centreline of the boat, hence the several Finns being deliberately heeled to windward in this international race. But if the boat is rocked backward and forward at the same time the sail is moved in and out, particularly in light winds, an artificial wind effect is created and boatspeed is increased. In the nearest boat here, the helmsman's right arm is busy doing just that with his mainsheet as he rocks the boat. The technique is known as 'rocking', and there are racing rules setting out what is permitted and what is not.

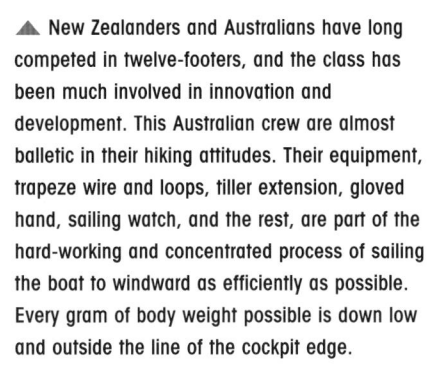

▲ New Zealanders and Australians have long competed in twelve-footers, and the class has been much involved in innovation and development. This Australian crew are almost balletic in their hiking attitudes. Their equipment, trapeze wire and loops, tiller extension, gloved hand, sailing watch, and the rest, are part of the hard-working and concentrated process of sailing the boat to windward as efficiently as possible. Every gram of body weight possible is down low and outside the line of the cockpit edge.

◀ The long, catenary slope of Rangitoto Island provides the background for this Contender sailor as he keeps an eye on the sail. Everything is led out to where he is perched on the rail, and the control lines for mainsheet, cunningham, and kicker are thus ready to hand on both sides of the boat. Bare feet and a short wetsuit are indications of the balmy, light-wind conditions in Auckland on this occasion.

simply leaning further outwards – very much in defiance, it must be said, of the old-fashioned, good-behaviour, good-seamanship customs inherited from the past, but of necessity if the lightweight boat were to be kept in planing mode off the wind and near-flat when going to windward.

Not only did hiking make the planing boat sit flatter in the water, and therefore go faster when sailing both on the wind and off it, but rapid movement in and out, and forward and aft, was soon seen to add further to boatspeed, provided it was done in a way which worked in harmony with the movement of the boat through and over the seas in the appropriate wind conditions. The techniques had to be learned out on the water and applied there.

Such vigorous behaviour has long been part of the New Zealand small-boat sailor's racing technique. Indeed, it has long been part of his or her fun-sailing activity. Working the boat to maximise the fun and thrill of planing has been part of non-racing behaviour ever since just mucking about was what one did on spare Sundays and appropriately windy days, several decades before such occasions came to be recognised and introduced in modern times as formal training sessions.

An essential factor on such non-racing occasions was, and still is, the immediate lesson learned if mistakes were made in boat handling, whether in helming, crew activity, or whatever – that is, capsize, or loss of control and near-capsize. This lesson is repeated all too often for most young sailors, and for all ages when the conditions become marginal. It has influenced sailors who stuck with the sport in all their later sailing careers, in big boats and small, despite the embarrassment and ignominy of such lessons, which are all too often very publicly learned.

To have learned these lessons, generation by generation by generation since 1920–21, in boats capable of planing, is without doubt part of the New Zealand sailing psyche. Truly international competition has, in such boats, been faced and mastered by some of the best New Zealand has produced.

Trapezing, the business of putting one's feet on the edge of the deck and hanging out from there on a hook at the end of a wire from high up on the mast, takes this agile approach literally one step further. Adopting the technique became one of the ways in which the administrators of each of the three more senior stepping-stone classes attempted to meet the challenge of the newer boats when they appeared on the sailing scene and threatened the future of the traditionalists.

The 7-foot, single-handed P-class was too small for such acrobatics (though no doubt some adventurous young skipper tried it out one non-race summer's day to impress the others – tiny spinnakers have certainly been tried). The class administration made sure that self-bailing was not allowed. This meant sailors had to learn to bail as they sailed along when sea conditions sent water into the cockpit, whose floor was in any case several inches below sea level and thus incapable of self-draining.

But the other three, Z, I, and X-class, changed their class rules to allow the use of trapezes very late in their development. It was too late to save them, but not too late to introduce more speed and new thrills to those who sailed the classic centreboarders in the declining years before their national championships ran out of contestants.

By 1955, both the Sanders Cup and Moffat Cup contest conferences had permitted trapezes to be used. The latter championship was sailed in light winds on Lake Brunner and the new technique made little impact, but the first race of the Sanders Cup in strong winds in Dunedin that year was marked by near tragedy. One crew member, Ross Telford, now a well-known yachting commentator, was taken to hospital after spending some time under water, having been caught by the legs in his half-released modified parachute harness following a capsize not long after the start.

▲ This is the way a Moth is righted after capsize. The boat is nearly but not absolutely head to wind, so that it doesn't round up and go about and capsize again. One foot of the fully-wetsuited crew is on the centreplate, the other is raised and ready to slide across the deck into the cockpit as the boat comes upright.

▼ This trapeze crew-member's gloved hands held out above the head are not a greeting, as might be thought by the uninitiated. By this means, the absolute maximum leverage is obtained from the body weight being carried by the boat. It seems from the look on his face that the trapeze artist knew he was being photographed.

▲ **International starts in big fleets are intensively competitive, with everybody determined to be in the most favourable position right on the line as the gun goes. So almost everyone sails slowly along on starboard tack, maintaining their right of way over anyone foolish enough to approach the line on port tack without that right. In an international Finn contest, scenes such as this occur every time fleets of highly-competitive sailors prepare for an on-the-wind start. The start line must be laid at right angles to the wind, or very nearly so, in order to avoid a very bumpy crush at the most favoured end.**

Starts and courses

If any proof were necessary for the contention that New Zealand clubs, class administrations, and class associations had developed sophisticated contest management skills by the 1960s, it was provided by a US competitor at the New Zealand Finn-class championships at Tauranga in February 1969. He is reported in the October 1969 issue of *Sea Spray* as saying, 'In spite of limited facilities and a tiny race committee, the Finn class ran the regatta with precision. The skippers' meeting was short because the sailing instructions were self-explanatory. Starting lines were square, the courses were well laid out, and the races even started on time.'

If the custom in the 1920s and 1930s at the Worser Bay Boating Club is typical of such clubs, small-boat racing was for some time conducted on the basis of Mark Foy starts, in which boats leave the start line according to the time allowance they had been given on the boat which started last – the scratch boat.

At that club's AGM in 1933, Alf Harvey, its founding commodore, persuaded the club members to use a five-flag start system instead, but the sailing committee only did so for every second race on the programme, preferring the excitement to be at the finishing line rather than at the start. In addition, under the Mark Foy system, the big-handicap boats sailed by less able skippers spent the early part of the race at or near the front of the fleet which, if the handicapper was generous to them, often meant they finished first or nearly so.

Even when one-class fleets began to dominate sailing at the club, from the mid-1930s, when club Idle Along numbers racing there reached 10 or more, it was still the habit to use the staggered start. Alf's advice, which had been given in the interest of improving fleet starting skills, took a long time to be heeded.

Alf Harvey also encouraged the club to have on-the-wind starts, another thing the sailing committee had difficulty with. But he continued to attend and influence Worser Bay annual meetings, even though he lived way across the harbour at Petone after 1928.

For many years, the Highet Points formula (200/N + 1) held sway in most national contests decided on a points system, though a much more primitive system had been in use before that. In 1968, the International Yacht Racing Union adopted what New Zealand reports called a 'new Olympic Points system', with 0 points awarded for first place, and 3, 5.7, 8, 10, 11.7 then place plus 6 thereafter, with the lowest total score being the winner. Local clubs and classes were told that they could, if they wished, adopt the new points scoring system, with or without a dropped race option.

▲ There are occasions in single-handed boats where there are too many things to be done and not enough hands to do them with. Hauling in ropes is best done hand-over-hand if any length of slack is involved, and a ready substitute can be found in the sailor's teeth. This young Starling skipper is about to use his teeth to hold the mainsheet, while his left hand grabs another length of rope.

Sailing schools

Encouraging young people, and the not so young, to take up sailing by running sailing schools and staging regattas for schoolchildren might seem a recent idea. But it was part of the Heretaunga Boating Club's promotional arrangements way back in the 1930s.

In 1975, a group of teachers and parents in Wellington's eastern suburbs interested in sailing put together a series of weekly instruction sessions during the winter, to be followed by a building programme and training videos. The underlying reason seems to have been a fall-off in centreboard sailing numbers and a perceived demand for reasonably knowledgeable people to crew on keelers. The latter reason has fundamental implications for sailing in New Zealand.

Women on the water

Sailing clubs have traditions concerning the part played by women, whether they are members or not. For a long time the place of women in a club's programme was largely defined by the existence of 'ladies committee' or the activities of the social committee. But these days such an arrangement is no longer taken for granted, as in the past.

Penny Whiting began what *Sea Spray* called 'ladies' sailing lessons' in late 1969, using her father Darcy's boat *Coruba*. Of the lessons, some consisting of theory and others of practical sailing work, the October 1969 issue of the magazine said, somewhat condescendingly, 'This is a wonderful opportunity for women to learn how to be useful on a boat and it seems the men will have to look out or they will soon find themselves fighting for crew positions.'

Isobel Hazeldine was elected Commodore of the Otago Cruising Club in July 1974, and two years later Jan Vaudrey was elected Commodore of Torbay/Taiotea Yacht Club. In so doing, they became the first and second women commodores of New Zealand yacht clubs.

In the period between these two appointments, at its AGM in 1975, Auckland's Royal New Zealand Yacht Squadron opened its membership to women – though it seems the change was brought about by the need to think well ahead when planning its new clubhouse about to be built at Westhaven rather than by the news about the new Otago Commodore.

Elsewhere in New Zealand, Leslie Egnot was the first woman to win the P-class Tauranga Cup at Christchurch in 1979. The Naomi James Challenge Trophy for first woman to finish in the Tanner Cup contest, named after another famous New Zealand sailor, was first awarded to Leanne Soper at the contest at Christchurch in 1981, and several other of its winners have gone on to excel in the sport, notably Michelle Baker and Sarah Macky.

With Jan Shearer, Leslie Egnot won a silver medal in the 470 class at the 1992 Olympic Games in Barcelona. They were the first New Zealand women to win an Olympic yachting medal. In 1994-95 Leslie helmed *Mighty Mary*, Bill Koch's all-women entry in the America's Cup defender trials, and in 1998-99 she was tactician for Dawn Riley's Young America syndicate.

Barbara Kendall MBE began sailing in P-class, Starlings, and Europe dinghies, and turned to windsurfing at age 16. She won her first world boardsailing title at the age of 20, and a gold medal at the 1992 Barcelona Olympic Games, the first New Zealand woman to win gold since 1952. In 1996, Barbara won a silver medal at the 1996 Olympic Games at Atlanta.

▲ Jan Shearer at the helm of this 470 has Fiona Galloway on the wire in a moderate breeze off Auckland's Musick Point. Both women sailed in smaller centreboarders before getting together in the demanding 470 – this boat showing on its topsides evidence of Whitcoulls' sponsorship.

Sailors' dress

What sailors consider best to wear when sailing has a long and varied history in New Zealand – no doubt it has elsewhere too. But the freedom from conventional expectations provided by the sport, especially for those who know they are most likely to get very wet (and that the jacket and cap of the big-boat men is not for them) has, since the advent of fast light boats, provided opportunities for unconventional dress.

Sea Spray, worried about the standard of clothing seen being worn at recent national contests, said in an editorial in 1951:

> It seems to be a tradition amongst the majority of yachtsmen to save and wear their oldest and scruffiest clothes when they get afloat ... Old football jerseys, ragged shorts of indeterminate hues are NOT the most suitable clothes when sailing in the public eye. We feel that many people would regard yachtsmen with a kinder eye were their dress not so unsightly. Parents of youngsters who are keen to take up yachting, are not very likely to view with favour, a sport that presents such a ragged and down-at-heel appearance to the public gaze ... Oilskins are inevitable when the weather is bad, but they are no excuse for untidiness and slovenliness ... It is odd that while time and money will be lavished on a boat to keep up appearances, clothing is neglected. ... Action must of course start with the clubs. It would not be difficult to instill some regard for appearance into the worst offenders, and discredit the myth that 'toughness' is indicated by rags and tatters.

Needless to say, the magazine editor was fighting a hopeless battle, but fashionable sailing gear was eventually to find its place on the small-boat scene. Purpose-made sailing clothing found its New Zealand originator just a few years later in one of the country's successful small-boat sailors, when Barry Wilson, winner of the Moffat Cup at Napier in 1953, developed his clothing business into the Line 7 brand of wet-weather gear.

Sensing the impact of wind and water on the body is very much a part of the way small boats are sailed in competition, and this fact has had a major effect on the way small-boat sailors have dressed for their sport. Going bare-footed as children and youths has long been part of the Kiwi holiday attitude. Doing so out sailing was for decades *de rigueur* for P-class kids and Zeddie youths alike (though few would have used the expression!).

The way the boat meets the water is transmitted through the hull and to the brain by way not only by the seat of the pants but also through the soles of the feet. Sensitivity to it is thus

▲ The Westlake College team has been successful on several occasions in the annual secondary-school national team-racing series. Their Sunburst carries the name of the sponsors of the contest on its stern and sails. Sponsorship is vital to the series, and its secondary-school competitors take the racing very seriously, as is indicated by the fully-matched clothing worn by this two-man Westlake crew – caps, jackets, wetsuits, wetboots, sailing gloves, and all. In the 1950s, by contrast, one Wellington small-boat sailor wore a knitted dress upside down as a proto-wetsuit.

lessened by footwear. This attitude to competition information-gathering, though, seems to have been diluted by the wide use of fancy wetboots in more recent times.

Certainly in light airs, but just as importantly in stronger winds, the feel of the wind past the ears and cheeks of both skipper and crew is also full of information, and wearing hats and caps doesn't help in this process – hence the equally long-standing tradition of going bare-headed in serious small-boat competition.

A justified concern about the effects of too much sun on the skin has led to the wide use of sun-hats and sunblocks, but sensitivity to the environment in which the boat is being sailed is the less for it.

Though no one has yet invented a pair which lasts long enough, which is a measure of the hard tasks they have to perform, sailing gloves have much reduced the wear and tear on the hands of small-boat sailors. Even with them though, the very painful destruction of the soft pads on the undersides of the fingers still goes on when the competition is fierce, the wind is blowing hard, and the hands are continually wet.

Ivan Real wrote about wet-weather gear for sailors in the August 1970 issue of *Sea Spray*, beginning, 'Ever read how the old square-rig sailors made their oilskins? After hand-sewing in calico the garment was treated with successive coats of a mixture of raw and boiled linseed oil garnished with ground black lead for colouring.' The colouring may not have still been in vogue in centreboard sailing in the 1940s and 1950s in New Zealand, but there must still be many who can remember the smell and feel of the linseed-oil-soaked, kapok-filled lifejackets that were in use well into the late 1950s. Most who do remember them will also recall their quick decay into useless and sodden hazards to life.

Heat-seamed PVC, seam-taped nylon, hooded jackets, bibbed trousers, wetboots, and foam-fabric wetsuits have in more recent times made strong-wind, cold- and wet-weather sailing much less unpleasant, but complete cover-up is much more the need of big boats than it is of small ones, where the pressing need for each crew member to keep constantly in touch with the elements still applies.

Sailing for the fun of it?

The New Zealand Sailing and Motor Yacht Federation was formed during the 1951–52 summer, with four provincial Associations, Auckland, Wellington, Canterbury, and Otago, as its foundation members. *Sea Spray* reported its formation, saying:

> Now each one of us must see that International contests become an important part of our yachting, and to this end we must think as New Zealanders, not as Aucklanders, Wellingtonians or any other provincial types.

▲ If the capsized boat is included, there are at least 50 Lasers ready to start here, virtually every one of which is on starboard tack with the main eased, drifting slowly along the line waiting for the gun. Experience in such fleets is vital for Kiwis heading overseas and expecting to do well in international Laser competition, where the numbers can be more than double those seen massed here.

In its twenty-first birthday issue in Dec/Jan 1966–67, *Sea Spray* had a number of things to say about what had taken place over the period and what the prospects were for New Zealand yachting, amongst them this:

> In common with the small boats, terylene and nylon sails and synthetic cordage have made a great difference in keelers, and they are now following the centreboarders in developing bendy or partly bendy rigs, and alloy masts are becoming commonplace …

The Kiwi transfer of the bendy-rig and light-displacement ideas from the new breed of small boats to even newer breeds of bigger and bigger boats was to become a most significant element in New Zealand's contribution to international yachting.

In addition, the transfer from small to big boats of not only the way such boats were sailed but also of many of the people who sailed them so vigorously was to transform the international big-boat sailing scene, somewhat to the consternation of the northern-hemisphere international establishment.

In time, the sponsorship which made full-time sailing affordable also made professionalism possible. Not only did sponsorship allow increasingly expensive boats to be built and sailed in frequent and wide-ranging competition by relatively modestly-financed skippers and crews, but it also made professional boatbuilders and sailors out of many of the best of them.

But all this was in the future. Professionalism had not infected sailing to any significant extent by the end of the 1950s. In October 1958, just as the sailing season began, under the heading 'Just For Fun', *Sea Spray*'s editor reflected the mood of the day when he expressed the view that local sailors can be thankful professionalism is absent from their sport. Near the beginning of the editorial he said:

◀ Glen Sowry and Phillip McNeil of New Zealand have their boat more than three-quarters airborne as they cross the finishing line very close to the committee-boat end in the 470 Worlds. The bendy mast used to flatten the mainsail in such windy conditions is very much in evidence, as is the agility of both members of the crew in coping with the extreme liveliness of the boat when sailing to windward in big seas. Rank Xerox obviously put some money into the championship series.

When one looks at other sports these days, it often seems that we are better off as we are, even if yachting as a whole does at times seem to be ratherpoverty stricken. Professionalism has invaded most sports and is trying to cash in on still more. Those who become paid performers cannot possibly enjoy their chosen sport as much as when it was only a game, even if they have found a quick way to make a fortune. ... If a man doesn't run, play or otherwise perform when and where his followers expect him to, there is an immediate public outcry, official scoldings and headlines in the press, usually bigger than those devoted to an impending war. ... it is no longer simply a means of relaxation and enjoyment to many of them. Boating in all forms seems likely to be last to suffer from this trend. ... we can be thankful that we still go yachting just for fun – and not at the dictate of the ticket holders and managers.

There are, given the events of recent years, some prophetic phrases embedded in this editorial, and its concerns and expectations invite thought about the long-term outcome for sailing in New Zealand.

Expensive boats, built and equipped with many of the products of high technology, many of which have been either invented or developed by New Zealand designers, builders, riggers, sailmakers, and sailors, had by the 1970s and 1980s become a very successful part of the international sailing scene.

▶ The sponsored, annual 24-hour race on Lake Pupuke, on Auckland's North Shore, is run nowadays in Lasers, each entry being sailed by a two-person team taking turns at the helm. Oki are major sponsors, as is shown by the course buoys, and in addition each boat is individually sponsored. The result is a brightly-coloured, lively sailing weekend on the lake, with activity right through the night and all very much in the public eye.

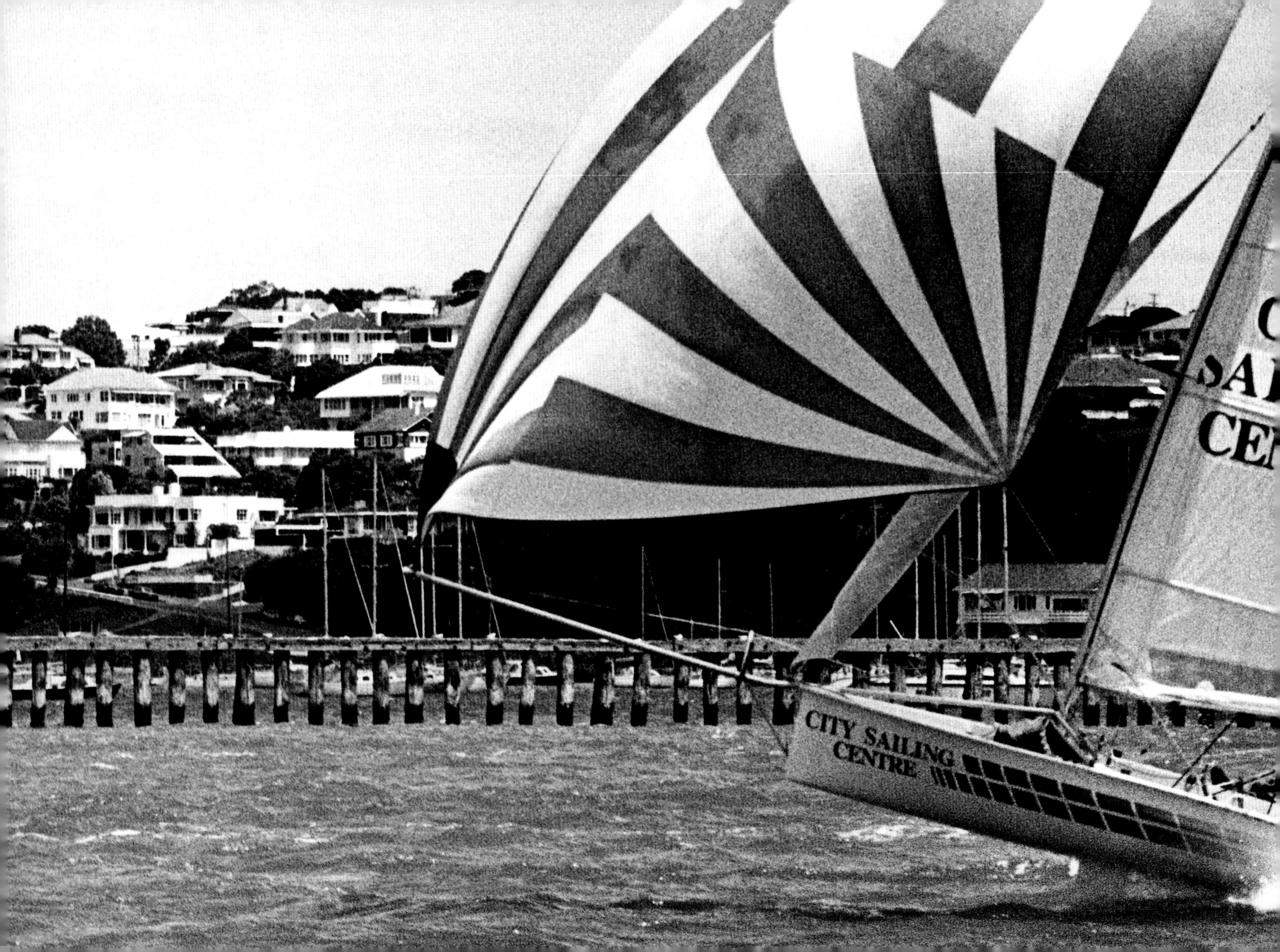
CITY SAILING
CENTRE

Chapter 5
Innovation and interweaving

While the PZIX system had suited many sailors who were happy to experiment within its limits, there were also some free spirits who felt constrained by the rules governing the one-design and restricted classes. This chapter is about how the innovators and those treading the stepping stones came to terms with each other and with the wider world of sailing.

Although they had gone from strength to strength in the 1950s, the next decade brought major changes to the stepping-stone classes. Some of the changes must have seemed insignificant at the time, as wooden boats were replaced first of all by ones made of marine plywood, and later by moulded fibreglass.

The most significant changes at this time were at the level of design, and they ranged from small modifications to the development of completely new classes based on light displacement principles. Not only did the innovations spread from small boats to larger ones, but the next phase of the design revolution saw the wholesale introduction of new classes that had been developed in other parts of the world. The flood of new classes, both local and imported, greatly increased the range of choices for local sailors at all levels. Though there were more sailors out on the water, fleet sizes dropped overall, and some established classes struggled to survive.

> The southerly is blowing hard enough out of Auckland's Okahu Bay for this 18-footer to have a reef in the main, but not so hard that it prevents the crew from using every ounce of wind pressure to keep the boat planing in a most impressive manner. About a quarter of its hull length is touching the water and just enough of the centreplate is in the sea to keep the boat under control.

▲ There are ten R-class boats in this busy scene at the top mark. One of them is already around the flagged buoy and heading out of the picture, but the others are all fighting for room as they approach on both tacks. The dark-hulled boat in the centre of the bunch is on port tack and will have had to give way to all the others.

◀ The 18-footers have long been associated with sponsorship. This picture of a Queensland boat on a tight reach reveals the speed achieved when sails, weight, and course are so balanced that planing seems deceptively effortless and easily controlled – until a moment's loss of concentration on the part of any one of the three-man crew reveals otherwise! Small-boat performance capability such as this would make any sponsor feel pleased about their decision to get involved in sailing.

The influence of innovators

The PXIZ stepping stone classes were a demonstration of the Kiwi 'Number 8 wire' approach, in that sailors could build and rig and fit out the boats themselves, largely out of basic indigenous materials. For many, though, they limited innovation, because of the controls that the various class rules placed on hull shape, timbers, construction methods, sails, and spars.

But there were always alternatives to the designer-constrained PZIX-series available to those New Zealanders for whom innovation was paramount. Indeed, the traditional PZIX-classes had developed haphazardly in the midst of a range of local choices, even though that range did not always manage to provide even-handed time allowances for those who chose to race them, and usually lacked widespread fleets beyond the home clubs.

Even before Alf Harvey had first sailed his prototype *Idle Along* at Petone, a free-spirited development class, the R-class, had come into being in Canterbury. More than any other boat, indigenous or introduced (except perhaps the Qs) the R-class was to lead the way in innovations which transformed small-boat sailing in New Zealand. More about it later.

The Q-class had been in existence in one form or another since at least the 1930s. For a time, it seems, it was the classification into which those Idle Alongs that failed to pass measurement descended – at least that was the case in Wellington. The Q-class was aptly described in its later years by Jenny Farrell in a 1973 issue of *Sea Spray* as 'a testbed of design theories, crew combinations and sail innovation'. She added that the class came into its own in the 1950s as a cheaper alternative to the flying 18-footers, and that Q-class boats 'have often been a stepping-stone to that class'.

That description of the Qs nicely fits the Rs also. Between them, these two classes have profoundly influenced the development of fast light boat concepts over some sixty years now. Within each designer-constrained class, as every possible legitimate competitive edge was pursued in order to win first local representation and then the class national championship, the constraints set down in drawings and specifications were closely studied and stretched to whatever limits were thought likely to be accepted by class administrators and, on occasions, beyond. That the controls were intended to provide class racing in which the competition was to find the best crew in near-identical boats did not stop innovation, but it certainly limited it. In time, because time passed them by, the original virtues of three of the stepping-stone classes, that is, their essential similarity, was to become the cause of their downfall.

For those who found the limitations irksome – and there were many whose competitive sailing experience included both the PZIX-series, especially in their younger days, as well as the unrestricted classes – it was frequently in the latter that their small-boat sailing career continued and their innovative ideas found an outlet.

But the interweaving of developments between the two types, one free and the other much less so in design terms, was multi-directional. It should not be thought that all the innovative ideas flowed one way. The limitations on boats, sails, and rigs led to a concentration on developing improvements in the way the traditional classes were sailed. On occasions, this led to very close-fought representative trials and national championships, in which race techniques and contest management methods became finely honed.

Because of this, and because the venue clubs applied the new methods to club racing, especially in centres where there was strong class racing in good-sized fleets, it was said on more than one occasion that it had been harder for the representative crew to win the local trials than it was for them to win the subsequent national contest itself.

▲ Two on the wire in a 12-footer on a reach under spinnaker makes an excellent platform for the marketers of Life Savers, and the boats provide an excellent example of sustained planing. The tiller extension is longer than the skipper is tall, and the spinnaker boom is almost as long as the boat itself. The braced frame off the stern allows the skipper to place one foot out beyond the corner of the hull, and thus get his weight even further aft to keep the bow well out of the water and the boat planing.

▲ The demanding complexities of the P-class are well illustrated in this light-weather view of four of them rounding the weather mark in close proximity to each other. Note the wind indicator bracketed out from the mast at eye level on the right-hand boat, the reverse-hand hold on the tiller of the young man in the foreground, the combination of mainsheet, cunningham, and kicker control lines led aft to both forward corners of the cockpit and free-swinging tiller extension — all to be managed by one pair of hands not yet 16 years old. Such complexity goes some way to explain the effectiveness of the class as an introduction to competitive sailing in bigger boats.

The later years of PZIX

Just before Peter Mander and Jack Cropp won their (non-planing) International Sharpie-class gold medal in the 1956 Melbourne Olympics, the New Zealand Yachting Federation, the national organisation formed during the 1953–54 sailing season to co-ordinate the activities of the four provincial yachting associations then in existence, had agreed on standards for what it called Established Classes and National Classes.

In order to make less chaotic the already burgeoning class diversity, those considered to be of Established status had to be well established in at least one sailing centre, to be affiliated to and recommended by at least one of the four member associations, and to have sound and adequate administration with fully set-out class rules. Recognised as National classes were those Established Classes considered by the Federation to be strong numerically and of such widespread popularity that they warranted the higher status.

Despite its inclusion in the National category, by 1955 the X-class was in deep trouble, having become the smallest of the recognised National classes in terms of boat numbers. In an endeavour to recover the position, the Sanders Cup conference that year asked the NZYF to arrange a design competition for a replacement boat. The eventual outcome of this was the decision to abandon the class's 34 years of largely amateur, but wholly wooden, construction and to have Graham Mander's winning design commercially built in fibreglass in order to ensure the production of identical boats from a master mould – a decision with which the Canterbury sailor disagreed. To the consternation of some, and to the ultimate detriment of the class, amateur hull construction was not to be permitted.

By then, the still thriving P-class had introduced plywood construction and aluminium masts, with ply boats and alloy spars first being used in the 1957 contests. Jack Williams and Garry Denniston were responsible for the drawings used for the change to ply approved by the Tauranga Yacht Club committee. Kitset ply P-class boats were first available, from several suppliers, in the early 1960s. It was not until 1976 that the class administration allowed fibreglass hulls, all from a master mould. These boats are available nowadays for some $7000, which buys one of everything, except a lifejacket, ready to sail.

Well-sailed, gaff-rigged P-class boats were light enough to be capable of sustained planing from the outset, and a minimum weight of 85 lbs. was introduced in 1985 for all forms of construction, which left the older boats still competitive. Carbon-fibre composite masts were approved in 1998 and were first used at the 1999 contests in Tauranga.

The Tauranga Yacht Club has owned the copyright for the class plans since 1924, and the latest fibreglass boats still conform to the original hull shape drawn up by Harry Highet in the early 1920s.

Famous sailors in the P-class include Graham Mander (twice winner), Des Townson, Jon Gilpin (three times winner), Murray Thom, Mark Patterson, David Barnes, Chris Dickson, and of course Russell Coutts. In addition, both Peter Blake and Peter Lester competed in the class, not very successfully, and this aspect of P-class competition – later success in sailing after lack of it in the class – is one of its legends.

From the outset of the Z-class national championship, under an original class rule not unlike those for modern match racing, crews drew for a different boat in each race, and the skipper and forward hand had to finish first in three races before being declared the winner of the Cornwell Cup.

On one famous occasion, it took nine races to find the winner at the contest on Evans Bay in 1932. Three years later the New Zealand Monotype Cup Championship was added to the contest programme, competed for by skippers sailing the boats single-handed, without the use of spinnakers, and open to all comers. This freedom of entry was a very early sign of things to come in New Zealand.

John Spencer had prepared drawings for plywood Zeddies in 1960, marconi masts were allowed by 1961, and by 1968 there were good fleets of plywood boats racing in the Paremata Easter Regatta, after cries of doom for the class four years earlier. Those warnings were only a few years premature, however.

The year 1971 was in many ways the last truly representative contest for the Cornwell Cup. The following year, when the championship series was held on Otago Harbour, it was clear that the class had become outdated. Though plywood boats built to a new minimum weight of 200 lbs and with aluminium marconi masts were noticeably quicker – it was claimed, not unreasonably, as many who have sailed the boat on a reach in a blow will

▲ P 331, reefed down, is about to break through a wave and plane down its front surface – the purists would call it surfing, rather than planing. But all three boats in this heavy-weather picture demonstrate the potential that seven-footers have to plane downwind. Each sailor is clearly concentrating his attention on the performance of his boat in the testing conditions, and each knows that a moment's lapse can lead to a capsize. All great experience and something to talk of with pride back in the clubhouse.

▼ This scene must be at the outside end of the starting line, opposite the committee boat, just after the gun has gone. Long seas are sweeping down on to the seven-footers and the pin-end buoy as most of them make their way up the course on starboard tack. The advantage for P-class boats of waves this big is that, in the main, they can sail up and down them. Such big waves seldom crash on to the boat and into the cockpit. Bailing and sailing will nevertheless still be the order of the day for everyone.

attest, that one of them had achieved a speed of 22 knots – the once predominant Zeddie had failed to match the popularity of the newer, lighter, and faster two-man classes now being campaigned by increasing numbers of young sailors.

The last Cornwell Cup to be contested for by representatives selected by local trials in each port was held at Lake Reserve in Featherston in 1973 – the first time it had been competed for on a lake. After that year, the Z-class contest was for a new trophy open to all comers with no club representation requirement, and no age limit.

But there has been a modern revival of the Z-class. Though they were prevented from calling their contest a 'world championship' in 1990 by the New Zealand Yachting Federation, the Z-class continues to have good fleets of plywood boats racing at Paremata and elsewhere.

Nowadays, the Cornwell Cup is awarded to the winner of the national two-handed youth trials, sailed in Laser IIs, and the Z-class Monotype Cup goes to the single-handed youth trial winner, sailing a Laser.

Well-known Z-class champions included George Brasell; Warren Wagstaff; B and C Armit; Peter, Graham, and David Mander; and Ralph Roberts.

In their turn, in order to meet the challenge of newer and faster classes and falling interest in their national contest, the Idle Alongs had been redesigned by John Spencer for plywood hull construction and full-length sail battens by 1960. But the reincarnation came too late for this class too, and only kept the championship alive for another nine years.

Significant I-class champions include the father and son G and P Carter (from a Tauranga family which also competed in Zeddies); Evan Julian; Peter and Graham Mander; Jack Cropp; Barry Wilson; Hugh Poole; and Bob Williamson.

The last national Idle Along contest for the Moffat Cup took place at New Plymouth in 1969. Since then, however, much as happened a little earlier in the Zeddies, there has been a revival in the class. A new open-entry championship was held in Northcote at Auckland's Anniversary Weekend in January 1999, in which 10 boats competed for the newly-created Alf Harvey Trophy.

Class distinctions

In what might quite properly be called the diversity decade, the period between 1951 and 1961 saw some fourteen new small-boat classes introduced in New Zealand. Most of them were introduced in the last few years of the 1950s. Two-thirds of them were indigenous designs; the remainder were international in origin.

Interest amongst local sailors in small boats designed overseas, such as the Sharpie, Finn, International 14, and Flying Dutchman classes, came about at first from Peter Mander and Jack Cropp's Sharpie success at the 1956 Melbourne Olympics, and was reinforced by Geoff Smale and Ralph Roberts' win in the Prince of Wales Cup in International 14s at Cowes in 1958.

But the many new and innovative local designs, most of them based on plywood construction, had a profound influence on small-boat classes and the way they were built and sailed in that decade and afterwards. One of them was not at all a planing type, but nevertheless had a profound effect, because it introduced families to inexpensive sailing.

Sea Spray, in an editorial in 1951, some 15 years before Richard Hartley produced details of his first Hartley 'trailer sailer', lamented what it called 'the gap that exists between the largest dinghy and the smallest keeler', and went on to advocate 'a small two-or-three-berth keeler that can be built cheaply and yet is sufficiently seaworthy to take part in races over existing courses and to cruise in'. What came to be known in England as the JOG – the Junior Offshore Group, comprising small keelboats between 16 and 20 ft

◀ Those white bands over the shoulders of this Finn sailor have nothing to do with his life jacket. They are connected to the water-filled weight bag he has strapped to his back to increase his leverage when hiking. The subtle thing about such a technique is that once the sailor is in the water after a capsize the bag is surrounded by sea water and weighs nothing. The catch is that as soon as the wearer rises out of the sea in righting the boat the weight tells again and increases the effort required to carry out that demanding task.

▼ With a tiller extension and the skipper and crew crouched well forward, windows in the main, and the jib sheeted hard in, this Hartley 16 is being sailed hard on the wind, epitomising the competitive attitude brought to the class by the establishment of regional and national championships once its numbers had built up.

▶ The Hartley trailer-sailer was very much part of the revolution in the way New Zealanders got to experience recreational sailing. The 16' 5" version shown here began life as the sort of boat in which members of the family, male and or female, could go sailing, racing, or cruising as their inclinations led. In the cabin there is just enough room to sleep, to prepare a meal, and to provide shelter for those who have had enough of the conditions out in the cockpit. More recently, competitive attitudes have made the class something of a racing machine. Not surprisingly, given the Kiwi sailor's pursuit of it, lightness has become one of the preoccupations of trailer-sailer enthusiasts.

▲ Inevitably, given the nature and history of New Zealand small boat sailing, the pursuit of speed overcame the original purposes of the trailer sailer class to the point where it changed the way they looked. This Farr design has much more the appearance of a racing machine than of a family cruiser on a road trailer, though the class requirement that such boats carry an outboard while racing serves as a reminder of their genesis. It is blowing hard here, in the lee of the hills in the background, and both boats in this picture have reefs in.

▼ The most prominent feature on the stern of this Cherub is the pair of large top-hinged flaps which, when their shock-cord control lines are released, will drain the cockpit of any water which comes aboard. The apparent tangle of ropes lying about the cockpit in fact conceals complex and well thought-out order. Just visible amongst it, either side of the keel, are two pivoting venturis in the up position, keeping them out of harm's way while the boat is lying on its cradle on the beach.

waterline length – was referred to in the editorial. But for many boat-owners in New Zealand the solution, though it took quite some time to materialise, was to be rather different and much more mobile than the English version.

Eight years later, in a 1959 letter to *Sea Spray*, an advocate proposed 'standardising and mass-producing a light displacement trailed yacht' in order to overcome the problems the family man faced with the lack of and costs of anchorage and haulout facilities, and the time involved in passage-making at sea between ports. Richard Hartley first publicised his double-chined plywood Hartley 16 Trailer Sailer (actually 16 ft 5 in long) in 1966. Four years later, there were 19 entries in the first national championships for TS 16s in Wellington. Over 300 boats had been built in the first two and a half years of the class coming into existence. In them, many newcomers to sailing became involved in the sport. Whether they did so as cruising or racing enthusiasts did not matter, since the sailing experience left its impression on all of them.

John Spencer's seminal Cherub class began the decade of diversification when it appeared in 1951. The first New Zealand-designed centreboarder to achieve world-championship status, this 12 ft plywood design was recognised by the RYA in 1959, and then, rather belatedly, as a National Class by the NZYF in 1966. There were fleets racing in Auckland, Hamilton, Whakatane, Wellington, and Cowes in 1957, and by 1958 there were over 200 registered in New Zealand, by which time the boats were also being built in the USA.

▶ In this view of the start of a Cherub race there is at least one Australian entry visible, identifiable by the letters KA on its sail. The trapeze hands are beginning to get out on the wire as the boats gather speed. All fifteen competitors are still on starboard tack, and Cherubs 1944 and 1990 would seem to be the only two free to go about on to port without risk of colliding with boats which have right of way.

Three years later, John Spencer designed the 3.85 m two-person Frostply to be sail-, oar-, or motor-driven. Its popularity as a plywood family sailing dinghy, especially in the Hamilton region (with Neil Wing leading a hard core of enthusiasts), was legendary. By 1974, there were 80 boats registered, half of them in Hamilton, sailed there by what Jenny Farrell in *Sea Spray* called 'the lake men'.

Peter Mander and Jack Cropp's 1956 Sharpie success in Melbourne first awakened local sailors to the fact that some in New Zealand had reached an international standard. The non-planing International Sharpie never created widespread interest, and very few boats were built and raced here. The only intense Sharpie-class competition in New Zealand occurred in the Olympic trials in 1955. At the end of the trials, Peter and Graham Mander were almost inseparable on points. But after that series, the boat, whose looks in hull and rig were strange to locals, faded into obscurity – though more than one is undergoing the small-boat restoration fashionable in the late 1990s.

Right at the beginning of the 1958–59 southern hemisphere summer, in October at Cowes in the Isle of Wight, Geoff Smale and Ralph Roberts from New Zealand won the Prince of Wales Cup in *Atua Hau* and gave further

▶ New Zealanders' won their first Olympic gold medal in 1956, but it was in a boat most unlike their fast, light Kiwi kind. The International Sharpie in which Peter Mander and Jack Cropp, shown here hiking hard on the wind, won in Melbourne was long and narrow, gaff-rigged, and relatively heavy. The sails in this photo are perfectly shaped, except for the crease at the top batten in the main, and Peter's glass eye, the result of an accident with a toy wooden propeller in his childhood, is glinting in the sunshine.

▲ Both these Flying Dutchman class boats are racing hard despite the threatening stormy look of the sky and the sea. Andy Ball in KZ 61 appears to have rounded the top mark and eased sheets on his way out to the wing mark, without setting the spinnaker (not surprisingly, given the conditions). Geoff Smale in KZ 50 is still heading upwind, snatching a glance to see how far they have still to go to reach the mark.

▲ The handsome, simple Frostply planes readily in quite light winds, as this sunny flat-water picture shows. This boat's fully-battened mainsail appears to be so loading the mast as to be the cause of the slack forestay, made highly visible by the curve in the luff of the jib. The forward hand looks very young, and seems to be enjoying the high-speed sailing experience.

proof to add to Peter Mander's 1956 demonstration of local abilities in international small-boat classes. The New Zealand team at the Cowes regatta was only just beaten by the highly-regarded Canadians for the team trophy. It was not just those two, whose names were to become famous in small-boat racing, who proved themselves able to match the international standard: others did so too. The New Zealanders set up their mainsheets in what they called 'the old-fashioned New Zealand way' – led from the boom down to a block in the cockpit and up to the hand, and cleated sometimes, even in strong winds, to the horror of the Englishmen. Geoff Smale said that this series:

◀ International competition in the Flying Dutchman class is both fierce and colourful, as this downwind scene in the 1991 FD World Championship series shows. Boat number 30 has begun to take down its spinnaker and is reaching across on port tack towards the next mark. The crew of the boat at the right-hand side of the picture will have been keeping a sharp lookout to see whether there is any risk of collision with FD 30 as they come together there.

...proved that our yachtsmen are better than we usually think ... we need have no compunction in challenging the best overseas men who we have always though of as way above our level – provided of course that we have had reasonable experience in the class.

There was class racing for these International 14s in the Auckland Anniversary Regatta in 1959. Stan Bacon, Commodore at Worser Bay Boating Club and winner of the Moffat Cup in 1952, built and raced one in Wellington at about the same time. But by 1968, the class had faded away locally. The solid-silver Duke of Edinburgh Cup for which the International 14s had competed in New Zealand was made a Flying Fifteen trophy instead – not a surprising choice in view of the Duke's interest in that keelboat class, by then thriving in New Zealand.

The NZYF declared the two-man Flying Dutchman, designed in 1951 by Uus van Essen and Conrad Gulcher, an Established Class in 1954. It arrived on the local scene virtually untried by most New Zealand sailors, though Geoff Smale and others had taken turns sailing one in Holland while they were in Europe in 1958. Several European-built hulls were imported into Auckland in that year, and support for the class was voiced in Wellington, after

◀ Russell Coutts is at the helm of KZ 1 in this group of Finns approaching the leeward mark in the 1984 Finn Worlds. Ivar Ganahl is sailing Finn Z 383 just ahead of him, PZ 6 is Henryk Blaszka, and the Irishman Bill O'Hara is sailing IR 1. Several boats astern are 'rocking' vigorously to improve boat speed in the light conditions, most noticeably the skipper of Finn 21 E.

▲ Clive Roberts, the brilliant New Zealand small-boat sailor, is shown here in the classic Paul Elvstrom hiking fashion, sailing a Finn upwind with eased sheets in sunny, moderate conditions. Roberts was New Zealand champion in the class in 1975 and was later tragically killed in a motor-vehicle accident.

▲ These Flying Fifteens, though keelboats, are trailerable and can plane in moderate winds, which has made the double-handed class a popular one in many parts of New Zealand – especially in Wellington, where for some years international class rules were bent a little to allow trapezes to be used in order to cope with the harbour's strong winds. In this picture of a national contest, ff 560 is the Wellington boat *ffandango*, ahead but to leeward of the fleet. The contest was held in Napier, a stronghold of the class and the home port of Barry Finlayson, winner of the ff Worlds in the 1970s.

it had become one of the two-man classes adopted by the IYRU for the 1960 Olympics. Class racing for FDs was included in the Auckland Anniversary Regatta in 1959, two years after it had been chosen for the Olympics. The first local FD trials for the games were held in 1960.

The Finn was introduced to New Zealand when, after the customary selection trials, the country was represented without medal success in the class at the 1956 Olympics. Designed in 1949 by Rickard Sarby of Sweden, this 4.5 m one-man class was the outcome of a design competition. Paul Elvstrom won the Finn gold medal in the first three Olympics in which the boat competed. There was fleet racing for Finns in the Auckland Anniversary Regatta in 1959, by which time it had been declared an Established Class by the NZYF. By the 1961–62 season, there were several sailors racing them regularly in Wellington. That summer, in a gale-battered contest sponsored by Rothmans with an annual $500 grant, Ralph Roberts won the Pall Mall Trophy, as he did again in 1963. Peter Mander sailed in the 1964 Finn Olympics, Ralph Roberts having done so in 1960.

The Flying Fifteen had been designed in 1948 by Uffa Fox, allegedly while relaxing in the bath. The first Flying Fifteen in New Zealand was *Buttercup*, Sam Mason's first boat, built at Kawau. Sam was a former winner of the Sanders Cup, and it was the long life and formidable reputation of his later boat, *Pinkie*, also built there, that profoundly influenced the progress of the class in New Zealand.

For at least a decade, these elegant two-man keelboats of classic design did not race as a class in Auckland. The enthusiasm for the class of a group led by Ben Fuller at the Evans Bay Yacht & Motor Boat Club in Wellington found its expression in a group-building scheme in 1959. With the same sail area as the International 14, a 400 lb cast-iron keel, and planing capability, the elegant Flying Fifteen appealed greatly to Wellingtonians for its strong wind kindliness (particularly in the years when international dispensation was obtained for the use of trapezes, on the basis of evidence provided by Barney Scully and other Wellington enthusiasts about the high average wind strengths on the harbour). Some dozen boats were soon on the water there, all amateur built. The first national championships, for the Anderson-Wilkin Trophy, were won by *Pinkie* in 1963. Sam Mason won again in the same boat in 1966, 1967, and 1968.

Flying Fifteens achieved NZYF National Class status in 1964 and IYRU International Class status in 1981.

The Javelin class, a 1958 design by John Spencer, evolved from his Cherub experience. It was a development of a square-bilge, plywood International 14 he built for himself. It really got going in 1960 after Spencer worked on developing and fine-tuning its design and rig, and the performance of the best boats and crews in open competition proved its capabilities. The first national championships in the class were held at Paremata in 1964. This event brought together the Canterbury and Auckland boats and aroused the interest of Wellington sailors – as it was no doubt intended to do.

◀ The real joy of sailing dinghies at high speed shows on the face of Gary Wiig of Auckland as he planes his Finn in big seas off Plimmerton in the class national championships. Lots of spray, bright sunshine, and a stark, almost treeless, background coastline all add to the drama of this scene.

◀ Boat names reflect popular interests of the day, and the song *Mr Bojangles* must have been getting airtime when this Javelin was named. John Spencer's plywood two-man invention, well sailed, revels in windy conditions. It is doing so as it is driven hard to windward in this Wellington harbour scene. With the jib cleated (considered very bad seamanship in earlier times), the trapeze hand controls the mainsheet. In typical two-man fashion, he enables the skipper to concentrate on getting the best out of the boat by easing and hauling in the main according to the sequence of squalls and lulls, which he can see best from his position out on the wire.

▲ Devised, as its name makes clear, as a junior version of the Cherub, this Junior Cherub looks as though it is sinking as it sails upwind on Wellington harbour. The forward hand is off his trapeze and crouching inboard, busy with some adjustment in the cockpit. The skipper is looking intently forward, his left hand on the tiller extension. His head is in an apparent halo which must have been the cause of merriment when the photograph was first passed around in the clubhouse.

▲ The Mistral class was never widespread, but it has always had a reputation as a 'family' class. Like the Frostbite, it has a timeless quality about its lines which shows up well in this apparently relaxed scene on Auckland harbour. Relaxed or not, the well-clad forward hand is keeping an eye on the sails while the skipper watches the launch moving away in the background.

New Zealand Javelin owners were invited to sail against the Australians at Manly Yacht Club in December 1967. There were 18 entries in the 1968 class national championships at Kohimarama, won by Helmer Pedersen (later an Olympic yachting medallist for New Zealand).

The new intermediate-class Junior Cherub, proposed by Peter Mander and created by John Spencer by attaching a reduced rig and sail area to his Mark II Cherub hull, arrived on the scene in 1959, some eight years after the introduction of the Cherub itself. It was intended to fill, the designers said 'what is probably the biggest gap in New Zealand yachting at the moment. A lack of a popular and modern junior class could prejudice the whole future of the sport in New Zealand.' The first national championships for the class were won by Graeme Woodroffe at Evans Bay in 1961, though there were none racing there at the time. The innovative winner's trophy was Peter Mander's framed certificate from his 1956 Olympic win in the Sharpie class. Twenty boats took part in the open-entry class national championships in 1966.

What someone called 'the friendly Mistral', because of the family atmosphere amongst owners of the boats, was a 3.7 m, one-design, two-person, moulded-ply centreboarder designed by Des Townson. Eighty-nine hulls were built in radiata pine, using resorcinal glue, by the boat's designer, the first of them in 1959. Most fleet racing has taken place at Tamaki Yacht Club. Forty-three Mistrals sailed in their class championship at Tamaki in 1983.

The New Zealand Moth Owners Association was formed in the 1961–62 season. Some 70 boats took part in the first

▲ The helmsperson's facial expression reflects the joy of sailing an International Moth at speed on a reach in strong winds. The proximity to sea level one has when sailing such boats has prompted a Moth enthusiast to say that, though they might not actually be faster than bigger boats with more freeboard, they certainly seem so! Details such as the bare feet under the hike strap, the mainsheet and left hand silhouetted against the dark trousers, and the hair blowing in the breeze add greatly to the liveliness of this picture.

▲ Out on his foam- padded hiking frame, Wayne Cook is sailing his Moth in the class World Championships. The embodiment of planing-capable light, fast boats, his boat is about one third in the water and moving at high speed on a reach. His mainsheet is eased a little and his relaxed bodyweight nicely maintains an efficient angle of heel with the minimum of effort.

Moth-class national championships, won by Jon Gilpin at Auckland in 1962 – Helmer Pedersen was sixth. The second Moth nationals saw a remarkable 100 entries. 'It's not how fast you're going, it's how fast you think you're going!' has been said of the class, and this perhaps explains the widespread enthusiasm for the boat. It was developed from the 3.35 m Australian Moth, and designed in plywood by Len Morris in 1946. The Moth was once described as 'matchbox-like with its slab sides, flat bottom and snub scow bow ... an acquired taste'. The New Zealand Moth is basically one-design, with some latitude in rig, deck, cockpit, rudder, and centreplate arrangement.

▶ The boat is a Moth and the helmsman is Bruce Farr. He is sailing the first Moth he designed and built. Amongst other innovations, including of course its shape and lightweight construction, the boat has roller reefing, as can be seen by the roller claw on the boom, to enable the mainsheet to be operated under reduced sail – not original to Bruce Farr but innovative in such a small boat.

▲ The R-class in this picture is not quite planing as it proceeds down-wind out of Wellington's Worser Bay Boating Club, and its crew seem relatively relaxed as they peer under the boom at something attracting their attention to leeward. They are wearing trapeze harnesses, which demands great agility of them when both are out on the wire.

In contrast with these new and influential designs, the R-class had been sailing in Canterbury since 1928, developing along traditional lines until the end of the Second World War. After 1945, the class and its adherents – most notably Brian Wall, who has been described as 'a genius at gear and rigging for racing yachts who typifies all that New Zealanders have done for themselves in this line over the years' – became a leader in its development. The R-class introduced many of the post-war innovations which so profoundly influenced small-boat sailing in New Zealand. The trapeze was first used in R-class boats by Brian Wall in *Impact* and by Graeme Wilson in *Havoc* in late 1953. Brian Wall, very much the R-class 'inventor', pioneered the use of venturis at about the same time as he did trapezes. His boat *Impact*, built in 1952 with two skins of cedar, the inner one diagonal and the outer laid fore and aft, weighed some 79 lbs and was the first moulded-ply R-class. *Fresco*, Brian Treleaven's boat, was the first to use two trapeze wires, doing so in the 1959-60 season.

Canterbury enthusiasts had begun promoting the class throughout New Zealand in 1951. Their *Sea Spray* notice that year carried a summary of what they called its 'specification'. From that specification, they quoted its objects as: 'To give yachtsmen the opportunity of developing fast racing centreboard yachts by putting into practice their own ideas in design and building.'

It was an attitude whose day had arrived, both in the class and in the wider sailing scene, and the southern sailors sensed its timeliness. The long-familiar stepping-stone boats were perceived as too constrained and too slow. Younger sailors were beginning to prefer the less-familiar paths of design inventiveness, variety, construction ease, greater lightness, and greater speed. The revolution was at hand.

The first contest for the Leander Trophy was held on the Christchurch Estuary in March 1951, and the R-class began to move north in the mid-1950s. In 1956 the national contest for the Leander Trophy was held in Wellington at the Evans Bay club, for the express purpose of creating interest in the class, and was won that year by Peter Mander. The first AGM of the Wellington R Class Squadron was held in 1958, and the R-class was declared a National Class by the NZYF the following year.

Something of the lively debate which accompanied the spread of the R-class beyond its home province is to be found in the *Sea Spray* issue of July 1951, the first year of that remarkable decade of change and diversification. Several letters to the editor argued the strengths and opportunities for inventiveness of the class, notably those from Peter Mander, his father Stan, and Hal Wagstaff. Peter's response to disbelief expressed at the speed the boats were capable of reads, 'I can understand ... doubts as to speeds attained, but as 'Z's have been timed at 14 knots and ' 'R's' have no difficulty in showing them a very clean pair of heels, I believe that under favourable circumstances they will even exceed the speed given.' The speed given was fifteen miles per hour.

Succinctly and with precision, Peter Mander summed up the reasons why the International 14 would not thrive here in New Zealand (and this writer's experience in crewing in one in windy conditions on Wellington Harbour leaves no doubts about the matter)

> The International 14 ft is open, and as pumps are barred, this class would have no hope, with a 2 man crew, of racing successfully in some of the weather we encounter in Lyttelton.

He goes on to say of the R:

> It is a keen competitive class in which ability to sail a boat will count for more than it does in most of our National classes, as it is obvious that a finely balanced boat requires more skill and attention to keep going at its best, than does a powerful craft ... To my mind they offer more than any other class in New Zealand – low cost, light weight, seaworthiness, speed and perfect handling, and above all freedom from restrictions of construction and design.

As much as any other boat, and there were to be many others in the years of diversification, the innovative R-class and the spread of its enthusiasts was at the heart of the transformation of small-boat building and racing in New Zealand in the following decade.

Since *Sopranino* was mentioned more than once in the debate in *Sea Spray* about how to fill the gap between the centreboarders and keelers for those who wanted to travel beyond their home waters and couldn't afford a boat big enough to do so, it seems right to mention the boat here. She was English in origin and not conceived of as a trailer-sailer of the sort soon to become widespread in New Zealand as a solution to the problem. But the design of *Sopranino* – clinker built, with chart table, galley, toilet, self-draining cockpit, and gear-storage space all fitted into her 19 ft 8 in length, along with a fin and bulb keel, a skeg-hung rudder, and a trapeze for one of her two-man crew – was a considerable step in the direction things were to go in New Zealand once the idea of fitting it all onto a road trailer had been seen to. And she planed!

The Zephyr-class spread from their home port of Auckland in 1958, though the greater number raced there, where they were used as a training class for the Finn. Terylene sailcloth was approved for the Zephyr in 1959. The New Plymouth Anniversary Day Regatta provided class racing for them in 1961, and there were 40 entries in the 1971 Auckland championships.

The passing of PZIX

Jack Brooke succinctly summarised the progress and fate of several classes racing in the Auckland Anniversary Regatta over the years up to 1970:

> The P class seven footer has gone from strength to strength and is at present the strongest numerically of any small boat class in New Zealand ... The Zs are struggling, Idle Alongs have given up the struggle ... I wish I could point a moral from this ... I find I can not, but there are a few positive points for class enthusiasts to think about. First the 'one-design' classes such as Zs and Ps. 'One designs' must in the long run become dated. The P class updated construction methods in good time to allow use of new materials. The Zs, I am afraid, missed the opportunity and left their run too late.

He could have said exactly the same about the Idle Alongs, of course, but made no mention of the reasons for their passing from the scene. In referring to the restricted-design classes he did, however, mention the Xies:

> The restricted classes, with more latitude within the rules, could have been in a better position with good management to progress with the times, both in design, sail plan and materials. The X class ... went too far and opened hull shape restrictions to give designers and builders a field day. With the Sanders Cup at stake some of our best designers took this opportunity, with startling results and the contest, as many have done throughout the world, deteriorated into a battle of designers. The class died.
>   Overall length classes, dependent on large crews, powerful boats and a tremendous spread of sail, were unable to compete with lighter, livelier and, at the same time, cheaper two-man boats. They also died. International competition, particularly in Olympic classes, then changed the pattern of small boat racing.

▲ Zephyrs, like Frostbites and Mistrals, also have a timeless look about them. Like the others, they have never had widespread support or great numbers, but the class obviously attracts a goodly fleet on occasions, as this 18-boat start illustrates.

Writing to the editor the September 1971 issue of *Sea Spray* about the rapid changes that were taking place all over New Zealand, Ian Treleaven noted that:

> … the outmoded X class has lost its popularity to the more sophisticated contemporary designs and so, too, has the venerable Takapuna punt … the Sanders Cup, indeed, at one time did have the status of the Ranfurly Shield, but this was in the days when the leading skippers and crews in New Zealand competed for the honour of representing their province in the prestigious X class dinghies. It is several years, however, since this was the case and this old-fashioned boat has dragged to a dismal end, sailed by, perhaps, enthusiastic crews but who are by no means the top-line yachtsmen in New Zealand. Our leading dinghy sailors have moved into Olympic classes and other modern designs … Today the popular contests are open contests, and this is what we should foster, because every New Zealander who has raced overseas will tell you that the one thing we lack experience in is racing in large fields.

The Ranfurly Shield that Treleaven referred to is New Zealand's most coveted inter-provincial rugby football trophy. In daring to compare the status of the Sanders Cup with that of the Shield, he was, in the eyes of rugby enthusiasts at least, taking a liberty.

Helping hands

In the very early days of yachting in New Zealand, in the latter part of the nineteenth century, it was a rich man's sport in big boats – just as it had been in Mother England. The less affluent typically took part as paid or unpaid crew, rather than as owners and skippers in their own right. But by the 1920s, as we have seen, the antipodean attitude to sailing had changed, and there were few financial barriers to entry.

Perhaps as a consequence, professional skippers and crews were ill-thought of by many involved in recreational sailing in New Zealand. They smacked of the moneyed advantage which yacht ownership had implied before the simplified construction of small boats enabled those with little money to build and crew and compete on something like even terms. Amateurism was deeply connected with the Kiwi 'do it yourself' ethos. It was thoroughly honourable, particularly if it included making your boat with your own hands. For a similar reason, when the idea of sponsorship began to spread, it too was disapproved of.

Don Tempest put the case well, though rather naively it seems now, in his contribution to *Sea Spray* in October 1966 ('Sponsored Yachting – a Bogey or a Blessing?') when he said:

▲ Early on in the sport, cigarette advertisers saw the potential for marketing that sailing provided out on the water in busy recreational areas, and the 18-footer class proved a spectacular mobile platform for such promotion. Of the three men in this Okahu Bay launching ramp scene, two are keeping the boat upright while the skipper sorts out some minor problem with the rudder. Soon they will be...

▼ ...all out on trapezes. Their boat standing out in bright sunshine against the bush-clad profile of Rangitoto Island, the crew of B&H are enjoying a breeze just about strong enough to get the boat planing on a reach tight enough to require the spinnaker pole to be very close to the forestay.

Sailmakers and shoemakers also found boat sails a good place on which to put their advertisements, and the performance capabilities of the Q-class made its boats a most noticeable feature of harbour sailing, especially when the wind got up, as it has done for this picture of two boats on the wind. For the moment, Q 5 is pointing higher than the Bally boat, and her just visible forward hand is using every ounce of weight to keep the boat flat, and sailing fast and high.

This R-class also fits the hull and rig requirements of the 12-foot skiffs, and can compete in either class. Less than a third of the boat was in the water at the moment this picture was taken off Worser Bay, yet Stephen Hogg and his crew seem to be well in control as they plane at very high speed.

Sponsorship, with the spectre of professionalism lurking in the background, has long been the province of the 18 footers and Q class yachts. However it has become increasingly apparent that sponsored yachting in one form or another has become the accepted thing in most of the highly competitive classes today. The primary object of sponsorship in any of its many forms is to enable yachtsmen who may not have the financial means to compete on an equal footing with those who have unlimited resources – in a class in which they may not otherwise have the opportunity to compete.

This was obviously not the primary aim of the sponsor, which was improved sales, of course, though it was of those who received it. What had slowly waned over the years between the end of the First World War and the 1960s was the strength of the belief that restricted design controls not only meant more or less equal boats being sailed in races to find the best sailors, but also that equality of boat was ensured because money didn't necessarily buy a better one.

As the community at large became more sophisticated and worldly-wise, those who participated in small-boat building also became more sophisticated and aware of the nuances that led to lightness, strength, and speed. Money spent on achieving these nuances began to make a difference out on the course.

In his *Sea Spray* article, Don Tempest quotes New Zealand sailor Don St. Clair Brown as saying, 'Sponsorship, whereby financial assistance is given to provide a boat or part of the cost of a boat fully or partly equipped without any ties or mention of the owners, except perhaps in club records or on official entry forms, may be better described as assisted yachting.' In the light of more recent events, such an arrangement would be better described as a most unlikely development – especially when it is recognised that the very determined tobacco industry was much to the fore in those early years.

Anyone who doubts the fairness of such an observation need only flick through issue upon issue of years of *Sea Sprays* to see the intensity of tobacco advertising placed there by the several companies marketing the product in New Zealand.

In his report to the NZYF annual meeting in 1974, its president Ian Treleaven said of sponsorship in general:

We are all fed up with selling raffle tickets and cadging … Today, sponsorship of sport is world wide, even for sports with a gate. It is time we discarded the old-fashioned Corinthian outlook and instead took a realistic look at the matter.

Naturally commercial interests will want as much mileage as they can get from their investment and I think that as long as we steer clear of Rule 26 (advertising on yachts) we must go along with them.'

By 1976, the UK government and the tobacco companies had agreed new laws that banned cigarette brand names from boats, though they didn't actually forbid cigarette sponsorship. It just mustn't be seen, and sponsors' names were still allowed to be mentioned in media reports.

The tobacco company Rothmans insisted in an article in the October 1966 issue of *Sea Spray* that their 'unobtrusive yet very direct help' for classes such as the Flying Dutchman, the Dragon, and the Finn was to be 'looked on in its true light – that of teaching and encouraging our younger yachtsmen'. That the company also 'got behind the Murray's Bay Father and Son class to help raise funds for better facilities' was a very blunt advertising instrument when the word Rothmans was incorporated in the class name (it was originally called the Rothmans Father & Son class), but became more subtle after their name was taken out.

Though it seems unbelievable now, Rothmans said then, and were not challenged in saying it, that in sponsoring young New Zealand yachtsmen they were 'proud to feel that they are assuming the responsibilities of citizenship in the community which owns them'.

No doubt the sponsorship deal still helped young sailors to learn to smoke tobacco when they were not sailing, even if the old-fashioned habit of doing so while competing had been given up. It was by then almost impossible to do so, given the vigorous way small boats were sailed downwind as well as up. (It is interesting to note that, in the late 1940s certainly, and no doubt earlier, some experienced centreboarder crews set their spinnaker, and then sat across the stern of their boat and had a cigarette as they sailed the downwind leg of the course. Yachting must in those days have seemed ripe for encouragement to those keen to sell the weed. Unlike most sports, some sailors actually smoked tobacco while they competed!)

Interestingly, though it was unfortunate for young British sailors, the London marketing manager of Dunhill claimed in the March 1969 issue of *Sea Spray* that his company had 'been keen supporters of British Olympic yachting for over three years now ... notably the sponsorship of the Poole Bay Olympic Training Regatta ...'

▲ It no doubt seemed innocuous at the time, but the Rothmans Father & Son class can now be seen as blatant tobacco advertising aimed right at the young sailor and his father. The sponsored 24-hour race on Lake Pupuke was for some years sailed in RFS boats, though it is now sailed in Lasers. Individual boat sponsors were also involved, just as they are nowadays, though Rothmans obviously insisted that other advertising be kept off the sails, where their own logo-turned-sail-symbol was left to stand out clear above everything else.

Clearly, tobacco companies have long known just where to strike, and they still loom large as sponsors in international yachting. They are not active domestically in New Zealand these days, even though they were still providing advertisement-covered mobile race-control centres for regattas at small yacht clubs here in the 1980s.

The Dunhill Cup was that tobacco company's way of getting their name further into New Zealand sailors' minds. Dunhill was innocently called 'The Godfather of New Zealand Yachting' by *Sea Spray* editor David Pardon in August 1975. That was the year they 'donated' the $1000 cup with their name on it for a mixed-rating offshore keeler series that included the Hobart–Auckland race. A total of $7750 in Dunhill prize money was involved, which the company said it hoped would attract a number of overseas entries.

◀ Presumably these three boats are racing. If so, the single-handed Moth whose hull is barely visible beyond the wake of the boat in the foreground is doing well, because the others are two-handed boats, one a 470, the other an R-class. Perhaps the race was a one-of-a-kind event started on the Mark Foy system, and the bigger boats are in the process of politely overtaking the Moth to leeward.

Dashing downhill rides

How small boats led the way to innovative developments in bigger ones was a feature of the special 1966 *Sea Spray* review issue:

> In local racing the most significant change in keel boat design has been the swing to light displacement and fin keels, best typified in the designs of Bob Stewart and John Spencer – the Patikis and Scimitars, *Northerner* and *Infidel*.
>
> In common with the small boats, terylene and nylon sails and synthetic cordage have made a great difference in keelers, and they are now following the centreboarders in developing bendy or partly bendy rigs, and alloy masts are becoming commonplace in the Auckland fleet.
>
> Boating in New Zealand has really come of age in the past 21 years and a book could be written in tribute to the many who have made the period so significant – the builders and designers and club officials as well as the boat owners.

Jack Brooke, the Auckland yachtsman and designer, in a *Sea Spray* article contributed on the occasion of the magazine's twenty-fifth birthday in 1970, summed up the post-war developments in sailing, as he saw them after examining his collection of *Sea Sprays*:

> We see the evolution of new classes, introduction of new materials and construction methods and increased efficiency of sails and sail trimming gear. We also see increasing complexity of equipment and cost of construction and maintenance. At the same time, a rapidly improving standard of living has brought more and more people into the yacht-owning category.
>
> Reading on, through 1950 to 1960 and 1970 we find not only a change in design and construction, but many more yachts of all types and an annual figure for new construction of 10 to 20 times the volume of pre-war building, and at a rough guess at least 50 times the value.

The two-person Sunburst dinghy is perhaps Jack Brooke's most well-known and long-lived centreboarder, and a class still thriving throughout New Zealand. Despite the inflation in prices that Brooke complained of in 1970, it is to this day a cheap boat, and one that can still be built in the back yard or shed.

Speaking very much from the designer's point of view, Brooke went on to consider other aspects of the changing scene and summarised them in a way which nicely captured the trends of the times:

▲ Starlings have a bendy rig, and their flexible masts have caused some anxiety at times, especially when their national championships were held on Wellington harbour on one windy occasion. The fashionable wrinkled luff area, believed by the young sailors to be a sign of quickness and an idea borrowed from the international classes, is evident in this picture, as is the shock-cord line from bow fitting to boom, which is used to keep the mainsail out against the sidestay when running downwind.

▶ Judging by their relative sizes, the crew of this Sunburst are likely to be father and son, or some such combination of youth and age, and the high sail number gives some indication of the popularity of the class. Life jackets are clearly being worn, and it is equally clear that the wind strength warrants such precautions. The camera has caught the instant the hull almost leaped out of the water and the thrill for the young forward hand of sailing on a reach in such conditions can be imagined.

▲ This Moth is spinning out of control without anyone at the tiller. Somewhere in the left-hand half of the cloud of spray is the sailor involved, and soon the boat will be lying on its side in the midst of it all. Sailing a low-wooded Moth downwind in such windy conditions – the state of the sea surface bottom right gives a clue as to how hard it is blowing – is full of thrills and of the possibility of capsize.

▼ Hard on the wind, the crew of this Flying Dutchman are almost obscured by the spray off the wave-top they have just driven through. The boat is clear of the water to a point well aft of the centreboard, and the hull and rig will be severely tested when it meets the next wave.

In larger classes and fields where there is keen international competition, such as the Olympic classes, overseas measurement rules have been adopted, but in the development of local classes the New Zealander is a rugged individualist and has in general developed his own classes and rules. It is evident in reading on from 1945 that the driving force has been speed, and most new classes developed since the war have had this in mind. Planing hulls, lighter construction and introduction of the multihull are the result, and if we have lost something in seaworthiness or length of life, who cares? The thrill of that dashing downhill ride, the liveliness and ease of handling in and out of the water, are the thing. If the craft falls to bits under hard driving, we can build another, better one tomorrow. We are in a changing world and change is progress ... Some of these [changes] have been gradual, some sudden and almost catastrophic.

But there were developments at other levels, too. An earlier issue of *Sea Spray* had some trenchant things to say about administrative advances in sailing the faster lighter boats which had resulted from the revolution:

In sailing, the major factor in class development has probably been the greater interest in international competition and the acceptance of international classes with their very great influence on other local developments. ...Coupled with our Olympic aspirations was the formation of the N.Z. Yachting Federation in 1954. This was formed primarily to ensure a national body to speak on Olympic affairs but has later taken on many more of the duties of a national body, but it has had to fight its own members who still want too much local control and provincial government. The Federation has not had a happy history. Perhaps the best thing that has happened in administration is the growth of class owners associations which keep control of class affairs firmly where it belongs – in the hands of the men who own the boats and sail them.

The magazine's view about class owners' associations was not a universally held opinion, especially amongst those at the national body headquarters, but was an astute observation nevertheless.

Specialising in speed

The single-minded, specialist racing-dinghy sailor, a breed that was soon to become the primary source of the specialist big-boat sailors and crews, first came into being during the late 1950s and 1960s. In the twenty-first birthday issue of *Sea Spray*, Peter Mander described the young sailor of the 1960s:

By the time he is 20 a yachtsman has probably been through Ps, and Zs or Junior Cherubs, and possibly Cherubs, R class dinghie or Javelins, and he is generally a much more experienced and competitive skipper able to talk 'learnedly' on the subtleties of his current class – but he may not even be able to row a dinghy.

Exactly. No longer was a general education in the old-fashioned arts and mysteries of 'good seamanship' considered necessary or desirable in the attributes of a competitor in fast light boats. The R-class, for instance, became the sort of boat which gave the appearance of having to be held upright when launched, otherwise it might fall over – not at all a seamanlike characteristic!

For success, experience in small boats requires that the whole boat be understood as a high-speed mechanism of which the crew is an equally high-speed part. The limits to its stability and performance must be instinctively recognised and responded to in competition. The extreme example of this point of view has to be boardsailing, a skill even some very successful small-boat sailors have difficulty in mastering. Boardsailing is the yachting equivalent of barefoot waterskiing, just as planing is the equivalent of breaking the sound barrier.

Vigorous operation of the mechanism, and equally vigorous responses to its behaviour by skipper and crew alike, are now simply taken for granted as racing skills long ago learned and honed to high levels in childhood and early youth. In most cases the training took place in that series of lightweight, planing centreboarders, both old-fashioned and new-fangled, that has long been available to New Zealanders of modest means but great enthusiasm for competitive sailing.

Over the decade or so from the mid 1950s to the mid 1960s, with the beginning of the transfer of their ideas into bigger boats, the cross-breeding between the classes, between the new-fangled and the old-fashioned, simply intensified the sense of competitive ability amongst designers and builders, skippers and crews, administrators and race officials. It proved to be excellent preparation for what was to come once New Zealand sailors went offshore, beyond their habitual club and small-boat courses, and started competing internationally.

▲ It soon became the thing in the big-boat sailing scene to sail keelboats like dinghies. KZ 2222, hard on the wind, has seven of its ten visible crewmembers out on the windward rail, four of them with their feet and legs dangling, and some of them, it seems in this picture, with their whole body outside the safety rail – a definite racing safety rules no-no. Soon, big boats came to not only be sailed like fast light small boats but also to look like them.

▼ Bendy rigs, just like stiff ones, find their limits when conditions get really tough. This fact can be dramatically brought home in many classes. This dismasting occurred in sunny but ferocious conditions during the trailer sailer National Championships in 1983. The crew have tidied up the ensuing mess, secured the broken spar aboard, and are now making their way slowly downwind amidst waves whose tops are being whipped off and turned into sparkling white spume. Rig failures and their analysis are one of the ways in which mast and other spar design developments evolve, in big boats as well as in small.

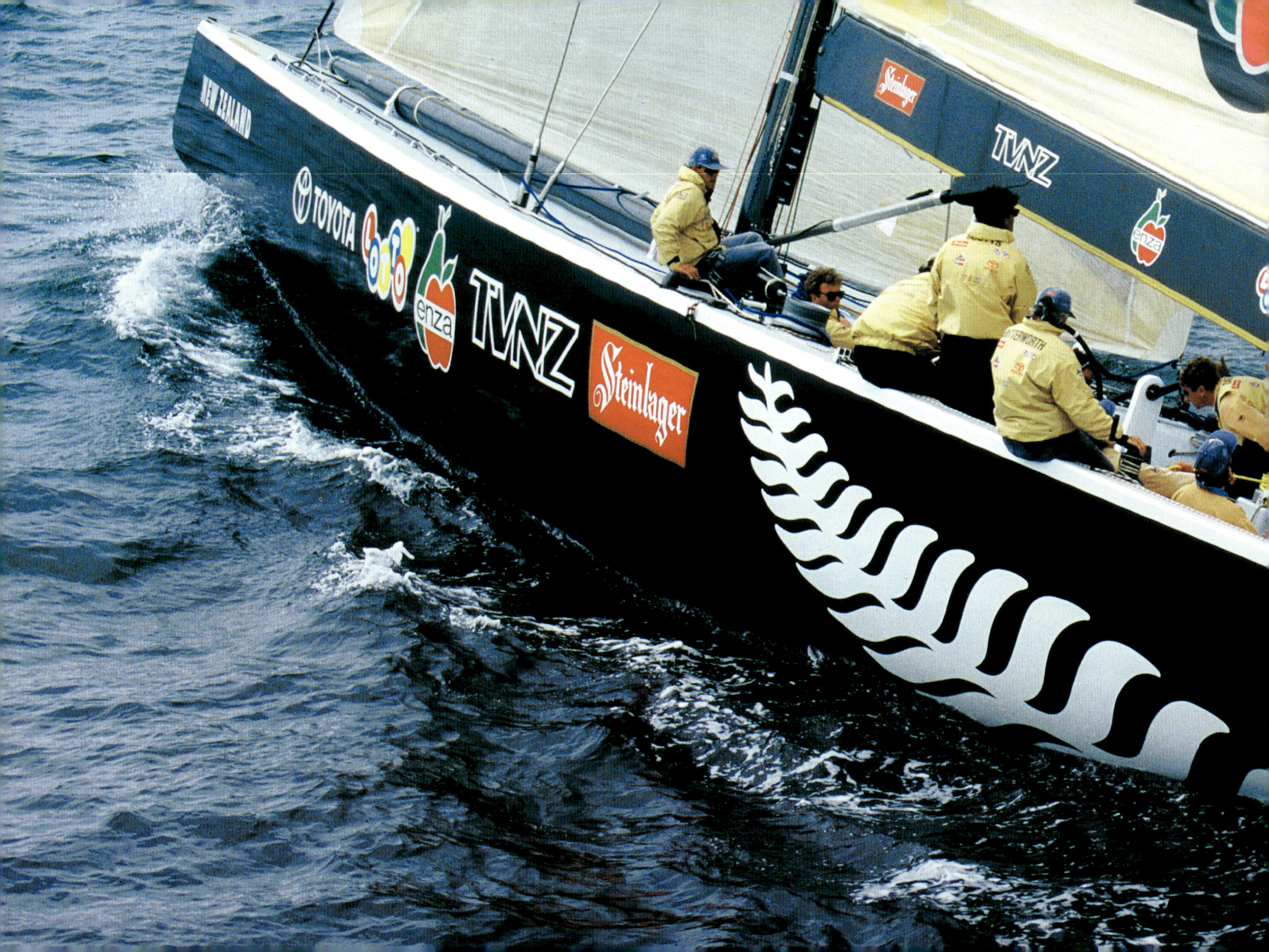

NEW ZEALAND
TOYOTA
LOTTO
enza
TVNZ
Steinlager

Chapter 6
Small boats writ large

> The ideas behind *Kiwi Magic*, and the skills of its crew, are the product of 100 years of thinking about, designing, building, and racing boats that stretch the boundaries of convention. The big black boat, decorated with sponsors' logos, is shown here on the wind, in the light conditions and big seas that are typical of San Diego – but unlike those in Auckland.

My first boat was a P-Class: the national youth boat and an amazing little craft. It is seven feet long and until recently was usually home-built out of plywood. It has one sail, a short mast, a long boom, a low aspect sail plan and it has the mast stepped well forward. The cockpit has no self-draining system and you have to bail the water out continuously when sailing in strong winds. They are much more demanding boats to sail than the Optimist or Sabot and they are one of the most difficult boats to sail downwind in strong winds because they frequently nose-dive. I look back at all the technology involved and the thinking behind it and it's such a complicated boat in terms of balance, sail shapes and tuning that there's no doubt that if you can master it you can sail almost any boat.

Russell Coutts, in *Course to Victory*

A great many of the Kiwi sailors who have succeeded in all sorts of international races and regattas, in Olympic competition in dinghies, in 'Ton Cup' races, in open-sea team events such as the Admirals and Kenwood Cups, and in the several round-the-world races held over the years, had developed their enthusiasm for racing under sail by first becoming involved in the New Zealand way of doing things in small boats.

The apparently huge difference between the seven-foot long, single-handed P-class which begins it all for many Kiwis and the present day America's Cup boats is, as Russell Coutts' observations reveal, not as

▼ If a single illustration could show the sport of big-boat sailing on the Waitemata Harbour in the middle years of the century, it would have to look something like this. The legendary *Ranger* makes her way past Rangitoto Island in a moderate breeze, her crew in white shorts and shirts, attending to tasks about the boat, protected from falling overboard by a concession to the changing times – the addition of pulpit, pushpit, and lifelines.

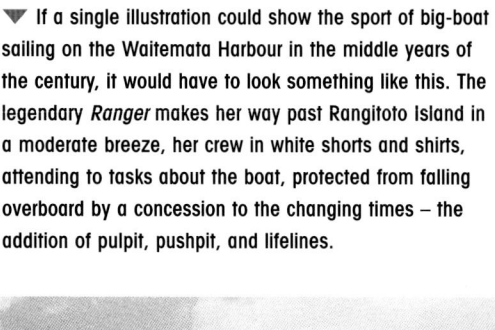

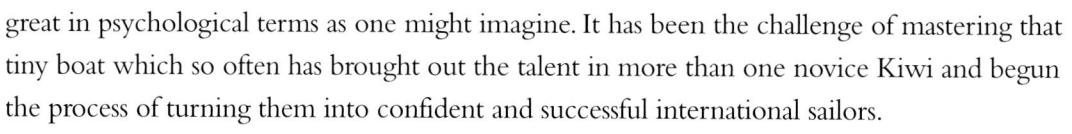

great in psychological terms as one might imagine. It has been the challenge of mastering that tiny boat which so often has brought out the talent in more than one novice Kiwi and begun the process of turning them into confident and successful international sailors.

Decades of experience in designing small fast light boats could have only one outcome once the designers' (and sailors') thoughts turned to applying their skills and enthusiasm to bigger boats. That turning point occurred in the 1960s, not all of a sudden, but by stages, and took the big-boat scene rather by surprise.

There were many people involved in this transfer from small to big boats. Designers, builders, riggers, sailmakers, and a host of sailors had taken their understanding of the needs and possibilities of fast light boats out into the wider world of sailing, where convention still reigned. The opportunity was there to employ that understanding and win.

The most widely known of these enthusiasts for lightness and speed is the renowned designer Bruce Farr, who has attributed New Zealand's design success to the do-it-yourself, inexpensive boat-building phenomenon. It was not matched anywhere else in the world, and it overwhelmed traditional thinking.

Over the decades when small boats had been undergoing great change, most of those involved in the design, construction, and sailing of big boats had continued along very much the old ways that good seamanship demanded of them – for good reason, since the demands of sailing at sea remained paramount for reasons of safety. In what were called 'keelers', strong, wooden (and therefore heavy) 'seaworthy' hulls, and equally strong, durable, and heavy rigs and sails, together with the traditions of good seamanship that went with it all, remained predominant in New Zealand for much of the period when the small-boat revolution was taking place.

For a very long time, at least until the decade of the 1950s, the sailors who graduated from the small-boat scene and built for themselves bigger boats took for granted the conservative shift in attitude necessary to adapt to the more sedate ways of big boats. Nevertheless, small-boat skills, especially those which came from sailing fast light boats to their limits and beyond, were much sought after – once it was realised that those skills made for faster big boats and the winning of races – because the former dinghy sailors knew instinctively the limits to which big boats could be taken.

Along with the introduction of rigs, fittings, and controls from small boats that enabled big boats of conventional design to sail more quickly, the small-boat sailors who went on to race in big boats also introduced their lively and athletic ways of crewing. By this process, big-boat crews came to operate their boats in small-boat ways, and some of them inevitably came to think of designing and building big boats which responded more quickly to those small-boat ways of sailing them.

Making boats sail faster

Boats driven by the force of the wind on their sails move more quickly through the water if they are lightly built than if they are of heavy construction. This must have been well understood by boatbuilders a very long time ago – long before recreational competitive sailing began. Simple physics teaches the sailor that.

▶ Sheets were once the only ropes handled as the boat went along. But as the significance of sail shape and setting became better understood, making adjustments as the race proceeded became the norm. A variety of control lines began to appear in the more competitive small boats, and became distinctly complicated when the crew moved outboard on to trapezes, taking the control lines out there with them. The resultant cats'-cradle is shown here, elegantly organised in this case.

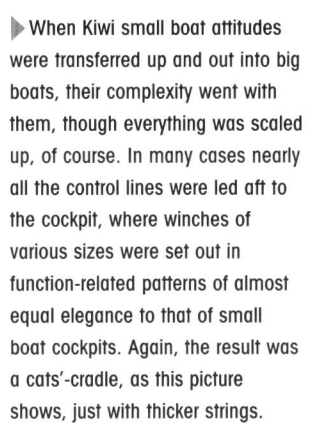

▶ When Kiwi small boat attitudes were transferred up and out into big boats, their complexity went with them, though everything was scaled up, of course. In many cases nearly all the control lines were led aft to the cockpit, where winches of various sizes were set out in function-related patterns of almost equal elegance to that of small boat cockpits. Again, the result was a cats'-cradle, as this picture shows, just with thicker strings.

But it was not until the advent of competitive small boat sailing that the fragility that accompanies lightness ceased to be a hazard to life out on the water. Once they started to make boats that were used only for racing, designers and builders were relieved of the absolute necessity to build strong durable vessels that would be capable of surviving the worst that seagoing duties could impose on them. Instead, they could concentrate on those factors that made for lightness and speed.

It was the same with sailing. Small-boat racing is a matter of sailing in company with other boats close to the shore in sheltered waters. Once sailors realised that sailing light boats required different crewing techniques, the traditional rules of good seamanship were set aside in the pursuit of boat speed.

Keeping boats from heeling excessively whether sailing upwind or down makes them sail faster, since they present a more efficient hull shape to the water when sailed upright. This fact applies whether the boat in question is light or heavy, big or small. Capsizing was once thought of as a disaster, but in small boats with built-in buoyancy it became only a moderate inconvenience. To make light boats sail faster, as well as to keep them from capsizing, it became necessary on occasions for the crew to extend their bodyweight out beyond the perimeter of the cockpit, out on to the deck and then outside the line of the hull. Similar techniques were later adopted in larger boats.

The enjoyment of this new way of sailing small boats far outweighed any sense of duty to the old rules of seamanship there might have been amongst the young sailors who indulged in it – and soon spread to those who might at first have disapproved.

The old distinction between 'centreboarders' (meaning small sailing craft) and 'keelers' (meaning big sailing craft) is now no longer a sufficient or accurate one. Some of the small fast light boats that entered the story in the last chapter have keels, and some of the big fast boats that will be discussed in this chapter have centreboards. The expressions adopted here to properly make the distinction are, simply, 'small boats' and 'big boats'.

▲ In the old days, spars and fittings had to be made very strong in order to survive the worst that the oceans could throw at them, as this picture shows. The sense of good seamanship that went with such massively-built vessels was almost impossible to overcome when lightness and rapid obsolescence took over in big boats as well. For some old-style sailors, adapting was even harder when it became obvious that it was antipodeans who were behind the revolution.

Designing Kiwis

At the end of 1966, Brian Wall, widely recognised as one of the more significant and lateral-thinking innovators in New Zealand's influential and free-spirited R-class, wrote a prophetic piece about what he saw as the likely direction of developments in Kiwi sailing in the coming decades:

> Since the war there have been changes in materials used for hulls, sails, and fittings. Rigging and fittings have been greatly altered and refined. I feel that the next area of major change may be boat design itself.

Brian Wall was right. The next area of major change was indeed in boat design, and it has been going on now for some thirty years.

Every present-day New Zealand designer of competitive sailing boats, both big and small, would admit to a debt to the ingenuity and inventiveness of all the Kiwis who designed, built, and sailed faster and faster small boats over the past hundred years or so. Some have said so in print, and all will surely have admitted to it in conversation at one time or another. The recognition of the quality of those early design ideas and innovative attitudes in the country at large, and amongst its sailing community in particular, pervades New Zealand sailing lore amongst those who think, research, and write about it.

As Kiwi design, construction, and competition ideas spread out into the wider sailing world through example, through debate, and through media interest, they become more and more complex in a more and more complicated world, to the point where by far the best way to examine them is by looking at several designers in more detail.

◀ There is an air of busyness and solidity about the fittings at the foot of *Corinthian's* mast, as this close-up shows. But there is no unnecessary weight, though the scale of the fittings and the thickness of the ropes is of an altogether different order to that of the innovative dinghies from which much of the design detail and thought derive.

◀ The scale of the gooseneck arrangement shown here is a little smaller than that of the *Corinthian* mast base arrangement shown above, but every part of it still has a look of substance. Each fitting has a particular task to do. Every one is of minimum thickness and maximum strength, with no wasted weight. Nevertheless, it is an aesthetically pleasing combination of hardwood cleat, aluminium spars, stainless-steel fittings, stranded natural fibre and braided synthetic rope, and satin-black winch-handle socket.

It is safe to say that every subsequent Kiwi designer of sailing boats owes something to John Spencer's ideas about design, construction, and materials. His design career began the day the sharp eyes shown here saw a tiny, strange-looking centreboarder under construction at Shelly Bay in Wellington and his lively mind appreciated the possibilities it presented. This picture was taken several years before John Spencer's death in 1996.

John Spencer's interest in the smallest of fast light boats continued all his life, as shown by this beach scene near the Tamaki Yacht Club, where he appears to be involved in a boat rigging exercise with a young Sea Spray representative.

John Spencer

Marine-grade waterproof plywood revolutionised small boat design and construction in the post-war years, and the transfer of the knowledge gained about its use in fast light small boats similarly revolutionised big-boat design and construction. John Spencer led these sequential revolutions, first with his introduction and development of innovative plywood small boats, and subsequently with his transfer of those ideas to bigger and bigger boats. According to Bruce Farr, John Spencer set other designers an example of innovative thinking: '... he did things that were quite different from the mainstream.'

Born in Australia, John Spencer began his involvement with sailing in the 1940s, sailing a hired EBYMBC-owned P-class out of Balaena Bay on the western side of Wellington's Evans Bay. As we have already seen, his interest in plywood construction dated from the mid 1940s, when he heard of a plywood boat being built at the Shelly Bay naval base across the bay from where he lived. Waterproof ply was a very new material at the time, untried in New Zealand, and Spencer's letter on page 68 to Barney Scully, one of the two brothers who built *Why Not* out of waterproof plywood, reveals something of this awakening of interest.

After his first seven-footer, Spencer sailed in Zeddies and Idle Alongs. He was a product of the PZIX stepping-stone sequence and expressed his on-the-water understanding of the Kiwi fast light boat philosophy in his radical new plywood designs.

In his January 1973 *Sea Spray* profile of John Spencer, David Pardon wrote: 'He knows damn well his ideas are going to work but won't say so until they actually do ... It's hard to imagine that you are talking to one of the most brilliant designers on the yachting scene, an ingenious mind that can push a sailboat through the water fast yet at considerably less expense than practically any other man in the game.'

That Spencer also designed very successful power boats, and understood their formidable high-speed planing performance and high-stress structural requirements, added greatly to his capabilities, and further explains his success when it came to designing and building big sailing boats.

It can be said without exaggeration that his use of marine-grade waterproof plywood revolutionised New Zealand small-boat design and construction in the years after the

Second World War, and that his transfer of the knowledge gained about its use in fast light small boats similarly revolutionised big-boat design and construction.

Following his development of radical plywood centreboarders, the Cherub in 1951 and the Javelin in 1959, Spencer became involved in big plywood boats such as *Adrienne* and *Scimitar* in 1959-60. Tom Clark's 37-foot *Saracen* was a tryout of Spencer's ideas for *Infidel*, the big fast boat for which he designed absolutely everything – just as he had for his centreboarders, and just as he was to do for *Buccaneer*, the 73-foot boat which confirmed his growing reputation as the 'plywood king'.

Building on the success of his several centerboarder designs, Spencer had gone on to design more fin-keel light-displacement big boats in ply. His 67-footer *Infidel* could beat *Ranger*, the hitherto unbeatable Auckland Harbour champion, to the consternation of the old guard.

His big boats were subtly scaled-up versions of his small ones, with hard-chined plywood hulls, short keels in the place of centreboards, and separately hung rudders. They were narrow, but still of relatively conventional hull shape when compared with the more extreme fast light big boats which were to follow them. Nevertheless, Spencer's inventive design and construction of keelers led the way for other New Zealand designers and builders.

By the early 1970s, Spencer was designing quarter-tonners and half-tonners – his 30-footer was the first boat he designed to a ton rule. This shift from fast small boats in plywood to fast big boats in plywood had its inevitable influence on other designers. Kiwi small-boat ingenuity began to spread amongst others who, like Spencer, had learnt the sport in the sort of boat which tested agility as well as sailing skill, and who were also beginning to design big boats.

'*Infidel* was a true ULDB ahead of its time,' said Gary Baigent of John Spencer's design in the June 1986 issue of *Sea Spray*, 'with its long narrow hull, long waterline, short rig and minimal displacement – it was the father of the movement to radical ultra light displacement boats like *Merlin*, *Kriter* and the Centomiglia yachts of the European lakes such as *Grifo*, *Farreticante*, *OPNI* and *DF Design*.' As Baigent pointed out, the influence of Bruce Farr in these later boats was considerable, though he noted that they harked back to Uffa Fox's somewhat derided sliding-seat canoe of the 1930s, and also pointed forward to the Aussie 18-footers of more recent times, capable of planing almost constantly, both upwind and downwind.

▲ In this slipway scene at Westhaven, *Gazelle*, one of John Spencer's early designs, looks pristine and brand new, and shows off his signature chined hull form while being inched into the water. The boat's fin keel and skeg rudder also reveal their centreboarder origins.

▼ Though the hull of *Ragtime*, originally known as *Infidel*, is almost out of sight as she runs under full main and big kite on a windy day, what can be seen of her cabin form and window shape is sufficient to identify her designer. The outstanding competition record of this Spencer boat over a long period and under both names, confirmed its significance in the Kiwi light displacement story.

▲ The low sun has silhouetted each foredeck crew on these Stewart 34s sailing on Auckland Harbour. Perhaps they are approaching the top mark and are about to drop the big genoas and set their spinnakers. Though not particularly quick-looking in this light air picture, the class became known for even performance in almost identical boats. For this reason Stewart 34s were chosen both for match racing and, later, for sponsored international competition amongst sailors of very high ability.

Bob Stewart

Bob Stewart, designer of the influential Stewart 34, was an Aucklander. Though the keeler he conceived in the late 1950s became known as the 'Stewart 34 Patiki', it owed much more to the 26-foot mullet boat, the heavier and stronger descendant of the fragile lightweight Patiki, than it did to the Patiki class itself.

Stewart's innovative design for Peter Colmore-Williams has been called 'the first true, native, light displacement monohull' by Gary Baigent (by which he meant the first *big* boat to warrant that title). Its three-skinned hull, built by John Lidgard, took into the big boat field the kind of construction that had been used in fast light small boats for a decade or so. The layers of quarter-inch kauri were glued with epoxy adhesives as in the smaller boats, but something of the traditional boatbuilding manner of doing things remained in the nailing, though it was a modern threaded form and not rivetting that was used.

Though it was not conceived as a planing boat, the Stewart 34 was shallow-drafted and looked positively dinghy-like when seen against the conventional keelers against which it raced. Its cabin height (dictated by the need for more headroom) above a generous freeboard made the boat look high-wooded and not quick, but its light weight and beamy hull gave it speed and stability both upwind and down, even if it did broach rather more readily than its heavy displacement competitors.

The masthead-rigged inboard sail plan devised by Bob Stewart had none of the overhangs of the mullet boats, but the Stewart 34's lightness of construction meant that the boat was easily driven by the smaller spread of sail. Its rudder was found to be too small, and a deeper one was introduced. The boat certainly felt as though it was planing at times, and the 10,000 lb lightweight easily left the big boats behind in off-the-wind starts.

Stewart 34s became an evenly-matched class of such quality that they proved ideal for the modern development of 'match-racing', and the class was used for that purpose right up until the 1997-98 season, after which the Citizen-sponsored match-racing series on Auckland Harbour was sailed in Farr MRXs.

Laurie Davidson

Laurie Davidson had crewed on Xies just after the Second World War, and at the age of 20 he upset the Auckland M-class establishment in the 1947-48 season with *Myth*, which he had built himself to his own design. *Myth* was painted black, fine-bowed, with a straight-up-and-down bow and stern, and its crew was dressed in matching clothing. It won so often that there was talk of having the boat destroyed. But it was not just the boat's looks and outstanding performance which caused the upset. It was her ingenious lightweight construction, carried out in a back-yard shed with a close if not scrupulous attention to the class rules, that established Davidson as an early exponent of that Kiwi approach to fast light boat design, construction, and competition that continually posed the question, 'Where in the rules does it say you can't do this?'

Davidson became a full time designer in 1970, and won the first NZ Half Ton championships with his *Blitzkreig*, designed for Tony Bouzaid. The beamy Davidson 28 was designed in 1975, and there were at one time more than 130 of them sailing in New Zealand. In 1976 Davidson's *Fun* was an internationally successful trailerable quarter-tonner, and his later *Pendragon* uniquely won both the 3/4 Ton Cup and subsequently the One Ton Cup after modification to suit the bigger class.

Davidson's *Outward Bound*, built for Digby Taylor, won the small-boat class in the 1981-82 Whitbread round-the-world race, and successful Davidson IOR boats included *Great Fun*, another *Pendragon*, and *Mad Max*. Significant Davidson 55s included *Starlight Express*, *Honkytonk Woman*, and *Emotional Rescue*.

Following his involvement with Bruce Farr and Ron Holland in the development of the fibreglass 12-metre boat for New Zealand's

▶ The Davidson M 20 trailer sailer, shown here on a light-wind day on Auckland Harbour, has something of the look of a scaled-down big boat. Its rig, including the adjustable permanent backstay just visible, and its efficient and well laid-out deck arrangements, also speak of its designer's big-boat understanding.

▼ Laurie Davidson's first *Pendragon* began life as a three-quarter tonner, in which form it won the Three-quarter Ton Cup, then the boat was modified, and won the One Ton Cup. This 1985 construction photograph is of the second *Pendragon*, designed to the one-ton rule. The boat's dinghy-like form, with its long planing after-sections, by then typical of most of the leading Kiwi designers, is clearly displayed as the boat lies upside down in a shed in Whangarei, the fairing of her hull almost finished.

challenge for the America's Cup in 1987, he moved his office to the United States in 1989.

The Davidson Ultimate 30 design, much influenced by the early Logan skimmers, with a scow-type bow, a short mast and long boom, and with outriggers for several of its crew, excelled in the sponsored circuit racing in San Francisco in 1990.

When it was all over at the America's Cup in San Diego in 1995, Laurie Davidson said of the whole exercise, as quoted in *New Zealand Boating World,* 'My greatest surprise, was that it was such a complete victory. We always thought we could win, but never by such big margins.' Davidson is involved in the 1999 New Zealand America's Cup defence, and at the time of writing his latest IACC boat had recently been launched in Auckland.

Des Townson

Like several other New Zealand designers, Des Townson began sailing in a P-class, and went on to crew for his father, first in a Frostbite and later, from the age of 16, in keelers.

Townson began building glued laminated-construction dinghies, having attended a symposium on the subject run by Jack Brooke, one of his mentors. He designed and built small boats, of which the Zephyr and Mistral are the most well known, for a decade or so. But then came Bob Stewart's Patiki, the boat Des Townson called 'a major breakthrough ... a complete reversal of the way keelers had been going ... a return to the 1890s really ... I remember Jack telling me that there was a 27 foot boat down in the shed and he could remember two men lifting it ...'. He later designed and built the 27-foot *Serene*, very much influenced by the lightweight Patiki idea, using a moulded technique.

Not originally intended for racing, having been conceived in 1971 as a Hauraki Gulf cruising boat, the Townson-designed *Moonlight* shook the One Ton Cup selection trials in 1971 when, sailed by Peter Mulgrew, it almost headed off *Wai Aniwa* and *Young Nick*, the specialist One Tonner trialists. Next to come along in the series of Townsons was *Starlight*, followed by *Twilight*, into which he put the best features of the previous two and in which he developed the ideas he had about comfortable but fast mid-sized Hauraki Gulf cruisers to produce the first Townson 32. The 22-foot Pied Pipers that followed were designed as a stepping-stone racing boat to bridge the gap between dinghies and keelers.

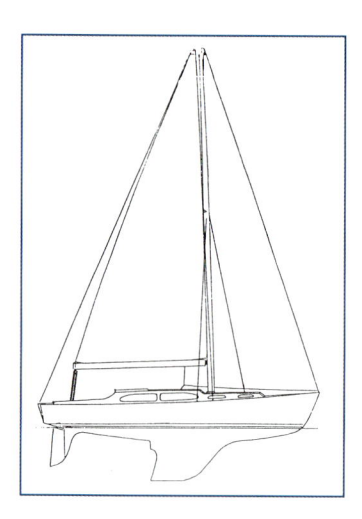

▲ The simple, classic lines of the Townson 32.

▲ Des Townson's influences came from men such as Jack Brooke and the Logan brothers, from early vessels such as the elegant Viking longships, and from the music of Albinoni and Beethoven. He has said, 'In expressing form, there is a certain rightness to things – and where it comes from I don't know.'

Bruce Farr

For Bruce Farr, it all began when he was an infant, in the Farr family keelers. He started sailing in dinghies at Leigh, north of Auckland, at the age of seven. His interest in mathematics, science, and technical drawing at school seems to have come from his grandparents. At about the time he began designing boats himself, with the help of his father he built a John Spencer-designed Flying Ant and began his racing career. Moths were his next interest, beginning with *Mammoth*, his own version of the International Moth class, designed and built during his time at secondary school, by which time he was also building boats for his friends.

After he left school, Bruce Farr began working and drawing for Jim Young. He had no formal training as a 'naval architect' – but then neither did John Spencer, Ron Holland, or Laurie Davidson. In 1970, after his job with Youngs had disappeared, he began designing and building his own versions of inexpensive fast light small boats on his own account, at first concentrating on very well drawn and very successful 18-footers.

In the early 1970s Farr became involved in designing inexpensive fast light big boats. The considerable success of his beamy-sterned light-displacement quarter-ton, half-ton, three-quarter- and one-ton designs led to the offshore racing rules being changed by northern-hemisphere conservatives, on the pretext that such boats were unseaworthy and unsafe.

Bruce Farr was a member of each of the three-man teams of Kiwi designers who produced the New Zealand boat for the 1987 challenge for the America's Cup in Fremantle, and

▲ Bruce Farr's big boats still looked like small boats, which fact upset the establishment, whose members thought big boats should be somehow different. They were. They were slower. Boats like this one, the 22ft 8in fractionally-rigged *Fantzipantz*, built by Alan Porter, typified the sort of Kiwi-designed boat, seemingly too dinghy-like to warrant the pulpit and lifelines adorning her rails, that could beat them.

▲ While big boats came to look more and more like scaled-up small boats, trailer sailers began to resemble scaled-down big boats, especially when, as in the case of this Farr 5000 being pushed hard, its crew well forward and out on the rail, on the wind in something approaching 20 knots of wind, they were sailed by people who knew how to extract the best out of them.

▲ Sailing in light winds somewhere out near Rangitoto Island in Auckland's Anniversary Regatta in 1985, Bruce Farr's *Swuzzlebubble V* shows here something of her underwater lines, as well as her bendy mast, fractional rig, and part-Kevlar mainsail, as she heels to a puff.

subsequently for the unsuccessful 'big boat' challenge in San Diego in 1988.

The Farr maxi *Longobardi*, designed for the Italian Gianni Varasi, which won the maxi World Championship in Palma in 1989, had hull shapes which had been developed using VPP computer programs, as well as information gathered from Whitbread race design studies carried out in his office. For this design there was much emphasis on weight location and reduction and on the tank-testing of alternative foil shapes and keel configurations. The boat was a very convenient test-bed for the development of fast light boat ideas where their application was not exposed to the risks and dangers to be found out on the open ocean.

This fast light boat theme was reiterated for Farr's *Steinlager 2*, designed for the Whitbread Round the World Race in 1989-90. Mark Oram, a crew member, said of the campaign:

> ... there was an almost fanatical attention paid to the distribution of weight in the building and sailing of *Steinlager 2* – the interior layout was extremely weight conscious ... the front and back 20 feet were stripped out shells ... the rig, hardware, and fittings were subject to the same kind of fanaticism as the hull ... the strongest and lightest of everything was researched and sourced during the building phase ...

About this boat, its skipper Peter Blake said: '... it is one of the ugliest in the world but looks like being one of the fastest ... it's something very different ...'. 'Ugly Different and Fast' is how the October 1988 issue of *Sea Spray* headlined its article on the boat, signalling a further step in the Kiwi attitude to sailing boat design, which no longer insists on beauty before performance!

His firm produced a design for a fast light boat especially devised to meet the newly formulated rules for the 1992-93 Whitbread Round The World Race, and eight of the ten entries sailed boats built to this design.

The two identical boats which formed the New Zealand challenge at San Diego in 1992 were Farr designs to the new IACC requirements, one built by Cooksons and the other by Marten Marine. At almost the same time, Ross Field used two Farr-designed boats in his campaign for the 1993-94 Whitbread race, his *Yamaha* design being the first of the new Whitbread 60 type to be built. 'An out and out racer with clean and fast lines ... with a fine entry progressing aft into huge saucer-like sections ... devastating to sail downwind ... and the question was, how long can we steer her for?' was Ross Field's comment on the boat.

Bruce Farr and his team now operate out of offices in Annapolis USA, where computer-aided design methods are much in evidence.

The Farr office was responsible for the Chris Dickson entry *NZL 39* for the 1995 America's Cup, and has more recently been busy working on design development for the latest version of *Young America*, the New York Yacht Club's 1999-2000 entry for the America's Cup challenger series.

Jim Young

Jim Young was a Wellingtonian by birth who grew up in Auckland. He sailed P-class boats there, followed by Zeddies, then Xies and Silver Ferns. Young did an apprenticeship with Shipbuilders Ltd and attended boat-designing classes at night school. He began his own boatbuilding business just after the Second World War, and won the X-class national championship, the Sanders Cup, following a memorable heavy-weather first race win in Wellington in his light-weight *White Heather* in 1949.

His drop-keel *Fiery Cross* was the first of many Kiwi boats to be built in glued double-skinned construction, and in his 1979 trailer sailer he pioneered water ballast for such boats. Jim Young was also responsible for the introduction of the winged keel to New Zealand.

Among his most successful designs are the Young 88 and Young 11. He no longer builds boats himself but still designs from his home office.

▶ The Young 88 *la quintessence* is being sailed in the Auckland Anniversary Regatta in classic light-displacement on-the-wind fashion in this 1984 photograph. Amongst the five members of her crew sitting along the weather rail with their legs over the side is a young girl, without a life jacket and looking quite at ease in her role as part of the boat's movable ballast. Such crew behaviour, especially with someone so young, would once have had traditionalists apoplectic.

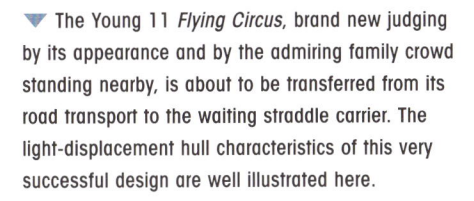

▼ The Young 11 *Flying Circus*, brand new judging by its appearance and by the admiring family crowd standing nearby, is about to be transferred from its road transport to the waiting straddle carrier. The light-displacement hull characteristics of this very successful design are well illustrated here.

Murray Ross

Murray Ross began his sailing career in Auckland in the late 1960s and early 1970s in Javelins and Flying Dutchmen, later crewing with Jock Bilger in the 1972 and 1976 Olympics, coming second in 1976. While working with Paul Whiting, Murray Ross began designing on his own account. He handled the aspects involved with assembling *Magic Bus* to Paul's lines and calculations and then developing its performance potential.

Ross went on to design a series of trailer sailers beginning with the Ross 780, a 'big dinghy' drawn to the limits of permissible trailer sailer rules and measurements. The boat combined very light displacement (1000 kg) with maximum sail area. His 930 version stretched out the earlier 780 ideas, and the Ross 40, built in 1980, took those ideas into big boats. His main design emphasis has been on creating fast reaching and running boats with long fine entries and wide U-shaped stern sections, though his very successful *Urban Cowboy* went well to windward also.

Murray Ross's approach to the profession reflects his self-taught status, something he has in common with almost all New Zealand designers. The methods he uses are essentially intuitive, and his designs don't get tank-tested. With a drawing board in an office at home, he has a drawing filing cabinet there, along with pictures of boats on the wall. 'I know what looks fast and what *is* fast,' he has said. Along with *Magic Bus*, winner of the Quarter Ton Cup in 1976, his *Newspaper Taxi* and *Higher Ground* have become part of the success story of Kiwi fast light big boats.

▲ The national championships for the Ross 780 trailer sailers were held at Easter in 1989, and the start of one of the races is shown here, with at least 10 boats taking part. Their designer may not have envisaged that his maximised trailer sailer, with its distinctive wide and upright stern, would be the precursor to a much bigger boat on the same lines, but his later Ross 40 was to be just such a boat.

◀ The bow sections of the big Ross *Pretty Boy Floyd* look like some exotic red-petalled flower in this 1992 picture of the boat on the hard at Okahu Bay. The long flat surfaces on which his boats sail so quickly downwind are well illustrated in this view, as are the deep keel and rudder necessary to control the performance of a boat with such a profile.

◀ Greg Elliott looks very much the Aucklander as he poses in Westhaven in this 1986 photograph with the successor to his trailer sailers, *Party Pro*, at a mooring in the background. His distinctive hull forms, and the lightness of the boat – the bow and stern areas not touching the water – are clearly evident.

◀ Tom Dodson, sailing *White Lines*, seems set to cross the whole fleet on port in this view of the start of this race in the Elliott 5.9 national championship series in Auckland in 1989. The Elliott hull forms, with their long entry and flared topsides in particular, show out well in the three boats in the foreground, against the long western slope of Rangitoto Island in the background.

◀ Bedecked with tiny flags, this pristine E 9.0, *E-nine*, hangs lightly on the straps of a straddle carrier at Westhaven. Her lines reveal both the boat's origins in the trailer sailers which preceded this design, and the reasons for its dinghy-like performance – truly a small boat writ larger.

Greg Elliott

Having grown up in Auckland in a sailing family – his father raced 12-footers and Moths – Greg Elliott competed in centreboarders at Point Chevalier as a youngster. He did his boatbuilding apprenticeship on big boats, ferries and the like, with Baileys in Auckland, then designed his light-displacement bulb-keeled 25-footer *Outsider* in the mid 1970s, just at the end of his time with the firm. The design was lofted out full size on the floor in traditional fashion, though he uses computers nowadays.

Elliott followed that boat with the bulb-keeled fibreglass Elliott 5.9 trailer sailer, of which some 200 have been built. In explaining his design approach, and in true Kiwi fast light boat fashion, he has said: 'If you keep the boat light, then maybe you don't need so much sail, and then you haven't got so much lead, and because of that the fitting sizes go down and the whole thing has a compounding effect … easy to handle … light on the helm, light on the gear.' A succinct and accurate definition of the fast light big boat philosophy.

The Elliott 5.9 led first to the design of *Party Pro*, to the development of *Pig Hunter* and *Peacemaker*, and ultimately to *Future Shock* – and the establishment of Greg Elliott as a fashionable young designer. Radical Elliott boats include *Excess* and *Gorilla Biscuits*.

There was much debate in earlier times between Jim Young and Greg Elliott about the design origins of such developments as flared topsides and bulb keels. The debate is apparently not resolvable, but is nevertheless of interest because of the profound influence, international as well as national, of such ideas in later years.

▲ The crew of *Inca*, and of the boat in the background in this picture, are all concentrating on the business of getting the spinnaker under control in strong winds. Times like this test crew-work and agility to the limit, and also reveal the difference between those who know, from bitter experience, what the limits are and those who do not.

▼ *Corinthian* is shown here with most of her crew, with the exception of the helmsman and the man on the weather rail, concentrating on the business of getting the coffee-grinder attended to as the boat picks up speed on the wind, perhaps just after going about. In big boats like this, enthusiastic and knowledgeable crew work makes a big difference to boat performance.

Sailing to the limit

From the mid 1950s, New Zealanders began by making their names in international competition and then went on to build a world-wide reputation, both as the skilled and energetic designers of fast light boats, and as sailors who applied their know-how to big-boat sailing as crew members on boats campaigned by others. As newcomers to the international scene, they at first did so on the terms imposed by relatively long-established international yacht racing organisations set up by countries for whom big-boat racing was based on the hallowed concepts of good seamanship, well-found yachts and, by and large, well-heeled yachtsmen.

Chris Bouzaid's impressive win in the One Ton Cup in the Sparkman & Stephens-designed *Rainbow II* in 1969 was a classic example of this scenario, except that on occasions during the cup series off Heligoland, especially in the stronger winds in the offshore races, the boat was sailed rather too much like a centreboarder than some thought proper. His success in the North Sea did as much to awaken Kiwi confidence in international big boat competition as had Peter Mander's win in the small-boat Sharpie class at the 1956 Olympics in Australia, even though both boats were of non-Kiwi design and neither were of the light planing type soon to dominate international yachting.

While small-boat competition continued apace at home and abroad, this big boat reputation developed as New Zealand sailors began crewing in senior positions on big boats. Kiwis were soon in demand as watch-captains and helmsmen for very competitive campaigners who recognised the value of the distinctive qualities they brought to the task.

From these positions of responsibility a significant number of New Zealand sailors went on to campaign their own boats – most of them Kiwi-designed, built, rigged, and crewed – in many international competitions, ranging from fleet racing to match racing, from Ton Cup competition to round-the-world races. Eventually, as the outcome of this process, Kiwis won what some regard as the most prestigious international competition of all, the America's Cup.

In making this transition, from innovators in home-grown boats to world-beaters in boats built with the very latest of inventive technology, Kiwi sailors have also turned from skilled amateurs into highly skilled professionals able to meet and beat the very best that can be devised by others.

It could be said that the essential transfer of the radical fast light boat attitude to sailing which had been evolving in the Kiwi centreboard classes since the end of the First World War, and which exploded into revolution in the 1950s, took place somewhere around 1974-75, when New Zealanders won the Quarter Ton Cup two years in a row. They did it in boats that looked and were sailed very much like the dinghies many of them (designers, builders, skippers, and crews) had competed in for years.

After almost 60 years of designing, building, and racing lightweight boats in increasingly ingenious and competitive ways throughout New Zealand, the proponents of the new ideas displayed a brashness and confidence both in their boats and in their own ability to sail them well. Even before they had been tested in races in some cases, their attitude antagonised the more conventional northern hemisphere sailors and administrators – not to mention those from across the Tasman Sea.

Not least of the attributes brought by the best of them to the big boat scene is the ability to recognise instinctively the limits to which a big boat can be driven. The truth of this is often brought out by the observable difference between those with it and those without, when things get marginal during races in strong winds – or at least in conditions which test fast light big boats to their limits and beyond.

That the big boat's limits are exceeded on occasions, and that gear failures, wipe-outs, dismastings, and worse occur to some is precisely the point – the attitudes which bring about such events are the ones which, applied to perfection in all aspects of design, construction, and competition, win races in big boats and small. The art lies in surviving all the vicissitudes of competition and finishing, first at best, well up the rankings at least.

Most big boat races take longer than those in small boats, and the fitness and stamina necessary to win in a seven-race national championship series in fast light boats stand such sailors in good stead when the going gets tough – and stays tough, for days or weeks on end, out on the water.

Fast light big boats are designed on the basis that the crew are an essential part of the stability and control factors built into the concept. Keeping up such a contribution to the boat's performance requires not only co-ordination of effort but great fitness also.

▶ Twenty years ago, Chris Dickson and Hamish Willcox won the 470 series in the New Zealand National Youth Championships. They are shown here just before the start of one of the races, with their illustrious racing careers still ahead of them.

▼ The wet-weather gear and warm headgear being worn by most of the people in this picture of the pre-start manoeuvring of a group of half-tonners indicate that it is a winter series race. But the life-rafts on the cabin tops and the sea conditions tell us it is a long-distance race that will be sailed in strong winds, in which the skill of the crews and the durability of the boats will be much tested.

▲ If it were not for the very well known name, this photograph might seem to be of some well set-up but innocuous trailer sailer, but it is Bruce Farr's quarter-tonner *45° South*, one of the most significant Kiwi contributions to the transfer of small boat ideas into the international big boat scene.

Doing the ton

In the 'Ton Cup' classes, New Zealand boats and crews began competing with much success in the 1970s and continued to do so in the 1980s. Bruce Farr's appearance with the dinghy-like *Titus Canby* in the 1972 Half Ton Cup showed the outside world just what might be expected from the Kiwi approach to bigger boats. Fine forward and with broad stern sections, a bulb keel, and a big main/small headsail 7/8th rig, the fast light Farr 'big boat' made a huge impression there.

In 1975, the Farr quarter-tonner *45° South*, designed to meet IOR specifications, took this philosophy all the way and became the single most important 'big boat' derivation from the Kiwi fast light small-boat scene. Its bendy 3/4 rig, bigger main, smaller jib, and greater beam aft, together with its deep narrow keel and all its control lines led aft to the cockpit, made the boat look and perform even more like the scaled-up dinghy it was than had *Titus Canby*. The northern-hemisphere establishment, at first scathing in their remarks about their appearance, had to eat their words when the two Kiwi boats built to this design came first and second in the series.

By 1975 it was clear that, after some 55 years of gestation in New Zealand, the fast light boat concept had now matured and ventured abroad, to the surprise and consternation of the rest of the sailing world whose international experts had barely heard of the country and had certainly not taken its international challenges seriously. That would not be the case in the years to come.

Of the 1975 contest at Deauville in France, in which he sailed a more conventional boat for Canada, Bruce Kirby, the creator of the single-handed quick-to-plane Laser class and thus no stranger to the phenomenon, said of *Genie*, sister ship to *45° South*:

> In the brisk beam reaching she was moving fast, with her light, dinghy-like hull picking up every wave while the medium displacement boats like ours only managed to grab every second or third one ...

Significantly his comments appeared in the magazine *One Design and Offshoresman*, not an apt description of the Kiwi approach to design and construction.

Bruce Farr's design successes in the 1974 and 1975 Quarter Ton Cups — a class of boat little bigger than the larger trailer-sailers that had become numerous throughout New Zealand, one should remember — brought to the fore other self-taught and similarly iconoclastic New Zealand designers, amongst them Paul Whiting, Laurie Davidson, and Jim Young.

The Kiwi light-displacement philosophy soon reached the One Ton Cup class, and thus had arrived amongst the truly sea-going boats where conventional thinking most certainly ruled. In Sydney, the Farr boat *Prospect of Ponsonby* (whose very name was a mocking play on the *Prospect of Whitby*, a much more staid and relatively heavy-displacement yacht from the UK) demolished the fleet in the One Ton Cup series there, beating the famous American sailor, Ted Turner, sailing the 1974 winner *Pied Piper*.

Now the Kiwi approach had well and truly arrived internationally, though it still engendered antagonism, at home and abroad, amongst those who considered it unsporting and possibly dangerous.

As it happened, one of the important developments in the 'big dinghy' philosophy came not from a New Zealander but from the American designer Britton Chance, whose boat *Resolute Salmon* was not as light displacement as the Kiwi boats, but nevertheless won the One Ton Cup at Marseilles. With a centreboard capable of being raised and lowered, Chance's boat could reduce wetted area and drag when sailing off the wind by raising the board, just as in a dinghy — though it paid the penalty for this attribute by being very hard to control downhill in strong winds.

▲ There is a launch just visible between the two windward boats in this picture of Farr 11s racing in heavy weather. Every boat is reefed down and each is making use of its fractional rig and bendy mast to flatten what mainsail is set, particularly so in the case of the boat to windward. Their main booms are pinned down well out to leeward to further reduce pressure, and each boat is making its way to windward very much on its headsail. All classic fast light big boat technique.

▲ French designers and sailors, unlike most in the Northern Hemisphere, quickly caught on to the Kiwi way of doing things, and this quarter-tonner exemplifies the approach. With the main reefed down and flogging, and its fractional rig being kept effective by three crew members sitting feet-foremost along the rail at its widest, this French boat is making its way upwind very much in dinghy-racing fashion.

In 1976 Laurie Davidson designed the lightweight quarter-tonner *Fun*, complete with a rise-and-fall centerboard, and this boat furthered the trend towards dinghy-like big boats. So too did Paul Whiting's quarter-tonner *Magic Bus* which, though not a centerboarder, was equally lightweight; an early Kiwi foam and fibreglass design, it won the Quarter Ton Cup at Corpus Christi that year.

Much of the local development of fast light big boats was from here on predominantly an Auckland preoccupation, with designers, builders, riggers, sailmakers, owners, skippers, and crews often in a high pitch of activity. But the essence of the philosophy they were pursuing and exploring remained a New Zealand-wide one, with small boat activity and development proceeding apace as it had done for decades. New Zealand designers, especially Bruce Farr, were now being commissioned by overseas competitors.

A notable early example was Farr's winning three-quarter tonner *Joe Louis*, sailed by the Frenchman Yves Pajot at La Rochelle in 1977. French designers were beginning to understand and develop for themselves their version of the big-dinghy approach. At La Rochelle, boats built for the more conventional designers were left in the wake of the antipodean boats and their adherents.

Both in design ingenuity and in the way their boats are sailed, and despite the very great cultural differences between the two countries, competitors from France and New Zealand seem to share a common attitude towards established ideas, essentially always posing that aggressive question – where does it say we can't do that?

In 1977, the designing and building season, in preparation for the One Ton Cup which was to be held in the Hauraki Gulf that summer, was one that brought the differences and dissatisfaction to a head. Sponsorship had reached the level of boat names identifying the products of the New Zealand companies paying the bills – Smirnoff and Lion – and added to the antagonism already being expressed by some, notably the Americans. (Their thinking was that if you couldn't afford such a boat you shouldn't be building and campaigning one!) But from that time on, sponsorship became the norm in such boats.

> They said it was just a whole bunch of whinging Kiwis and there was a real problem with that attitude …There was this idea that the Kiwis had somehow taken advantage of the rule …

So said Bruce Farr to *Sea Spray* in March 1989, about the comments of members of the Offshore Racing Committee of the IYRU when it changed the International Offshore Racing rules in 1989 to outlaw the New Zealanders' innovative fast light big boats.

Learning to win

New Zealand won the Kenwood Cup series for the first time in 1986 when the Fay Richwhite-sponsored team of three boats designed by Bruce Farr gave an impressive display of big boat team sailing, especially in the long race out on the Royal Hawaiian Ocean Racing Club's course. Michael Clark sailed *Exador*, Del Hogg sailed *Equity,* and Don St. Clair Brown was at the helm of *Thunderbird,* and they beat the two American teams present into second and third places.

Bruce Farr's design for the 62.3-foot *Brindabella*, commissioned by Australian George Snow for the Sydney to Hobart race, had more beam and more displacement than the American 'sled' ULDB's designed for the race from the West Coast of the US to Honolulu.

As if to celebrate the arrival of Kiwi attitudes and ideas on the wider sailing scene, there was a magical month in the southern spring of the 1988-89 summer when New Zealand sailors experienced a remarkable series of impressive performances in international competition. New Zealand boats sailed by David Barnes, Richard Dodson, and Russell Coutts won the One Ton Cup and came second in the San Francisco big boat series. Three sailors came away with

▲ The New Zealand Admirals Cup team boat *Shockwave* is shown here crossing the finishing line at the end of the 1983 Fastnet race. The scene is quiet and calm as she does so (witness the untroubled Laser spectator-boat almost hidden on the left), but the classic 605-mile race can be one of the toughest in the world.

This picture of Bruce and Barbara Kendall training before the 1992 Barcelona Olympics reveals not only something of their technique but also something of the sponsorship nowadays vital to the sport of sailing, with the television logo on each sail.

This competitor in Olympicsail '92, part of New Zealand's preparation for the 1992 Olympics, is in the process of gybing, a rather different process than is the case in 'normal' sailing craft, since here the sail is swung around in front of the board and brought into use again on its other side. Boardsailing is in some ways the sailing equivalent of barefoot water-skiing!

Chris Dickson is at the helm in this view of Paprika sailing in the 1983 Citizen Match Racing series on Auckland Harbour. His father Roy is sitting next to him, on a day when everyone is out on the weather rail, but it is not blowing hard enough for the sheets to have to be cleated off, and each is being hand-held off the winch and lazy block.

medals from the Olympic Games, Bruce Kendall winning gold in boardsailing, Chris Timms coming second in his Tornado catamaran, and John Cutler third in the Finn class.

Nor were the women far behind. Leslie Egnot and her crew, sailing unfamiliar but quick J 24 boats, won the Women's World Sailing Championship on New York Harbour in 1990, beating the Irish crew 3-2 in the finals of the series.

Matching skills

Match racing is based on the idea of pitting several pairs of crews against each other in a series of two-boat races (matches) which, by an appropriate points system, identifies the best two of them, and then having a final 'match race' series between those two. It is the absolute opposite of fleet racing. A match-racing series does not have to be staged in big boats to be successful, as New Zealand's annual secondary school event in Sunburst dinghies demonstrates.

At a grander level, skippers and crews in the several national and international match-racing regattas held in various parts of the world gain considerable prestige from winning, and frequently become contenders for places in even more prestigious match-racing events such as the America's Cup.

In recognition of the rapidly-developing significance of international match-racing to the sport, in 1984-85 the IYRU sanctioned the formation of a group it called the Match Racing Conference to administer it. In 1990 the same body set up a match-racing committee with New Zealander Richard Endean as its chairman, the intention being to promote match-racing, including the training of umpires and judges, in various parts of the world.

Russell Coutts ended a two-year domination of international match racing by Chris Dickson when he won the Kouros Cup in France in 1990, heading off 11 other top-class entries. He was the only one to beat Dickson in the opening 'round robin' series.

The 1997-98 Citizen match racing series in Auckland, sailed in Stewart 34s, was won by Chris Dickson from a quality list of entries which included Russell Coutts, Chris Dickson's father Roy, Peter Isler, and Tom Blackaller, as well as several other top sailors and crews. The following season the series was sailed in Farr MRXs, the Farr 1020 hulls replacing the Stewart 34s for this purpose.

▲ Not all that long ago, certainly no more than 25 years, a boat of this size would have been built right-way-up, and made of substantial timbers well and truly bolted to an even more substantial keelson. Here, upside down, the method of construction that makes it a light displacement boat is very clear to see, as is much of the hull form that makes it quick.

▼ The bow of this Farr 11 has been exposed by the boat rising off a sea as it beats to windward. Its largely Kevlar sails have a phenomenal strength-to-weight ratio, and contribute much to its all-up lightness, but they have a limited life and must be looked after with a degree of care which brings to mind old-fashioned sail-care advice.

The material world

At the beginning of the twentieth century, the new lightweight high-speed nautical phenomenon was the planing hull. At the end of the century the equally dramatic equivalent was the use of carbon fibre. Originally developed for the aerospace industry, where its remarkable strength to weight ratio was vital to space flight, carbon fibre eventually came into use in boats and enabled them to be made even lighter and faster than before.

Over the years, hulls made of plywood, of thin wood veneers laid counter to each other over moulds, of fibreglass fabrics laid over lightweight cores of cedar, balsa, foam plastic and the like, followed one after the other as developments in gluing, moulding, finishing, and fabric-laying made such techniques more and more available and more economical. New Zealanders made a name for themselves in developing and marketing such skills.

Carbon fibre, Kevlar, and other new materials with a similarly impressive strength-to-weight ratio all found their place in a sport where lightness and strength had been the goal of designers and builders for generations. By the 1980s, the application of such materials frequently went straight into big boats, without the introductory stage in small boats which had in the past preceded their use in larger-scale construction. By the 1990s, Kevlar, Mylar, carbon fibre, and foam core were being used extensively. In design, where computers have revolutionised the process, and in the fabrication and arrangement of hulls, spars, rigging, sails, fittings and ropes, as well as in the whole business of managing the boat during competition, altogether new possibilities are constantly being introduced and developed.

Always and in every way in the pursuit of lightness combined with strength, new materials and techniques are discovered, tested, and used in boats intended for competition where speed is not only important but absolutely critical to winning – though the price of going too far in the search for lightness is insufficient strength to last the distance.

▲ The crew of *Lion New Zealand*, with Peter Blake at the helm, are all concentration in this view of the after third of the boat they sailed in the 1985-86 *Whitbread*. Teamwork such as this, built up over the planning period, the construction phase, and over continuous months of competition, is an essential part of many New Zealand campaigns.

'Fragile, expensive, and dangerous' is how, on two very public occasions, the American Bill Koch described the IACC boats. The first time was after the world championships for the new class in 1991, and the second was at the press conference at the America's Cup in 1992. It may be significant that just prior to the second occasion his IACC boat *Jayhawk* was dismasted, with Bill Koch at the helm, at a cost of some US$1 million to repair.

Sprinting round the world

The idea of racing around the world has caught the imagination of many sailors from New Zealand and elsewhere over the years. Readers of *Sea Spray* felt only mild surprise when Peter Blake announced in its news page in November 1992 that he was teaming up with the renowned English sailor Robin Knox-Johnson in a sponsored attempt to win the lucrative Jules Verne prize. The prize was to be presented to the first boat to sail the distance in less than 80 days.

Any surprise Kiwi sailors felt about Peter Blake's announcement came from recalling his remarks at the end of the Round Australia Race he won in 1988 in his catamaran *Steinlager 1*. Back then he had said firmly, 'Never again', and described racing multihulls in the open sea in strong winds as dangerous and scary.

In an article in *Sea Spray* in April 1993, Peter Blake anticipated the exhilaration of the voyage, describing it as a high-speed, adrenalin-fuelled charge around the planet, a succinct and telling reference to what must be very nearly the ultimate in the transfer of the fast light small-boat round-the-buoys philosophy into a flat-out global sprint.

As it turned out, Blake's first Kiwi big-catamaran attempt in 1993 failed when damage to the boat cut it short when it was some 4 days ahead of schedule, but in 1994 he and his crew, in the 92-foot catamaran *Enza*, named after its Kiwi apple-marketing sponsor, stormed their way over the finishing line off Ushant to win the trophy with a 74 day 22 hour 17 minute 22 second elapsed time for the voyage, beating the previous record by some four days.

The story of round-the-world fleet-racing had begun in September 1973, when seventeen boats took part in the first Whitbread Round the World Race. The southern stopover was Sydney, and there were no New Zealand entries, but on Leslie Williams' 80-foot *Burton Cutter*, hastily prepared and unable to complete the race due to hull damage, one of the watch-leaders was Peter Blake. Competing hard down in the Forties and Fifties latitudes took its toll both on the boats and on their crews, with two men lost overboard on that leg of the race. From such experiences began the legends of the dangers and hardships of racing lighter and lighter big boats in the Southern Ocean, which have persisted ever since in the Whitbread.

Former paratrooper Chay Blyth observed that he thought of the race '... as an adventure, with the ocean providing one of the last great challenges. I thought I would teach myself as I went along – and I did, which got up the noses of the bar-room gin-and-tonic brigade, because it destroyed the cosy image that sailing is élitist and takes a lifetime to learn.' New Zealanders were soon to follow suit, with their own iconoclastic approach to big-boat sailing.

Dutchman Cornelis 'Connie' van Rietschoten won the second Whitbread, for which Auckland had replaced Sydney as the half-way stopover. On his Sparkman & Stephens-designed 65 foot ketch *Flyer*, van Reitschoten had only one aim – to win – and as part of his thoroughness of preparation he took the boat on two Atlantic crossings. Peter Blake took part again, this time on *Heath's Condor*, sailing it into first place on the leg into Auckland, but this boat also suffered, as had *Burton Cutter*, from lack of preparation. Blake was no doubt learning about the cost of such haste and storing the knowledge away for future reference.

New Zealand's first entries in the race came in the 1981-82 Whitbread, when two boats designed, skippered, and crewed by New Zealanders took part. Fast light small-boat thinking was beginning to infiltrate out on to the oceans of the world.

▲ With its headsail boomed out to weather, and the main eased right off and held down by the moderate vang tension, this Whitbread boat is rushing downwind through big, occasionally breaking seas. There is no snow on deck, but the Southern Ocean is a hard, cold place most of the time. In this view, nobody is on deck who doesn't have to be there!

Having campaigned for '... an entry of New Zealand design and construction, crewed solely by Kiwis [to] show the rest of the world what we really can do in the longest and toughest ocean race of the world', Peter Blake sailed Bruce Farr's 68-footer *Ceramco New Zealand* through the disaster of an early dismasting to a very close contest with van Rietschoten over the closing stages of the race. Wellington's Digby Taylor and his Kiwi crew sailed the 50ft Laurie Davidson-designed *Outward Bound*, though their efforts were constrained by a very limited budget, something New Zealanders found to be not to their advantage despite their long tradition of doing things that way. The eventual winner was van Rietschoten in his new *Flyer*, a 76ft Frers-designed replacement for his earlier boat.

By the fourth Whitbread in 1985-86, which again used Auckland as the southern stopover, the Kiwi involvement had increased dramatically. Of the sixteen entries taking part, five boats were designed by New Zealanders. Two were campaigned by the same pair who had taken part in the previous race. Peter Blake entered the Ron Holland-designed *Lion New Zealand*, a relatively heavy (76,600 lbs) and strong and well prepared 78-foot maxi in which he had just won the Sydney to Hobart race. Digby Taylor, in a typically low-budget campaign, sailed his fractionally-rigged Farr maxi *NZI Enterprise*.

In addition, Pierre Fehlmann sailed a similarly well prepared Farr 80-footer *UBS Switzerland*, Skip Novak competed in *Drum*, a Farr sister-ship to *Lion New Zealand*, and the

▲ The Farr boat *Ceramco New Zealand* was the country's first entry in the Whitbread Race, though by this time many Kiwi sailors had crewed on other countries' entries in earlier races. Though *Ceramco* was dismasted early in the 1981-82 Whitbread, she was responsible for taking a great deal of the Kiwi light-fast-big-boat philosophy into round-the-world racing. Something of that attitude shows in this view of the boat lifting her bow as she powers downwind in a blow.

▶ The two New Zealand maxi entries in the 1985-86 Whitbread Race sail alongside each other in this close-up view. Peter Blake is at the weather wheel of *Lion New Zealand* as she sails with *NZI Enterprise* just to leeward on a sunny day in a moderate breeze – by no means typical weather conditions in the Whitbread!

first South African entry in the race was another Farr maxi, Paddi Kuttel's 80-foot maxi *Atlantic Privateer*.

In this race Peter Blake finished second overall behind Pierre Fehlmann, the significantly lightweight composite construction (61,150 lb) Farr-designed Swiss boat having set a new 24-hour record of 374 miles and a new race time of 117 days, two days faster than *Flyer*'s previous best. The trends in ocean racing towards Kiwi design inventiveness and crewing skills amongst those determined to win were becoming obvious and compelling.

The pursuit of lightness without loss of strength was by now a major preoccupation amongst big-boat sailors. The news page in the February 1989 issue of *Sea Spray* said of *Steinlager 2*, that it was ' ... like a giant sailboard with a flush deck, two shallow cockpits and scant cover for a deck crew thrashing through the ice, hail, and snow of the Southern Ocean.'

Though it was not entirely the result of New Zealand's influence, the pursuit of lightness spread like a rash as far as the round-the-world racers were concerned. When 23 boats started in the 1989-90 Whitbread, amongst them were six Kiwi designed boats – not all of them brand new, but all of them considered to be serious contenders by their skippers and crews.

Pierre Fehlmann had *Merit*, a new Farr-designed maxi sloop, though all the other maxis were ketches. Peter Blake had the 84 foot fractional-rigged *Steinlager 2*, and fellow Kiwi Grant Dalton had the 82-foot *Fisher & Paykel*, both of them Farr maxi ketches.

Bruce Farr's *UBS Switzerland* was there again, under another name, Tracey Edwards' all-women crewed entry *Maiden* was a renamed nine-year-old aluminium Farr boat, and *NZI Enterprise* had been renamed and entered as *Gatorade*. In addition, the expatriate Kiwi Ron Holland had designed the heavy-displacement boat *UCB Ireland* for Joe English and his Irish crew.

By this time though, the race had become more even-handed as far as boat-for-boat competition was concerned, and the maxis were to race without time adjustment. In addition, led by designer Bruce Farr, the general opinion was that the race would be largely one involving reaching in conditions and under race rules which allowed a mizzen staysail to be set.

▼ The backstay adjustment system on Digby Taylor's 1985-86 Whitbread entry *NZI Enterprise* consists of four big matching stainless-steel blocks and associated wires and fittings, all set out with simplicity and symmetry either side of a smaller block with lighter tackle, across the boat's gently-raked transom. The boat was to sail again in the 1989-90 Whitbread as *Gatorade*.

▲ The bare, brand-new, undecked, unlabelled hull of Grant Dalton's maxi ketch *Fisher & Paykel* shows its hint of clipper bow and unmistakably quick underwater form in this view of the boat being craned onto a cradle in 1988.

▼ This is a trick photograph, which combines images of two boats being built at different locations. The one on the left is the Swarbrick-designed Whitbread 60 and the other is the Farr-designed one. The smiling man in the middle with his arms outstretched is Chris Dickson, and the boats were built to enable a choice to be made between them for his 1993-93 entry in the Whitbread.

Again the Kiwi entries were very well prepared and organised, and this time their pre-race behaviour in England was exemplary, professional and quietly confident. Grant Dalton had been watch-leader in *Lion New Zealand* and had Tom Schnackenberg as sail designer. Peter Blake, having finished ahead of *Fisher & Paykel* in the Fastnet race, reminded the crew of *Steinlager 2* at the start of the Whitbread that their entry obviously had boat speed, and that all they needed was crew-work to match it.

Steinlager 2 beat *Fisher & Paykel* for first place by six minutes in a dramatic finish to the sprint from Fremantle to Auckland, and by five miles when they rounded Cape Horn. Peter Blake's boat crossed the line at Southampton after 128 days of racing, some 36 minutes ahead of Grant Dalton's in a one-two Kiwi finish which gave *Steinlager 2* a first on every leg and the overall trophy for the 1989-90 Whitbread.

For the 1993-94 race, the rules were changed again, this time by the Whitbread 60 Rule, which provided for boats built to a Farr design. The first boat built to the new rule was New Zealander Ross Field's *Yamaha*.

The new 60s were to be sloop-rigged and fitted with watertight compartments. Water-ballast systems were allowed, and it was envisaged that these smaller boats would be capable of beating the maxis in some conditions.

Chris Dickson's Whitbread 60 entry in the 1993 round-the-world classic was a truly competitive one, as were his attitudes to the business of winning the race. After the Southern Ocean leg he made a famous remark about icebergs which put into perspective the dread with which they were thought of by competitors, saying to a reporter that he was glad they didn't come out at night!

In the twelve years between the 1981-82 Whitbread and the one in 1993-94, the New Zealanders' contributions to boat management had risen from occasional watch-leaders to skippers of the first and second boats to finish, and Kiwi designers were responsible for the majority of the boats entered.

In addition, the way such boats were campaigned had changed radically. No longer could any entry be considered seriously if it was not the product of thorough and intensive preparation by a team of individuals committed to success and absolutely familiar with the whole process from concept to final leg finish.

As far as the America's Cup was concerned, Whitbread competition was to prove an intensive training ground and test bed for the kind of approach adopted by many with great success several years later.

Sleight of hand

Though the much more conventional relationship of owner, designer, builder, skipper, and crew exists in the New Zealand sailing scene, for a very long time it was the exception. From the time of the introduction of those small boat classes capable of being 'home built' by skipper and crew together, up to the present day, the attitude which sees such work as a joint effort entered into by enthusiasts on an equal basis has flourished.

New Zealand's designers tend to have been fast light small boat sailors themselves, as do the country's boatbuilders,

▲ Digby Taylor's *NZI Enterprise* is shown here sailing off Cape Town, with Table Mountain in the background, during the 1985-86 Whitbread Race. Such races widened the breadth of experience of New Zealand sailors, and throughout the 1980s their big-boat command and watch-keeping skills were much in demand.

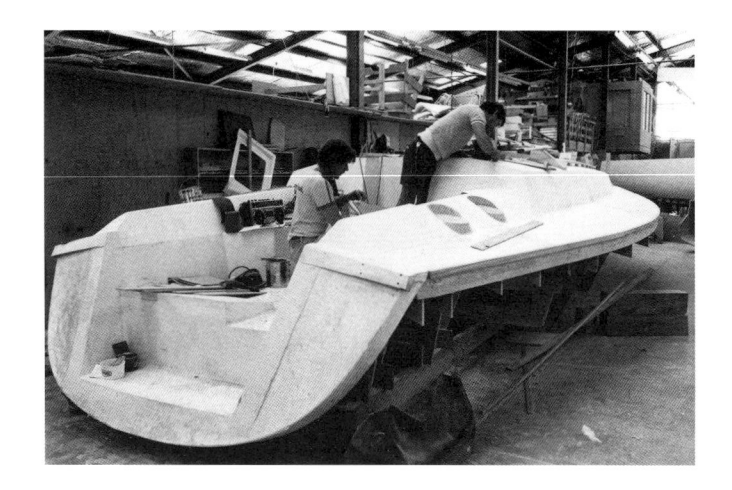

▲ This 1986 'deck plug' on which fibreglass deck elements were fabricated for Farr 1220s illustrates the vast changes taking place in the way boat hulls were being built. By this time much boat-building was considered to be a high speed assembly of pre-built parts, not a long drawn-out process, in which small pieces of laboriously custom-shaped and fitted elements were put together over many months.

▼ Sailmaking too has had to become a production line process, though something of the ancient art still remains, especially in the use of the floor to accommodate the huge spreads of cloth involved in big-boat sails. This scene is of a team of six sailmakers fixing the star-in-a-circle logo into the centre of a very big lightweight spinnaker that is taking up the whole of the sail-loft floor.

sparmakers, riggers, sailmakers, navigators, afterguard, grinders, bowmen, and so on, and many of them will have been involved in their earlier sailing careers in one or more of those gatherings of enthusiasts who built and sailed their own fast light boat.

In many fields of endeavour, the best engineers and designers use extremely well-developed intuition first and the virtues and patience of computers second, knowing them to be simply 'very very fast idiots', to check and confirm their intuitive judgement. So do the best designers of boats intended to sail fast.

Computer modelling of almost any aspect of design from hulls to sails and spars and 'appendages', and the computer analysis of tank testing of hulls and the wind tunnel testing of sails, does no more than report on the ideas of designers, and it is the origination of those ideas which makes the difference to performance.

That inventiveness has by no means run out amongst those who design fast light boats, whether of the small or the big variety, was made clear when Greg Elliott produced his big schooner *Elliott Marine* in 1994. Designed to meet his own requirements for an unrestrained, ocean-racing machine, the ultra-light-displacement boat was said to have achieved some 16 knots on a reach under working sails.

With its twin rotating carbon fibre masts, Kevlar standing rigging, and flared carbon-fibre-clad Divinycell hull, the big boat took the schooner rig to new heights of competitiveness. Its combination of high technology and outright pursuit of speed, put together almost exactly 100 years after the first planing small boats in the world were built and sailed in New Zealand, carried the Kiwi idea of fast light boats another dramatic step further.

Further recognition of the changing face of Kiwi sailing came at the end of the 1991-92 southern summer when the New Zealand Yachting Federation, founded some 40 years previously, with its administration for some time now very much involved in the marketing of the sport at home and overseas, announced it had changed its name to Yachting New Zealand. Not everyone agrees with the change, it must be said. There are many who are concerned about the future of the sport, believing that, despite the smart new logo designed by a well-known Kiwi small-boat sailor, the national body has drifted away from the true heart of sailing where small inexpensive boats built and sailed by enthusiasts began it all.

The business of large-scale sponsorship in sailing in New Zealand has come a long way since the days when tobacco company involvement was the norm and very little in the way of individual sponsorship of boats took place. *New Zealand Boating World* had something to say about the state of sailing sponsorship in its July 1993 issue where it made the point that: 'Yachting has risen from the depths of relative obscurity to become the biggest sponsorship game in town.' The story of New Zealand's challenges for the America's Cup that follows below will make the need for sponsorship abundantly clear.

That 100-guinea cup

New Zealand's involvement in challenges for the America's Cup began back in 1957, when Kiwi designer Arthur Robb, with access to tank testing and the ability to analyse the results, contributed to the English *Red Duster* campaign. Ten years later, in a July 1967 *Sea Spray* article by Don Tempest, Aucklander Jim Davern proposed the formation of a syndicate 'to design and build a 12-Metre yacht if Australia is successful in her challenge for the America's Cup in September'.

The Australians failed in their 1967 challenge, of course, and it was to be 20 years before Jim Davern's idea of a Cup challenge came to fruition in Fremantle, but Don Tempest's article ended with telling comment on the scale of the task and on the state of the sport in New Zealand:

> ... the strength of the challenge would depend entirely on the men who get behind it. Whether they supply money, and believe me large lumps of that would be required, or design and building equipment, or even if they just have good ideas that someone else could translate into reality – backing would be required not just from yachtsmen but from every sportsman in the country. New Zealanders have, in a very short period, shown themselves to be in world class in small boat yachting. If the same initiative can be shown in the big stuff I'm sure we'll never disgrace ourselves ... .

Three years later (but too early in his career to have the Davern idea in mind), the young Bruce Farr, having designed and built numerous small boats since he had won the

▲ The traditional sailmaking materials and methods are still very much in evidence in this 1964 picture of the mainsail for the 12-metre boat *Kurrewa V*, the Australian challenger for the America's Cup, being assembled on the cutting floor in Gosport, England. Narrow cloths of heavy material are pinned to the floor in the early stages of the process, and tape is being applied to hold the pieces together for stitching and fabrication.

▲ In 1967, the year after he won the Sydney to Hobart race in record time in *Fidelis*, Aucklander Jim Davern proposed that New Zealand should mount a challenge for the America's Cup if it were won by Australia that year. He is shown here in 1966, just after the Sydney to Hobart race, with his trophy.

Restricted Moth national championships in his own design in 1966, left his job as a boat-builder, and went into business as a designer-builder.

The Americans' 132-year hold on the Cup ended in September 1983, when the Australians won in Newport, Rhode Island. The first requirement for Jim Davern's bold idea had been achieved: the next challenge for the America's Cup would be in the Southern Hemisphere.

New Zealand sailors had taken no significant part in the 1983 event, though the Canterbury Clothing Company found itself suppliers of matching shirts for the Australians after an urgent request from their team at Newport. New Zealand's first challenge came in 1987, with a fibreglass boat built from a wooden plug made by an aluminium boatbuilding firm in Auckland, a sequence of events which not only achieved its intended secrecy but also unintentionally aroused the ire of some of its competitors.

The Kiwi approach to small boats frequently caused international agitation when transferred to big boats. It certainly did so in Perth, with the appearance of the fibreglass boat in 1987, and also in the period leading up to the controversial two-boat Cup contest in San Diego in 1988.

The product of a trio of Kiwi sailors-turned-designers, the three New Zealand 12-metre class boats built for the 1987 challenge were actually of composite construction made up of 'exotic' materials, epoxy-soaked fabric, and an unidentified core. The designers were Laurie Davidson, Bruce Farr, and Ron Holland. All three were by this time involved in international design commissions, particularly in the IOR field, and New Zealand-designed and -built boats had been involved in Admirals Cup, Whitbread, and Southern Cross Cup competition. The fast light boat philosophy had by the mid-1980s become a well and truly international phenomenon, more than capable of providing the design and construction know-how needed for an America's Cup campaign.

For the 1987 boats, the initial research and development funding came from Michael Fay, the merchant banker who later became syndicate chairman for the challenge. Ron Holland did much of the computer and tank testing work in his office in Ireland; Bruce Farr, along with his Kiwi associate Russell Bowler, concentrated on design aspects in his US office; and Laurie Davidson was much involved in the New Zealand construction side of the joint venture.

Chris Dickson was chosen as skipper, following a very successful performance as helmsman of KZ5 at the 12-metre world championships that had been held prior to the Fremantle challenge. By one route or another, many of them building their small-boat reputation into one as a highly skilled big-boat sailor by crewing and helming for overseas boats, almost all of the New Zealand crew came from the competitive and peculiarly Kiwi sequence of fast light small boats.

The Fremantle challenger series for the Cup in 1987 saw New Zealand's KZ7 beaten by the US boat and crew, and Australia beaten by them too in the contest proper. But it also saw the end of the use of the 12-metre class ('an expensive way to sail slowly', it had once been called!) for the America's Cup. Instead, the IACC class was devised by an international team of designers.

The innovative and provocative 1988 New Zealand challenge mounted by Michael Fay with a 130-foot boat, KZ1, named *New Zealand*, though unsuccessful – it never stood a chance against the equally innovative American catamaran – nevertheless elegantly demonstrated the 'show us where it says you can't do that' philosophy. This challenge, despite its outcome, left the international sailing world in no doubt about the New Zealanders' determination to succeed in its pursuit of the America's Cup.

When the new IACC boat specification was announced in 1989, *Sea Spray* in its February news page said it would produce '... a light displacement speedster of about 57ft waterline length ... representatives from 10 countries including New Zealand met to set up the requirements ... 76ft overall, 18ft beam, 2900 sq ft sail area and 35500 lbs displacement.'

Described at the time as 'high-tech and high-performance', the replacement design provided for boats that were longer, had more sail area, and were lighter than the 12s, and were to be constructed of 'space-age carbon-fibre composites' – criteria which particularly appealed to New Zealand designers and builders, given their long-standing interest in such go-fast characteristics.

New Zealand's performance at the end of the 1992 Louis Vuitton Cup challenger series with the bowsprit-boat *New Zealand*, helmed for all but one race by Rod Davis, was a bitter disappointment to its supporters. The Kiwi competitors lost to Italy in the challenger finals more by man-on-man psychology than by boat-on-boat performance. It was a reason for losing which went very much against the grain for Kiwi sailors.

▲ Although Chris Dickson is sometimes thought of as the *enfant terrible* of Kiwi sailing, his racing record is nonetheless a remarkable one. In the pursuit of lightness, too, he has been unremitting: the crew on his Whitbread 60 weren't allowed to bring their personal tubes of toothpaste along, because of the extra weight.

▼ Russell Coutts gives the appearance of great concentration in the picture taken at San Diego in 1995, but *Black Magic* was in fact not racing on this occasion.

Something like US$350 million was spent in challenging for and defending the 1992 America's Cup. Italy alone spent some US$85 million and Bill Koch committed US$65 million to his defence. For this reason, and as a result of events prior to and during the 1992 series, changes were made to the Cup rules. Each competitor may now build a maximum of two boats, with a wardrobe of no more than 45 sails, and must refrain from spying on others. In addition, the course was made a windward-leeward one, without reaching legs, in order to further reduce the need for specialist sails.

New Zealand Boating World, in its July 1992 issue, described the MIT-graduate Bill Koch's successful America's Cup campaign as a 'science-driven effort' with a 'scientist-led design team', pointing out that he had only begun competitive sailing in his mature years, and that 'he decided there were ways in which the existing traditionalism could be overcome by a more radical approach'.

Kiwi magic – but no superstars

In a very positive demonstration of its methodical approach to the task ahead, by mid 1993, almost three years out from the Americans' defence date, the general framework of the organisation set up for the Kiwi challenge had been announced, with Laurie Davidson and Doug Peterson nominated as the designers. Bruce Farr was still being mentioned as a possible member of the team, as were Greg Elliott, Jim Young, and Murray Ross. As everyone expected, Peter Blake remained as campaign manager for the 1995 challenge, Tom Schnackenberg continued as design-team co-ordinator, and Russell Coutts was to have charge of the sailing programme.

New Zealand was one of seven challengers for the America's Cup in 1995, and between these seven and the three defenders some US$200 million was spent. For the first time there was an all-women crew, and for the first time also there was an organised 'public keel unveiling' before the finals of the challenger series – and Internet coverage of the whole event.

The 1995 design team for *Kiwi Magic* was led by Laurie Davidson and Doug Peterson, and the boat showed it, of course. The IAAC class would never plane in a sustained fashion, indeed the Cup racing rules prevented competition taking place in the sort of conditions which would be necessary for such performance. But despite its colour, the boat they produced somehow looked light as well as fast, even though it was of necessity narrower than were the classic planing boats. It had no need for beamy planing capability because it would never be given the opportunity to use it.

Doug Peterson revealed much about the team approach to every aspect of the challenge when he said, 'When we started designing, the crew asked Laurie [Davidson] and me for a boat that would be equal to what everyone else had ... no breakthrough ... just solid all round.'

By far the majority of its team – from syndicate head through designers, builders, riggers, sailmakers, and crew – were the inheritors and product of New Zealand's long-running fast light small-boat philosophy, but the Kiwi syndicate also brought to its 1995 effort the hard-earned lessons of the previous three challenges.

When it was all over and the Cup was in New Zealand hands, Peter Blake summed up the New Zealand way of doing things: 'If we had a secret, it was in our attention to every detail through a team approach. The designers, builders, sailmakers, and crew all worked together. There were no superstars on the boat.'

Others in the team agreed: 'The secret is boring ... it's the teamwork ... everything we put into the boat works together – the hull, the sails, the rig, the crew, the shore team, the appendages ...'. The breakthrough was in the no-superstars teamwork ashore and afloat, rather than in some clever design difference. Innovative design development and team sailing had been part of the sailing life of each team member, and was part of the input each one made to the programme.

Though it may have sounded much too democratic and egalitarian to those from other countries where the old-fashioned relationships still persist, it came as no surprise to New Zealand sailors to hear Peter Blake describe the Team New Zealand approach to its America's Cup challenge as a team effort by equals. The scale of the task, the complexity of the technology involved, and the logistics of carrying out a successful big-boat campaign at an international level are of course several orders of magnitude greater than that of pursuing national championship success within New Zealand, but in the minds of Kiwi sailors the collective attitude required to do it is no different.

But the fast light idea had its limits. This was dramatically illustrated in 1995 by the

▲ Framed in this picture by the reinforced panel at the foot of the headsail, the bowman on *Black Magic* is attending to something on the forestay as the boat makes its way upwind. The profile of the bow of the New Zealand boat is, not surprisingly, reminiscent of that of the 470 – just a little more upright, perhaps.

▲ Bruce Farr and Russell Coutts are seen here in San Diego in 1992, concentrating on something Russell is reading (apparently not to his liking, judging by the look on his face). The outboard end of the deep rectangular-sectioned boom of the outclassed big boat, beaten in its mis-match series with the American catamaran, is just visible on the left of the picture.

Australians, whose boat suffered what one of their design team called 'a catastrophic failure' of its long narrow and very light AUS-35 hull and sank in 20-knot winds and moderate seas, by no means extreme conditions for such boats.

That they were competing against the New Zealanders at the time, and had already taken the only race of the series off the Kiwis, meant that this sinking added one more item to the legendary list of stroppy sporting occasions involving the Southern Ocean neighbours, the underarm-bowling incident of 1980 being perhaps the most infamous.

New Zealanders had entered two challenges for the 1995 Cup, of course, and the second was also very much the outcome of fast light boat attitudes. Chris Dickson was both syndicate head and skipper of the Tutukaka South Pacific Yacht Club entry, whose very name emphasises the significance of beach-front boating clubs in the Kiwi sailing scene, and his small boat reputation is as prodigious as it is in big boats.

Bruce Farr designed the Dickson entry *NZL-39*, a boat whose forward shape was described as 'a sharp slender bow that made the foredeck team operate like trapeze artists' and its crew included many Kiwi small-boat men.

Perhaps most significantly of all for 1995, the skipper of Bill Koch's boats *America^3* and *Mighty Mary* was not only a fast-light-boat New Zealander but also a very successful woman sailor. Leslie Egnot had been the first woman to win the P-class national trophy, the Tanner Cup, and her sailing reputation was such that she easily topped the 120 or so women who sought membership of the all-woman Koch team.

Leslie Egnot saw herself and the crew of the Koch campaign as true equal-standing competitors. At the outset of the defender series, she said: 'We don't want to be remembered as the first women's team. We want to be remembered as the defender.' She and her crew were very nearly just that, despite being infiltrated by a lone male crew member right at the end of the defender series.

New Zealanders were also to be found in the crews of several of the non-Kiwi challenger boats, their international reputations readily attesting to their agility, athleticism, boat-skill, and determination in whatever area of activity they were called on to become involved.

Kiwi Number 8-wire ingenuity, by the 1990s a tradition with a venerable history, will be much tested by the need to produce a successful end-of-century defence of the America's Cup. The future of international competition seems to lie with high-technology and a 'scientific' approach – but in what kind of boat, and at what cost? Certainly there is no shortage of new ideas, or of up-and-coming designers with a commercial approach. Of the new breed of designers of fast light boats, Greg Young has to be one of the most impressive. His Aqua Vitae-sponsored Bull series includes racing and cruising models, and overseas sales so far have been considerable.

A thought-provoking last word on fast light boats comes from designer Greg Elliott, in a bold claim about the future of monohulls:

> We will all end up with multihulls. Because they're just better. What do you want to carry this lump of lead round for? It's just a waste of time – an expensive waste of time. We will eventually end up there.

Whether these words will turn out to be prophetic, or merely wild surmise, only time will tell.

▲ The ubiquitous Hobie, in this case a spoonsored 16-foot version, demonstrates here the phenomenon known as 'flying a hull'. With both men on trapezes, and only one rudder in the water, the curved-keel Hobie catamaran epitomises the high-speed, lightweight multihull alternative for bored 'half-boat' sailors looking for one.

An illustrated checklist of small fast light boats

▲ **18 FOOTERS** The Aussie 18-footer is the fastest single-hulled sailing boat around today. They can plane all the way around the course, a feat which only they, boardsails, and multihulls are capable of. They are the inspiration behind the way America's Cup and Whitbread boats are designed, built, rigged, and sailed.

▲ **470** Designed in 1963 by Andrew Cornu of France, the 470, described as an overgrown Cherub, relies on agility of crew rather than strength and weight. It was selected as the two-man Olympic class for the 1976 Games, and by the mid 1980s there were 34,000 boats sailing in 42 countries. New Zealanders first made their mark in the class in 1981 when David Barnes and Hamish Willcox won the men's title; two years later Leslie Egnot and Michelle Holland finished second in the women's worlds. The class is strictly one-design; New Zealanders were prominent in the development of construction. Marten Marine achieved an international reputation in the 1980s for their strongly built fibreglass hulls, rig adjustment, and racing technique. There were 150 boats in New Zealand by 1984, when David Barnes and Hamish Willcox won the world title for the second time in a row from Chris Dickson and Joe Allen at Milford Beach on Auckland's North Shore.

▲ **3.7** Developed from a prototype designed by Bruce Farr in 1970 as the XL, the trapezing single-handed beamy hard-chined 3.7 m regularly beat the Auckland Q-class boats when sailed by its designer. The class owners association was formed in 1975, and NZYF recognition soon followed. By 1983 almost all were of foam-sandwich construction.

◀ **CATAMARANS** Polynesian sea-going multihulls are said to have achieved speeds of up to 25 knots, and it is this performance capability which attracts modern sailors to multihulls. The Shearwater Catamaran arrived in New Zealand in 1956, thriving in the strong winds of New Plymouth, Wellington, and Lyttelton. Cats joined the fleet sailing at Charteris Bay in Canterbury in 1957. Following the exclusion of catamarans from the previously unrestricted 12-foot class racing in Auckland, the 12 Foot Catamaran Owners Association was formed at a meeting at the Tamaki Yacht Club in 1959, with John Peet, whose *Kitty* won the international title for Australasia, as its chairman. There was a small fleet racing in Auckland that summer; six of the restricted-class boats were racing in Wellington in the 1959/60 season; and by 1966 they had become the most numerous catamaran class racing here. A lighter and faster 'second generation' revival began around 1964, with Barry Ryan's New Zealand champion *Hot Foot*, sailing out of the Evans Bay club, being one of the first. By 1966, they were building lightweight hulls and bendy rigs.

In 1964, the first catamarans built to the lightweight one-man international A-class in New Zealand were George Hoerr's *Falcon* in Wellington and Graham Stanton's *Kitten* in Canterbury. The A-class *Scat* achieved New Zealand's first truly international cat success when it came second in the World Championships in Melbourne in the 1965-66 season. By 1967, there were 48 entries in six classes in the Rothmans Cat week in

▲ **BOARDSAILS** The class is so different from all the others in this list that descriptions of the various types sound more like surfboards than sailing craft. Boardsailing was first included in the Olympic Games in 1984. New Zealanders have excelled in the sport for some years, most recently through the successes of Barbara and Bruce Kendall and Aaron McIntosh, both in world competitions and in the Olympics.

Wellington. Engineer-designer Graham Stanton in his particularly innovative bendy-rig A-class boat *Saracen* was outstanding in a regatta in which International B-class, Shearwater, Kitty, and Yachting World boats took part.

International recognition for New Zealand in centreboard multihulls came in 1970, when David Peet won the Paper Tiger class at International Cat Week in Melbourne. In 1971, there were some 120 of Aucklander Ron Given's 1967-designed 4.26 m Paper Tigers at their Australian National Championships. By the following season, there were 220 registered in New Zealand, with over 126 entries in National Cat Week at Torbay in Auckland. Given had designed his 14-ft lightweight, low-cost, easily-built catamaran in 1968, and within two years, controlled by tight class restrictions, it had spread across New Zealand and to Australia.

By 1973, the arrival of the Hobie Cat with its multicoloured sails was beginning to transform the catamaran scene. When the Tornado was adopted as an Olympic class in 1976, the catamaran had come of age as a performance racing centreboarder. The Canterbury Catamaran Squadron's challenger *Miss Stars Travel*, designed and built by Cliff Papps and Bill Hende, also involving West Coast enthusiasts, and sailed by Brett de Thier against Australia for the Little America's Cup on Port Phillip Bay in February 1974, was unsuccessful, being well beaten by the wing-sailed *Miss Nylex*. In 1976, a new world sailing speed record of 31.8 knots (the first time a speed of more than 30 knots had been certified) was set in the UK Speed Week at Weymouth by Timothy Coleman in the proa *Crossbow II*, a specialist outrigger catamaran capable of sailing in one direction only. The hydrofoil A-class cat *Mayfly* achieved 21.2 knots at the same trials.

165

◀ **CHERUB** Designed by John Spencer in 1951, the Cherub is a 12-ft plywood design, and was the first New Zealand-designed centreboarder to be granted world championship status. There were fleets racing in Auckland, Hamilton, Whakatane, Wellington, and Cowes in 1957; by 1958 there were over 200 boats registered in New Zealand, with boats being built in the US. It was recognised by the RYA in 1959, but was not recognised as a National Class by the NZYF until 1966. The first Cherub World Championships took place in Perth in 1970, the growth of the class owing much to the introduction of synthetic sail materials, bendy masts, full-width travellers, and double-luff spinnakers, which all improved the performance of a boat that was already very quick. The 15th class national championships in Nelson in 1970 used the Olympic points system. When describing the changing role of the class, from a senior to an intermediate boat, Jenny Farrell commented that 'the drift towards more expensive and more difficult boats to sail, at an earlier age, is doing New Zealand yachting a power of good, because younger sailors are more capable of winning in international or Olympic events than older men. Their easily attained fitness ... is an advantage and the knowledge they have gained in good intermediate boats like the Cherub sees them quickly taking the lead in senior boats once they graduate. About 80% of the highly competitive New Zealand Olympic 470 fleet consists of one-time Cherub class stalwarts.'

◀ **CONTENDER** The winner in a design competition for a boat to replace the Finn, Australian Bob Miller's plywood prototype Contender convincingly won a seven-race IYRU trial series. The 16-ft lightweight trapeze dinghy proved to be exceptionally fast. There were 44 entries in the first world championships for the class in 1970.

▶ **EUROPE DINGHY** The Europa Moth, a European Moth design from the early 1960s, broke away from the International Moth Class Association and formed the one-design Europe Dinghy class. It has a carbon-fibre mast and the dinghy itself only weighs 45 kg. The Europe was introduced as the women's Olympic Games single-hander in 1992 and will be so again in Sydney in 2000. With certain modifications, the Europe Dinghy can race as a Classic Moth Boat.

▶ **FINN** A 4.5 m, one-man, Olympic-class monotype, the Finn was designed by Rickard Sarby of Sweden in 1949. The class was introduced into New Zealand after the 1956 Olympics, where New Zealand was represented in the Finn class, but failed to win any medals in it. The Finn had been declared an Established Class by 1959, and a fleet raced at the Auckland Anniversary Regatta that year. Ralph Roberts sailed the class in the 1960 Olympics and won the Pall Mall Trophy, sponsored by Rothmans, in 1963. In 1964, Peter Mander represented New Zealand in the class in the Olympics. By 1966, there were 48 starters in the class national championships, at a time when the Sanders Cup could only muster six boats. In 1970, New Zealanders gave further indication of their international standing in the class when Jonty Farmer won the Finn Interdominion contest against Australia. 'Pumping' began in the Finns at the 1960 Olympics and 'ooching' in 1970 – both techniques causing intense debate and rule changes then and since.

▶ **FLYING DUTCHMAN** Designed by Uus van Essen and Conrad Gulcher in 1951, the Flying Dutchman was declared an Established Class by the NZYF in 1954, even though it was virtually unknown to local sailors when it arrived in the country. Sailors in Auckland imported several European-built hulls in 1958, and class racing for FDs was included in the 1959 Auckland Anniversary Regatta. Amateur construction in cedar began in Auckland in 1959, and fibreglass boats were introduced in 1961. The class gained support in Wellington after it was adopted by the IYRU as a two-man class for the 1960 Olympics. The first New Zealand trials to select representatives in the class for the Games were held that year. Class rules allow experimentation in materials (the FD was the first international class to allow the use of Kevlar without restriction), gear, and rig, but the major elements of the boat are one design. In the 1960s and 1970s, there were often up to 25 racing in Auckland, and in the mid-1980s there were over 100 registered in New Zealand.

FLYING FIFTEEN Uffa Fox designed the Flying Fifteen in 1948. Their 400 lb cast iron keel gives them a distinctive look out of the water, especially when dangling from the hoist that is required to get them in and out of it! Sam Mason built the first one in New Zealand, *Buttercup*. A group-building scheme in Wellington in 1959 soon saw twelve amateur-built Flying Fifteens on Evans Bay. With special dispensation from the UK, Wellington crews were allowed to use trapezes for the first few years – at home only – and those years saw impressive FF planing performances on reaches on the harbour in strong winds. Sam Mason, a Sanders Cup winner, won the first national championship, the Anderson-Wilkin Trophy, in 1963 in *Pinkie*, and again in three out of the next five years. Flying Fifteens achieved NZYF National Class status in 1964 and IYRU International Class status in 1981. Barry Finlayson and Ian Norrie of Napier won the class World Championship at Hayling Island in England in 1980 and the 1982 FF Worlds were held at Napier.

FROSTBITE Developed by the Wakatere Boating Club in Auckland in 1938, the class was designed to meet the need for a general purpose sailing dinghy which would be light enough to lift out of the water easily, yet strong enough to stand the strain of rough weather racing or of transporting to inland centres by car or trailer. Quite deliberately it seems, and in contrast to the advocates of the stepping-stone classes, the club made no organised attempt to spread the Frostbite throughout New Zealand by means other than the suitability of the boats for the locality concerned.

FROSTPLY Designed by John Spencer in 1954, the Frostply is a 3.85 m plywood dinghy that can be driven by sail, oar, or motor. By 1974, there were 80 boats registered, half of them in Hamilton.

◀ **INTERNATIONAL 14** An open 14-ft centreboarders class, the International 14 has been the springboard for many New Zealand sailors and designers. Geoff Smale and Ralph Roberts won the Prince of Wales Cup in *Atua Hau* at Cowes in 1958. They attracted international interest, particularly for their mainsheet set-up and their habit of cleating it, even on a reach. There was class racing at the 1959 Auckland Anniversary Regatta. At the same time, the Commodore of the Worser Bay Boating Club, Stan Bacon, built and raced one there. By 1968, however, local support for the class had disappeared, and their national trophy, the solid-silver Duke of Edinburgh Cup, was competed for by Flying Fifteens instead.

▼ **JUNIOR CHERUB** Created by John Spencer by attaching a reduced rig and sail area to his Mark II Cherub hull in 1959, some eight years after the introduction of the Cherub, the Junior Cherub was proposed by Peter Mander as a new intermediate class. 'A lack of a popular and modern junior class could prejudice the whole future of the sport in New Zealand,' the designers said. The first national championships for the class were won by Graeme Woodroffe at Evans Bay in 1961, though there were none racing there at the time, the winner's trophy being Peter Mander's certificate from his 1956 Olympic win in the Sharpie. Twenty boats took part in the national championships in 1966.

◀ **JAVELIN** Designed by John Spencer in 1958, the Javelin drew on both his Cherub experience and that of building a square-bilge plywood International 14 for himself. The class took off in 1960 after showing off its performance capability in open competition. The first national championships in 1964 brought Canterbury and Auckland boats to Paremata, which caught the interest of local sailors. The lines of Peter Nelson's *Profile*, from 1972 a most successful version of the Javelin, illustrate its essential form. In the 1975-76 season, 11 boats entered the first Open Sanders Cup on Lake Te Anau, and the Javelin won easily. Thirty Javelins contested their national championships in Auckland that summer, and several boats came from Perth for the series.

▲ **MISTRAL** Designed by Des Townson, the Mistral is a 3.7-m one-design, two-person moulded-ply centreboarder. Townson built 89 hulls in radiata pine with resorcinal glue, the first of them in 1959. Most fleet racing has taken place at Tamaki Yacht Club. Forty-three sailed in the class championship at Tamaki in 1983. A small number of fibreglass boats have been built in more recent times. Spars have become aluminium and the spinnaker double-luffed.

▶ **M CLASS** Over 60 of these classic 18-ft steel-centreboarded boats have been built since the first Emmy was launched in 1922. There has been class racing on Auckland Harbour for the Logan Memorial Trophy apart from the war years. In the early 1980s, there was a revival, with 11 Emmies racing there and several new boats being built.

▲ **LASER** Designed by Canadian Bruce Kirby and built by his industrial designer countryman Ian Bruce, both Olympic sailors, this strictest of one-design boats had some 7000 sailing in various parts of the world when it was introduced into New Zealand in 1973. With some justification, *Yachting* magazine has called it 'perhaps the most radical innovation in the history of yacht racing'. The international status of the class was much in dispute in the mid 1970s, with New Zealand vocal at the IYRU in the debate between its builders and the Union about applying the measurement rules used for other classes. In due course there were 38 entries in the second national women's championships for the class, won by Margaret Stanley, and its status in New Zealand became assured.

MOTH (INTERNATIONAL) Classic Moth Boats are a class of small single-handed racing sailboats that originated in the US in 1929. Classic Moths are a development class with a length of 11 feet, a maximum beam of 60 inches, a minimum hull weight of 75 pounds, and very few other restrictions. Over the years, various Moth classes have appeared around the world. In addition to the Classic Moth, one can find reference to the Australian Moth, British Moth, New Zealand Moth, and International Moth. All have 11-foot hulls, and all can trace their origins to either the US or Australian Moth (or both!). The Classic US Moth Boat was raced in the United States from 1930 until the late 1960s. The class was formally organized in 1932 as the National Moth Boat Association. In 1935, due to increasing overseas interest in the class, the name was changed to International Moth Class Association or IMCA.

MOTH (NZ) Designed by Len Morris in 1946, the NZ Moth was a development of the 3.35 m Australian Moth. It has been likened to a matchbox, because of its boxy shape and plywood construction. Although there is some latitude in the class rules for the arrangement of its rig, deck, cockpit, rudder, and centreplate, the NZ Moth is a one-design class. The NZ Moth Owners Association was formed during the summer of 1961-62. Some 70 boats competed in the first national championships in 1962, which was won by Jon Gilpin. The next year, there were 100 entries. Out of 1000 registered in New Zealand in 1984, only 50 were sailing.

MOTH (RESTRICTED) In 1964, the Restricted Moth was developed in New Zealand. A year later, a 16-year-old schoolboy, Bruce Farr, sailing *Mammoth*, a boat of his own design and construction, won the Restricted Moth national championships. Hal Wagstaff was influential in the early development of the Restricted Moth with his Puriri design, many of which were built.

MULLET BOATS Though no doubt capable of surfing, these Auckland clinker-built centerboarders ranging from 20 to 26 feet in length were too substantially constructed to plane consistently, but they were an economical alternative for those who could not afford a keeler. Originally built for the fishing industry – hence the name – they began their racing history in the decade before the turn of the century. Their sailing qualities and shallow-water abilities led to many being built. A big sail area meant that a crew of up to six was necessary, and this, along with the complexities and cost of clinker construction, eventually led to a decline in the class, though Mulleties are still raced on Auckland Harbour today.

▶ **OK DINGHY** Designed by Knud Olsen and promoted in Europe by Paul Elvstrom and others as a training class especially for future Finn sailors, the OK Dinghy is 13' 2" long, with a 90 sq ft sail on a rotating mast. It was introduced to New Zealand by enthusiasts in Canterbury, where Barry Stewart built the first of them, and by the 1962-63 season small fleets were racing in Canterbury, Auckland, Dunedin, and Nelson. By the summer of 1963-64, when Clive Roberts won the first National Championships at Kohimarama from 36 entries, there were over 100 boats racing in New Zealand.

▲ **Q CLASS** Also known as the 12-foot skiff, the Q-class is a 3.7 m high-tech unrestricted racing dinghy, with nearly 650 sq ft of sail area down-wind with the big rig on, sailed by two men on trapezes. The Q is said by enthusiasts to be one of the most challenging boats in the world to sail. It was introduced to New Zealand in 1951 by Dave Marks at the Glendowie Boating Club. The class grew rapidly and the Q-class owners association was formed in the 1955-56 season. Experimentation continued, and some prominent sailors experimented with fibreglass and foam, including Don Lidgard, Russell Bowler, and Bruce Farr. Rigs and sails now use exotic materials, with spars (including spinnaker poles and booms) commonly made of carbon fibre.

▶ **OPTIMIST** There were over 100 Optimists at their world championships on the Solent in 1969 – with parents on the shore using binoculars and walkie-talkies. The Kohimarama club announced in 1972 that it intended to promote the class, following its introduction to NZ by Clive Roberts, but it was to be a further four years before the New Zealand Optimist Dinghy Association was formed. It was headed by Paul Pritchett of Charteris Bay, who had built one for his children in 1975. Described in *Sea Spray* as `a cake box with pretensions, a small and unsophisticated 7ft 7in praam dinghy with a sprit-sail rig like a mishapen teatowel spreading to all of 38 sq ft', the boat was intended by its class association to `foster sailing for the beginner at low cost' – and in this it has succeeded.

▼ **R CLASS** The R-class was first sailed in Canterbury in 1928. It developed along traditional lines at first, but after the Second World War, the class and its supporters, most notably Brian Wall, introduced many of the innovations that have transformed small-boat sailing. The R-class spread north in the mid 1950s. The Wellington Squadron's inaugural AGM was held in 1958 and in 1959 the Rs were declared a National Class by the NZYF.

▼ **RFS** The tobacco-sponsored Rothmans Father & Son 4 m two-person dinghy was a joint design for the Murray's Bay Boating Club by Brin Wilson and Geoff Smale in 1965. In return for having their name on the sail, the tobacco company paid for distributing kitset plywood boats to other clubs in New Zealand and for the annual 24-hour race on nearby Lake Pupuke. In 1980, fibreglass hulls were introduced.

▼ **SHARPIE** A prize-winnning Kroger design, the boat is 19′ 8″ long, 4′ 8″ in the beam, with a steel plate and 165 sq ft of working sail on a gaff-rigged hollow mast. Although notable successes were made in the class, the International Sharpie never caught on in New Zealand. The boat's hull shape and rig were unfamiliar to locals and very few boats were built and raced here. Peter and Graham Mander created a stir when they finished the trials for Olympic Games representation in the class almost inseparable on points. Following NZ's success in the Sharpie at the 1956 Olympics, the class faded into obscurity here, though in Australia lightweight construction, a marconi rig, and trapezes have kept it alive.

SOLING Designed by Jan Linge as a day racer, the Soling first appeared as a National Class in Norway in 1965. It was selected as the Olympic three-man keelboat class in 1968 and still remains so. The Soling is raced in 41 countries on six continents. Due to its ease of handling and extreme responsiveness to hull and sail trim, it is the most commonly used boat in commercial sailing schools in the world. The Soling was the only gender-mixed class in the 1996 Olympics. It introduced match racing to the Games and is still considered to be the best introduction to match racing around today. It was introduced to New Zealand in 1969, when the Royal New Zealand Yacht Squadron imported moulds and promoted it, led by Don Colebrooke. The first national championships for the class were won by Ian Gibbs in a five-boat contest in Auckland in 1970, and Helmer Pedersen won the second nationals was won by Helmer Pedersen in Wellington in 1971. Leading New Zealanders who have sailed the class include Russell Coutts and Rod Davis.

STARLING Designed in 1969 by Des Townson, the creator of the Zephyr and Mistral, with the intention of it becoming 'the next step from P class', the 9 ft 6 in single-hander was seen as filling the stepping-stone gap between Ps and Zeddies. John Peet built and sailed the prototype – 'responsive, easy to sail and planes readily' was the reaction of those who tried it out – and by the 1970-71 season there were 20 sailing. Construction was kept simple, straightforward, and strong, with quarter-inch ply on quarter-inch frames. The class was discreetly sponsored by Fosters and there were nearly 300 plans sold in the first few years. A very windy, abandoned 1975 national championship in Wellington saw several masts broken, but there had been over 530 plans sold by then. Nearly 80 boats competed in the class nationals at Taupo in 1984. The home-built boats are still thought of as a single-handed intermediate class leading from Ps to OKs, Lasers, and Finns, for those who still want to sail on their own.

SUNBURST Designed as a plywood equivalent of the Frostbite in 1964 by Jack Brooke for the *New Zealand Weekly News* as its centennial project, this 11 ft 6 in restricted-class vee-bottomed plywood dinghy has been described as 'a sturdy, stable learner's boat that can be built from modern materials by an amateur'. Sponsored in the late 1960s by Auckland's Wakatere Boating Club as a trainer and for those who wanted competition, there were some 500 boats built by 1969. At that time their owners said they had no intention to form an owners association, saying 'Sunbursts are for fun ... and there is no intention of having national championships'. There have been national championships practically ever since, and the newer fibreglass boats are somewhat faster than the plywood originals.

TEMPEST Designed as a true one-design class in 1965 by Ian Proctor of England, the 22 ft two-man Tempest was described at the time as 'the first true planing keelboat'. The class held its first world championships at Weymouth in England in 1967 with 15 starters, but never took on in New Zealand, despite its advocates pointing out the advantages of its ability to perform well in windy places like Wellington.

◀ **TRAILER SAILERS** By 1959, there was seen to be a need for a type of boat that came between the centreboarder and the keeler, something inexpensive and easy to build that could be kept on a trailer, but was versatile enough to suit a range of uses. Richard Hartley responded to this need with his double-chined plywood Hartley 16 Trailer Sailer (actually 16 ft 5 in), which he first publicised in 1966. Within two-and-a-half years, over 300 boats had been built. The first national championships were held in Wellington in 1970 and attracted nineteen entries. The first of the more sophisticated fibreglass Noelex 22s appeared in 1970, receiving National status in 1976, the Hartley 16 having already done so by then. The New Zealand Trailer Sailer Association had been formed by 1972. The Elliott 5.9 pictured is one of the more sophisticated trailer sailers.

▶ **ZEPHYR** Used as a traing class for the Finn, most boats in New Zealand have been sailed in their home port of Auckland. They started spreading elsewhere in the country in 1958. There was class racing at the New Plymouth Anniversary Day Regatta in 1961. By 1971, the Auckland championships mustered 40 entries.

Glossary of sailing terms

about, to go, to tack across the wind to bring it from one side of the boat to the other.

aft, at or towards the stern of the boat.

afterguard, the group at the after end of the boat in command of proceedings.

ahead, a direction any distance directly in front of a boat (the opposite of astern).

amidships, in the middle of the boat, whether longitudinally or transversely.

apparent wind, the direction of the wind as it appears to those on board.

aspect ratio, the ratio between the length of the luff and the foot of a boat's sail.

backstay, a part of the rigging to support the mast. The leeward one is generally slacked off to allow the boom to move further forward in order to present the mainsail at a more efficient angle to the wind while running. In bigger boats with a permanent stay to the stern it is called a backstay and the pair either side are called runners. See also **preventers** and **runners**.

bailing, emptying out the water from a boat.

bare poles, the condition of a boat when all its sails have been taken in.

batten, a thin strip of wood or other flexible material fitted into long pockets in the leech of the sail to hold it out in a more efficient shape.

beam, the transverse measurement of a boat. Also used to indicate a direction in relation to a boat and to describe a transverse member of a boat's construction frame.

beam reach, to sail across the wind on a course more or less at right angles to it.

beat, to sail to windward by a series of alternate tacks across the wind.

Bermudan rig, a sail plan in which the main sail is of triangular shape, long in the luff and set from a tall mast. Now almost universal in modern racing boats.

bilge, that part of a boat on either side of the keel which approaches nearer to the horizontal than to the vertical direction.

block, a case in which are fitted one or more sheaves, around which ropes pass.

boat, in the context of this book, the generic name for sailing craft both big and small.

bolt rope, the rope which is sewn around the edges of a sail to keep it from fraying.

boom, the spar used to extend the foot of a sail.

boom vang, see **vang**.

bow, the forward end of a boat.

broach, to, a sailing boat's tendency to round up into the wind when running free.

broad reach, sailing on a reach at an angle to the wind greater than 90 degrees.

bulkheads, in small boats, the internal walls which form the watertight compartments intended to keep the boat afloat and capable of being righted in the event of a capsize.

bumps, distortions in hull form so as to affect its measurement favourably for rating purposes.

buoy, a floating object used to indicate one of the marks of a racing course.

buoyancy, entrapped air or fixed buoyant material used to ensure that a sailing boat remains afloat if capsized or damaged.

capsize, to, to upset or overturn a boat; once considered a calamity, but a matter of no great moment in fast light small boats.

catspaw, a ruffle on the water indicating the presence of a breath of wind during a calm.

centreboard, a device used to increase a sailing boat's resistance to leeway.

centreboarder, a boat, either big or small, fitted with a centerboard or centerplate.

centrecase, the slot at the centre of the boat in which the centreboard is moved up and down.

centreplate, a device, usually of steel, used to increase a sailing boat's resistance to leeway.

chine, the angle where the bottom of the hull of a boat meets the side. In a hard-chined boat this angle is pronounced; in a soft-chined boat it is rounded off.

chinese gybe, a wild and unpremeditated gybe which occurs when the main boom lifts over to the lee side of the boat while the upper part of the sail does not follow.

cleat, a two-armed fitting for making ropes fast.

clew, the lower aftermost corner of a sail.

clinker-built, a method of boatbuilding using narrow planks whose lower edges overlap the upper edges of the one below.

close-hauled, sailing with the sails so trimmed as to enable the boat to move upwind as close to the direction of the wind as possible.

close reach, sailing on a reach at an angle to the wind less than 90 degrees, but not as close to the wind as close-hauled.

clutch cleat, a form of cleat that locks the rope in its cleated position.

coaming, the raised edge around the cockpit to prevent water on the deck running down into the boat.

cockpit, the opening in the deck of a boat to accommodate the skipper and crew when not otherwise occupied about the boat.

consistent planing, achieving the state known as planing as a steady condition.

Corinthian, a mid-19th/early 20th century term used to describe an amateur sailor who sailed his own boat without the aid of a professional skipper, hence the Royal Corinthian Yacht Club.

crosstrees, light timber or metal spreaders fixed transversely to a mast and attached at their outer ends to the stays to give it support.

Cunningham hole, **Cunningham rope**, the gap and tackle at the foot of the mainsail used to enable the luff to be set up more tautly.

dagger board, a drop keel or sliding centerboard of wood or metal which can be raised or lowered through a slot in a boat's hull.

dinghy, from the Hindi, originally meaning a small rowing boat, but since the end of the First World War also used internationally to describe small racing sailing craft.

displacement, the weight of water that a boat displaces when it is afloat.

dynamic lift, lifting force caused by the increased pressure on a planing boat's hull from the water flow beneath it.

ease, to, used generally to mean to take the pressure off, as in easing the sheets to take pressure off the sail.

fast, to make, to secure, attach or fix in place.

fill, to, to trim the sails so that the wind can fill them.

flare, the outward curve of the sides of a boat, designed not only to throw the water outwards when meeting waves but also to enable the crew to sit out further from the center of the boat, thus hiking more effectively.

flukey, used to describe a wind when it is light and variable in direction.

foils, a term used by more modern sailors to describe centreplates and rudders, and also Kevlar sails.

foot (sail), the bottom of a sail.

foreguy, a rope leading forward from a boom to prevent it swinging out of control.

forestay, the part of the standing rigging which supports the mast or forward-most mast in a fore-and aft direction.

forward hand, the crew member whose normal position in the boat is most near its forward end.

freeboard, the distance, measured at the lowest point, from the water to the level of the deck.

gaff, a spar to which the head and forward edge of a sail is attached in gaff-rigged boats.

gale, a wind of between 34 and 47 knots, force 8 and 9 on the Beaufort scale.

genoa, a large jib or foresail.

ghosting, making headway without any apparent wind to fill the sails.

gooseneck, a fitting on the inboard end of a boom which connects it to the mast and allows it to swing sideways.

gunter rig, an arrangement of the mainsail in which the gaff to which it is attached lies almost vertical and against the mast in the fully hoisted position.

gunwale, the upper edge of the side of a boat.

gybe, the process, often hazardous in strong winds, by which the sails are swung from one side of the boat to the other when the wind passes across the stern.

halyard, the rope or wire by which sails are hoisted or lowered.

harden in, to haul in the sheets to present the sails at a more acute angle to the wind.

headsails, the name used to describe the sails set before the mast.

heavy displacement, the opposite of light displacement, a hull that displaces a large amount of water for its size. Traditional clinker-built dinghies are heavy-displacement boats.

heel, of a mast, the bottom end.

helm, another name for the tiller or wheel by which the boat is steered.

high aspect ratio, the opposite of low aspect ratio, where the ratio between the length of the luff and the foot of a boat's sail is high.

hiking, leaning out while sitting on or near the gunwale of a boat in order to influence the degree to which it heels.

hull, the main body of a boat.

IACC, International America's Cup Class.

IYRU, International Yacht Racing Union.

jammers, lever-mechanism fittings to hold ropes against slipping.

jaws, jaw-shaped fittings on the inside ends of booms and gaffs which fit loosely around the mast and allow relative movement.

jib, the triangular sail set on the forestay.

jibe, see **gybe**.

jib hank, fittings of metal or plastic by which the luff of the headsail is attached to the forestay.

jib-sheet, the rope attached to the clew of the jib and used to control the set of the sail.

jockey pole, a transverse spar used to prevent the spinnaker guy fouling the sidestays when the spinnaker is set well forward.

jury rig, a temporary arrangement of a boat's spars and sails used to continue sailing after they have become damaged.

Kahikatea, *Podocarpus dacridioides*, 'white pine' to boatbuilders, and lighter in weight than kauri.

Kaikawaka, *Libocedrus bidwillii*, southern cedar ('kaik') to boatbuilders, and lighter still in weight than white pine.

kauri, *Agathis australis*.

keeler, a big sailing boat fitted with a keel.

ketch, a type of sailing boat with two masts.

kite, see **spinnaker**.

knock-down, to, to roll a sailing boat over with its sails and rigging in the water, caused by a violent squall or mishandling of the boat.

lazy block, the block through which the mainsheet is passed.

leader, see **genoa**.

lee-o, the instruction usually given in a sailing boat when it is intended to go about.

leech cord, a cord, attached to the head of a sail and passed down the leech to the clew, used to adjust leech tension and thus the set of the sail.

leech, the after side, or trailing edge, of a sail.

leeward, to, in the general direction towards which the wind is blowing.
lifeline, a rope or wire stretched fore and aft along or around the deck of a boat so that the crew can clip harnesses to it in heavy weather.
lift, a change in wind direction which allows the boat to point higher than before.
light displacement, the opposite of heavy displacement, a hull that is wide and flat and displaces the minimal amount of water for its size.
line squall, a squally wind, the arrival of which is indicated by an approaching line of dark cloud.
loose-footed, a sail which is set without a boom or attached to the boom at its ends and not along its length.
low aspect ratio, the opposite of high aspect ratio, where the ratio between the length of the luff and the foot of a boat's sail is low.
luff, the leading edge of a sail.
luff, to, to bring the head of the boat up closer to the direction of the wind.
mainsail, the principal sail on a boat.
mainsheet, the rope used to control the mainsail.
mainsheet hand, the crew member whose task it is to control the mainsheet.
marconi, a one-piece mast.
mark, see **buoy**; may also be a course marker, possibly set into the seabed.
Mark Foy start, a staggered start system for handicap races which allows the slowest boats to start at intervals, with the fastest boat starting last.
mastbox, the part of a boat located and shaped to take the foot of the mast.
mitre, the seam in a sail where cloths which run in two or more directions are joined.
mizzen, the name of the aftermost mast on a boat rigged with two masts.
monohull, a boat with only one hull.
multi-hull, a boat with more than one hull.
Number 8 wire, the guage of mild steel wire (just under 3/16") much used in fencing in New Zealand. Its application in an infinite variety of uses (usually in the back shed) has seen the expression become synonymous with the Kiwi do-it-yourself attitude.
NZYF, New Zealand Yachting Federation.
off-the-wind, a boat sailing with eased sheets and the wind coming from broad of the bow.
one-design class, a class of boats all of which have been built to one accepted design.
on-the-wind, a boat sailing close to the direction of the wind.
ooching, sudden forward body movement, stopped abruptly.
outhaul, a rope or pulley system by which the outer end of a sail is pulled out along a spar.
overhang, the parts of the hull of a boat which extend beyond its waterline length.
pennant, the small, pivotting, feather-light material fitting used to indicate wind direction.
pinch, to, to sail a boat too close to the wind.
planing, attaining sufficient speed to cause the forward part of the hull of a sailing boat to rise and the boat to then sail along more quickly with only part of its hull touching the water.
Populars, in colonial times in New Zealand, those who were not Selects.
port, the left-hand side of a boat as viewed from aft.
port tack, the direction a boat is going in when the wind is coming from its port side.
preventer, the name given to any additional rope or wire set up to prevent any part of the rig or sails behaving in an undesirable way.
protest, an objection on behalf of a racing boat that some other party has broken the racing rules.
pulley, see **block**.
pulpit, a metal frame at the bow of a sailing boat.
pumping, moving the sail in and out in still air conditions in a regular fashion in order to achieve forward movement of the boat.
pushpit, the after equivalent of the pulpit.
quarter, the after corner of the boat
rake, the angle of a boat's mast to 90°.
rating, a calculation of a boat's expected racing performance relative to other boats, based on measurement of its hull, sails, etc.
reaching, **on a reach**, sailing with the sails full and the wind free.
ready about, the call given to prepare the crew for going about, after which the usual instruction is to say, loudly and clearly, 'lee-o'.
reef, to, to reduce the area of sail exposed to the wind.
reef points, short lengths of cord or rope, depending on the size of the boat and its sails, set into the sail and used to tie it to the boom when reefing down.
regatta, a term once used to describe a series of rowing races, but which now also refers to sailing races.
restricted class, a class of boat whose hull, sails, and rig are restricted within specified limits.
rigging, the term which embraces all ropes and wires used to support the masts of boats.
roach, the curve in the leech of a sail.
rocking, repeated rolling of the boat, induced either by body movement or adjustment of the sails or centerboard.
roll tacking, asssisting the process of tacking by movement of the body athwartships.
round-bilged, the expression used to describe a hull whose cross-section is curved and not squared off at its bilges.
rudder, the fitting, usually hung from or near the stern of a boat which alters the direction in which it is sailed.
runners, the adjustable stays, sometimes loosely called preventers, led from the mast to either quarter of the boat, and alternately slackened and made fast as the boat gybes when running downwind. See also **backstays**.
running free, sailing downwind.
sculling, repeated movement of the helm.
Selects, in earlier times in New Zealand, regatta participants of means.
shackle, a generally U-shaped metal fitting closed with a pin across its open end and used for securing sails, rigging, and fittings on boats.
shackle spanner, a tool for opening and closing the pin in a shackle.
sheave, the revolving wheel in a block.
sheets, ropes by which sails are controlled.
shrouds, the standing rigging of a sailing boat which gives its mast support.
sidestay, a stay led from the mast to the side of the boat.
sister clips, a pair of readily locked and unlocked metal fittings, each one of which is attached to the end of a rope.
skiff, a small fast sailing boat.
sky (the kite), to, allowing the kite to rise too high above the boat and thus risking the boat becoming unstable and difficult to control.
sloop, a sailing boat with a single mast.
small-boat racing, in this book, competition under sail in a dinghy or small centerboarder or other class of boat capable of planing.
snap-shackle, a spring-loaded self-closing shackle.
spars, a general term for masts, booms, gaffs, etc.
spinnaker, a sail which is usually set forward of a boat's mast, with or without a boom, when running before the wind.
squall, a sudden gust of wind.
square-bilged, the expression used to describe a hull whose cross-section is squared off at its bilges.
stacking, see **hiking**.
starboard, the right-hand side of a boat as viewed from aft.
starboard tack, the direction a boat is going in when the wind is coming from its starboard side.
stays, a part of the standing rigging of a boat which supports the mast.
steerage way, a boat is said to have steerage way when it has sufficient forward movement for its rudder to be used to apply pressure on the water passing it, and control the direction of the boat.
stem, the foremost part of the hull of a boat.
stern, the aft or rear end of a boat.
surfing, intermittent planing on wave formations which assist the action.
tack, to, to turn a boat head to wind and across it so as to bring the wind onto its opposite side. See also **about**, to go.
telltales, see **wools**.
tiller, the bar which fits onto or into the head of the rudder and by which it is moved as required.
tiller extension, a swivelling extension of the tiller whose purpose is to allow the helmsperson to sit further away from the tiller itself while continuing to control it.
traveller, a term used to describe both the pulley or other fitting which slides along it carrying a sheet and the fitting across the stern of a boat along which the pulley or the like slides.
trim, the way in which a boat floats on the water in relation to its fore-and-aft line as indicated by its design drawings or by its painted waterline.
tuck, a colloquial term common amongst Kiwi sailors of both big boats and small, used indiscriminately to describe both the stern of a boat and a reef in the sail.
ULDB, Ultra Light Displacement Boat
vang, in this book, an alternative name for the kicking strap.
wardrobe, the collection of sails carried on a boat.
watch, the system by which, during long periods of effort managing the boat, the crew are allocated times during which they are required to be on duty.
way, the movement of the boat through the water.
wear, to, to go from one tack to the other by gybing instead of by going about, usually due to stress of weather rather than by choice.
whisker pole, a short spar used to hold out the jib on the opposite side to the mainsail when running downwind.
windward, to, in the general direction from which the wind is blowing.
wools, short pieces of wool attached to sails to show the flow of air along them.
WPYMBA, Wellington Provincial Yachting Association, on which the region's sailing clubs are represented.
yacht, a sailing craft, but in the context of this book, a term seldom used (see boat).
YNZ, Yachting New Zealand, the present national body administering the sport of sailing.

Notes

Chapter 1

Page 7
The *Heemskerck* listed as a 'war-yacht': see Sharp, Andrew, *The Voyages of Abel Janszoon Tasman* (London, 1968) p. 28.
For Tasman's use of boats around New Zealand: see Sharp, Andrew, ibid. pp. 118-145.
For an account of Charles II bringing yachts to England: see Bradford, Emile, *Three Centuries of Sailing* (London, 1964) pp. 15-16.

Page 8
Anderson, Grahame, *Fresh About Cook Strait* (Auckland, 1984) p. 152 (the letter, written on 6 November 1840 by Edward Catchpool to a friend in England, appears in Louis Ward's *Early Wellington*).

Page 13
Garrett, Ross, *The Symmetry of Sailing*, (London, 1987) p. 33.

Page 16
Clive Highet was quoted by Hardham, Harry A, 'Why the N.Z. 14 Footers "Vamp" and "Impudence" won at Hobart', *Sea Spray* (Volume 3, Number 2), January 1948, p. 9.

Page 17
Whittenbury, Roy, 'The Making of Sailcloth', *Sea Spray* (Volume 27, Number 9), October 1972, p. 61.
The article on sail care was in *Sea Spray* (Volume 4, Number 1), December 1948, p. 29.
Leo Bouzaid on breaking in new sails: *Sea Spray* (Volume 4, Number 4), March 1949, p. 1.

Pages 19-25
Smith, Peter, 'The Race is to the Swift', *Sea Spray* (Volume 4, Number 10), September 1949, pp. 18-20.

Chapter 2

Page 34
'The Cradle of Yachting', *Sea Spray* (Volume 2, Number 9), August 1947, pp. 20-21.

Page 37
Carter, Ronald, *Little Ships* (Wellington, 1948) pp. 131-2.

Chapter 3

Page 51
Carter, Ronald, 'A Hundred Years of Yachting', *Sea Spray* (Volume 5, Number 1), December 1949, pp. 5-8.

Page 56
Sea Spray (Volume 30, Number 4), May 1975, pp. 20-22.

Page 59
Scandal dispute: see Papps, Clifford, 'The Facts about the "Scandal"', *Sea Spray* (Volume 4, Number 4), March 1949, p. 7.

Page 72
Wheatley and Reid, History of the Sanders Cup (1946), pp. 37-8.

Page 73
Letters to the Editor, *Sea Spray* (Volume 4, Number 10), September 1949, p. 22.

Chapter 4

Page 78
'21 Years ... 1945-1966', *Sea Spray* (Volume 21, Number 11), December 1966-January 1967, pp. 44-5.

Page 79
Book Reviews, *Sea Spray* (Volume 6, Number 5), April 1951, p. 33. The book that was reviewed, *20 Plywood Boats and How to Build Them*, had been published in the US by Rudder Publishing in 1947.

Page 80
'Plastic Hulled Sailboats', *Sea Spray* (Volume 4, Number 12). November 1949, p. 10.
Sea Spray (Volume 22, Number 9), October 1967, p. 68.
'21 Years ... 1945-1966', *Sea Spray* (Volume 21, Number 11), December 1966-January 1967, pp. 45-6.

Page 81
Pardon, David, 'Carbon Fibre – The Next Hull Material?', *Sea Spray* (Volume 24, Number 6), July 1969, p. 52.
Pardon, David, 'The Balsa Sandwich Story', *Sea Spray* (Volume 25, Number 5), June 1970, pp. 47-9.

Page 82
Sea Spray (Volume 6, Number 5), April 1951, p. 33.

Page 84
Shepherd, Gordon, 'How to Get a Go-Fast Bottom Finish', *Sea Spray* (Volume 22, Number 10), November 1967, p. 74.

Page 85
Norlin, Peter and Rosenow, Frank, 'Basic Yacht Tuning – No. 2: The Kicker', *Sea Spray* (Volume 28, Number 3), April 1973, p. 61.

Page 87
Sea Spray (Volume 10, Number 11), December 1954-January 1955, p. 8.

Page 88
Sea Spray (Volume 7, Number 7), August 1951, p. 51.

Page 89
'Was it Lawful to Rock the Boat?', *Sea Spray* (Volume 2, Number 6), May 1947, p. 22.

Page 95
Sea Spray (Volume 6, Number 5), April 1951, p. 5.

Page 96
Real, Ivan, 'So You Want to Buy Wet Weather Gear', *Sea Spray* (Volume 25, Number 7), August 1970, p.44.

Page 97
'21 Years ... 1945-1966', *Sea Spray* (Volume 21, Number 11), December 1966-January 1967, p. 47.

Page 99
'Just for Fun', *Sea Spray* (Volume 13, Number 9), October 1958, p. 15.

Chapter 5

Page 111
Sea Spray (Volume 13, Number 9), October 1958, pp. 30-31.

Page 117
Letters to the Editor, *Sea Spray* (Volume 6, Number 8), July 1951, pp. 34-5.

Page 118
Sea Spray (Volume 25, Number 11), December 1970-January 1971, p. 37.

Page 119
Letters to the Editor, *Sea Spray* (Volume 26, Number 8), September 1971, p. 73.

Page 120
Jack Brooke summarising the fate of several classes racing in Auckland Anniversary Regatta: *Sea Spray* (Volume 25, Number 11), December 1970-January 1971, p. 37.

Page 123
'21 Years … 1945-1966', *Sea Spray* (Volume 21, Number 11), December 1966-January 1967, p. 47.
Sea Spray (Volume 25, Number 1), December 1970-January 1971, p. 35.

Page 124
Sea Spray (Volume 25, Number 1), December 1970-January 1971, p. 36.
'21 Years … 1945-1966', *Sea Spray* (Volume 21, Number 11), December 1966-January 1967, p. 46.

Page 125
'21 Years … 1945-1966', *Sea Spray* (Volume 21, Number 11), December 1966-January 1967, pp. 48-9.

Chapter 6

Page 127
Coutts, Russell, *Course to Victory*, (Auckland, 1996), pp. 28-9.

Page 131
Brian Wall's article on rigging, *Sea Spray* (Volume 21, Number 11), December 1966-January 1967, pp. 54-5.

Page 132
The quote from Bruce Farr is taken from the undated transcript of an interview with Bruce Farr, held in the archives of the Museum of New Zealand Te Papa Tongarewa, Te Papa Archives MU Series 401.
Profile of John Spencer by David Pardon, *Sea Spray* (Volume 27 Number 1), January 1973, p. 31.

Page 133
Sea Spray (Volume 40, Number 6), June 1986.

Page 136
Laurie Davidson was quoted in *New Zealand Boating World*, June 1995, pp. 18-20.
Des Townson was interviewed by Sandra Gorter, 23 May 1998, published as 'Des Townson and Other Designers', *Classic Yacht Quarterly*, Issue 12, July 1998, and used with permission.

Page 138
Mark Oram was quoted on the 1989-90 Whitbread campaign in *Sea Spray*, June 1990, pp. 16-18.

Page 141
The quote from Greg Elliott is taken from the transcript of an interview with Greg Elliott in September 1995, Te Papa Archives MU Series 401.

Page 145
Bruce Kirby was quoted in 'The Light Brigade', an unpublished manuscript by Gary Baigent, held in the archives of the Museum of New Zealand Te Papa Tongarewa, and used with permission.

Pages 146-147
Bruce Farr was quoted in *Sea Spray*, March 1989, pp. 8-9.

Page 150
Bill Koch was quoted in *America's Cup '95: the Official Record*, p. 111.

Page 151
Chay Blyth was quoted in Bob Fisher and Barry Pickthall, *Ocean Conquest* (London, 1993), p. 29.

Page 152
Peter Blake was quoted in Fisher and Pickthall, ibid., p. 46.

Page 153
The description of *Steinlager 2* as a 'giant sailboard' appeared in an article on the Whitbread in *Sea Spray*, July 1990, pp. 16-18.

Page 157
The article about sponsorship appeared in *New Zealand Boating World*, July 1993, pp. 20-25.
Don Tempest's article appeared in *Sea Spray* (Volume 22, Number 6), July 1967, p. 52.

Page 159
The new IACC specification was discussed in *Sea Spray*, February 1989, pp. 8-9.

Page 160
Bill Koch's America's Cup campaign was discussed in *New Zealand Boating World*, July 1992, p. 47.

Page 161
Doug Peterson was quoted in *America's Cup '95: the Official Record*, p. 84.

Page 163
The quote from Greg Elliott is taken from the transcript of an interview with Greg Elliott in September 1995, Te Papa Archives MU Series 401.

Index

12 Foot Catamaran Owners Association, 165
45° South, 144, **144**
470 class, **12**, 94, **94**, **98**, **122**, 164, 166
  National Youth Championship (1979), **143**

A
A-class, 165
A-class World Championships (1965-66), 165
Admirals Cup, 127, 158
Adrienne, 133
Aerial, 11
'A Hundred Years of Yachting', 51
'aircraft carrier', 60
Akarana Winter Series, **27**
Alert, 19–20, 22, 22–3, 23–4
Alf Harvey Trophy, 106
Allen, Joe, 164
aluminium, 53, 59, 70, 81
America³, 162
America's Cup, 6, 17, 127–8, 135, 136, 137–8, 157–63, **160**, **162**
  changes to rules, 160
  cost of challenging and defending, 160
  all-women team, 162
  Australians' catastrophic failure, 162
America's Cup (1999), 136
  defence, 163
America's Cup challenger series (1999-2000), 139
Anderson, Grahame, **66**
Anderson-Wilkin Trophy, 113, 168
Andrews, George, **44**, **71**, 72
Aotearoa, **11**
Armit, B, 106
Armit, C, 106
aspect ratio, 88
Atlantic Privateer, 152–3
Atua Hau, 109–10, 169
Auckland Anniversary Regatta (1945), 59
Auckland Anniversary Regatta (1950), 77
Auckland Anniversary Regatta (1959), 111, 112, 167
Auckland Anniversary Regatta (1984), **139**
Auckland Anniversary Regatta (1985), **138**
Auckland Maritime Museum, 74
AUS-35 hull, 162
Aussie, **5**
Australia compared with New Zealand, 48
Australian 18-footers, 133 see 18-footers
Avenger, 11
Awatiri, 21

B
Bacon, Stan, 111, 169
Baigent, Gary, 133, 134
bailer boy, 82
Bailey, Glad, **31**, 39
Baileys (boatbuilders), 141
bailing, 82, **82**
Baker, Michelle, 94
Ball, Andy, **110**
Barnes, David, 6, 34–5, 105, 147, 164
Bartlet, Tim, 26
Benson & Hedges, **119**
Bermudan rig, 37–8
Bethwaite family, 6
Betty, **44**, **71**, 72
Bilger, Jock, 6, 140
Blackaller, Tom, 148
Black Magic, **161**
Blake, Peter, 6, 138, **150**, 150–4, **152**, 160, 161
Blaszka, Henryk, **111**
Blitzkrieg, 135
Blyth, Chay, 151
boardsailers, 125, 147–8, **148**, 165
boatbuilding, **156**
  amateur, 43, 51–2, **53**, 61, 72, 78, 80
  P-class, 57
  professional, 4, 72
  X-class, 52, 72
boat clubs, 27
Bouzaid, Chris, 6, 142
Bouzaid, Leo, 6, 17–18
Bouzaid, Tony, 6, 80, 135
Bowler, Russell, 158, 172
Brasell, George, 106
Brindabella, 147
Brooke, Jack, 88, 118, 123–4, 136, 174
Brown, RB, 35
Bruce, Ian, 170
Buccaneer, 133
Bull series, 163
buoyancy tanks, 51
Burton Cutter, 151
Butler, Paul, 9
'butterbox', 60. see also I-class
Buttercup, 112, 168

C
canoe sailing see Butler, Paul
Canterbury Catamaran Squadron, 165
Canterbury Clothing Company, 158
Canterbury R-class Squadron, 25
capsizes, 90–1, **91**, **124**, 130
capsizing, 51
carbon fibre, 81, 149, 159
Carter, G, 106
Carter, P, 106
Carter, Percy, 33
Carter, Ronald, 37–8, 51
catamarans see multihulls
Catchpool, Edward, 8
centreboarders, 27, 130
centrecases, **79**
centreplates, 88
Ceramco New Zealand, 152, **152**
Chance, Britton, 145
Charade, **72**, 74, **74**
Charles II (King of England), 7
Cherub class, 108, **108**, 113, 125, 133, 166, 169
  Mark II hull, 114
  national championship (1970), 166
Cherub World Championships (1970), 166
Citizen match racing series, **148**
Clark, Michael, 147
Clark, Tom, 133
class administration, 62
class associations, 67, 124
class distinctions, 3–4, 9, 29–30
Cloke, Frank, 39
coffee-grinders, **142**
Colebrooke, Don, 174
Coleman, Timothy, 165
Colmore-Williams, Peter, 134
computer modelling, 156
construction
  amateur, 167
  balsa-core, 81
  cold moulding, 80
  composite, 158
  double-skinned, 139
  fibreglass, 52, 57, 79–80, 80, 149
  foam sandwich, 80
  laminated, 136
  light displacement, **149**
  lightness, **78**, **79**, 79–82, 129–30, 135
  low cost, 30
  plywood, 52, 57, 59, 67, 79, 80, 107, 132–3, 133, 149
Contender class, 60, **88**, **90**, 166
Cooksons (boatbuilders), 138
Cook, Wayne, **115**
Corinthian, **131**, **142**
Cornu, Andrew, 164
Cornwell Cup, 36, **36**, 59, **60**, 63, 73, 105, 106
courses, 49–50, 66, 92–3
Coutts, Russell, 6, 34–5, 105, **111**, 127–8, 147, 148, **160**, **162**, 174
Cropp, Jack, 104, 106, 107, **109**, 109
Crossbow II, 165
C-Tech, 26
cunninghams, **45**, 56, **57**, **84**, **104**
Cutler, John, 147–8

D
Dalton, Grant, 153, 154
Davern, Jim, **157**, 157–8
Davidson 28 class, 135
Davidson IACC boat, 136
Davidson IOR class, 135
Davidson, Laurie, 6, 135, 137, 145, 146, 152, 158, 160, 161
Davidson M 20 class, **135**
Davidson Ultimate 30 class, 136
Davina, 73
Davis, Rod, 159, 174
Dawson, Barry, 106
Demon, **17**, 37, **37**
Denniston, CG, 57
Desert Gold, 39
design controls, 103, 120
Dickson, Chris, 6, 34–5, 105, 139, **143**, 148, **148**, **154**, 154–5, 159, 162, 164; enfant terrible, **159**
Dickson, Roy, 6, 148, **148**
displacement boats
  heavy, 10, 13, 16
  light, 16, **139**
  ultra light, 133
Dodson, Richard, 6, 147
Dodson, Tom, **141**
Dragon class, **9**, 70, 121
Drum, 152–3
ducts, flap-controlled, 83, **108**
Duke of Edinburgh Cup, 111, 169
Dunhill, 121
Dunhill Cup, 122

E
Edwards, Tracy, 153
Egnot, Leslie, 34–5, 94, 148, 162, 164
eighteen-footers, 5, **5**, 6, **6**, **15**, 15–16, **54**, **78**, 100–1, **102**, **119**, 120, 137, 164
Elaine, 85
Elliott 5.9 class, **141**, 175
  national championship (1989), **141**
Elliott 9.0 class, **141**
Elliott, Greg, 141, **141**, 156, 160, 163
Elliott Marine, 156
Elvstrom, Paul, 112, 172
  hiking fashion, **111**
Emmies see M-class
Endean, Richard, 148
England, Hugh, 64
English, Joe, 153
Enza, 151
Equity, 147
Essen, Uus van, 111, 167
Established Classes, 67, 104, 111, 112, 167
Estralita, 23, 24, 24–5
Europa Moth class, 166
Europe Dinghy class, 166
Evans Bay Yacht and Motor Boat Club, **11**, 66, 113, 132, 165
Exador, 147

F
Falcon, 165
Fantzipantz, **137**
Farmer, Jonty, 167
Farr 1020 class, 148
Farr 11 class, **145**, **149**
Farr 1220 class, **156**
Farr 3.7 class, **87**, 164
  class owners association, 164
Farr 5000 class, **137**
Farr, Bruce, 6, **115**, 128, 132, 133, 135, 137–9, 144, **144**, 146, 146–7, 147, 152, 153, 157–8, 158, 160, 162, **162**, 164, 171, 172
Farrell, Jenny, 102, 109, 166
Farreticante, 133
Farr IACC boat, 138
Farr MRX class, 134, 148
Fastnet race (1983), **147**
Fastnet race (1989), **27**
Fay, Michael, 158
Fay Richwhite, 147
Fehlmann, Pierre, 152–3
ffandango, **112**
fibreglass see construction, fibreglass
Field, Ross, 138–9, 154
Fiery Cross, 139
Finlayson, Barry, **112**, 168
Finn class, 60, 70, **89**, **92**, 92, 107, **107**, **111**, **113**, 121, 147–8, 166, 167, 175
  Interdominion, 167
  national championship (1966), 167
Finn World Championships (1984), **111**
Fisher & Paykel, **2–3**, 153, 154, **154**
five-flag starts, 92–3
floating judges, 65
Flyer, 151, 152, 153
Flying Ant class, 137
Flying Circus, **139**
Flying Dutchman class, **55**, 70, **78**, **87**, 107, **110**, 111–12, 121, **124**, 140, 167
Flying Dutchman World Championship (1991), **110**
Flying Fifteen class, **86**, 111, **112**, 112–13, 168, 169
  group building scheme, 113, 168
  national championship see Anderson-Wilkin Trophy
  Flying Fifteen World Championship, 168
Fosters beer, 174
fourteen footers, **22** see International 14 class
Fox, Uffa, 11, 31, 61, 84, 112, 133, 168
Fresco, 116
Frostbite class, 136, 168, 174
Frostply class, 59, **110**, 168
Fuller, Ben, 113
Fun, 135, 146
Future Shock, 141

G
gaff rigs see rigging, gaff
Galloway, Fiona, **94**
Ganahl, Ivar, **111**
Garrett, Ross, 13
Gatorade, 153
Gazelle, **133**
Genie, 145
Gestro, Clem, **65**
Gibbs, Ian, 174
Gilpin, Jon, **57**, 105, 114–15, 171
Given, Ron, 165
Glendowie Boating Club, 172
goosenecks, **131**
Grifo, 133
Gulcher, Conrad, 111, 167
gunter rigs see rigging, gunter

H
Half Ton Cup (1972), 144
half-tonners, **143**
Hartley 16 class, **107**, 108, 175
Hartley, Richard, 6, 107, 108, 175
Harvey, Alf, 37, 50, 60–1, 92–3, 102
Havoc, 116
Hayman, Bill, 34, **34**
Hazeldine, Isobel, 94
Heath's Condor, 151
Heemskerk, 7, **7**
Hende, Bill, 165
Heretaunga Boating Club, 37, 50, 61, 66, 74, 85, 93
Highet, Clive, 16
Highet, Harry, 6, 33, **33**, 55, **57**, 105

180

Highet points system, 63, 69, 93
hiking, 89–90, **90**
hiking straps, 54, 56, **56**, **84**
Hobart-Auckland race, 122
Hobie Cat class, 163, 165
Hodgkinson, Len, 38
Hoerr, George, 165
Hogg, Del, 147
Hogg, Stephen, **26**
Holland, Michelle, 164
Holland, Ron, 6, 135, 137, 152, 153, 158
Hot Foot, 165
Houdini Jnr, 34, **34**
hull finish, 83, 83–4
hull shape
    clinker built, 71, 73
    hard chine, 51, 59

I

IAAC class, 150, 159, 160–1
I-class, 29, 37–9, 43, 44–5, 52, 60–71, 63, 72, 73, 74, 78, 82, 85, 91, 93, 118, 132
    class rules, 63, 65
    construction, 67–9
    construction tolerances, 63, 65, 66
    crew, 53, **63**
    decline, 67
    drop-race clause, 69
    full-length sail battens, 106
    interprovincial contest (1936), 61
    minimum weight for plywood boats, 67–9
    modern revival, 106
    national championship see Moffat Cup
    plywood construction, 106
    pre-race debates, 66
    provincial residential rule, 67
    provincial districts, 63
    representative trial race (1949), **65**
    specifications, 63, **64**, 67
Idle Along, 37, 38, **38**, 61, 62, **62**, 102
Idle Along see I-class
Idle Along Association, 71
Illinoie, **14**
Impact, 116
Impudence, 16
Inca, **142**
Infidel, 123, **133**, 133
International Sharpie class, 104
International 14 class, 11, **11**, 16, 31, 107, 111, 113, 117, 169
International B-class, 165
International Classes, 113, 168
International Moth Class Association (IMCA), 171
International Moth Owners Association, 166
International Sharpie class, 107, **109**, 109, 173
International Yachting Racing Union (IYRU), 67, 69, 93, 111–12, 113, 148, 167, 168, 170
    Offshore Racing Committee, 146–7
Iron Duke, 40, **40**
Isler, Peter, 148
Italian America's Cup team, 159–60

J

J 24 class, 148
japara *see* sails, japara
Javelin class, 74, **74**, **83**, **113**, 113–14, 125, 133, 140, 169
    national championships, 113–14, 169
Jayhawk, 150
Jellicoe, Lord (Governor-General of NZ), 39, 40–1
Joe Louis, 146
Jules Verne prize, 150–1
Julian, Evan, 106
Junior Cherub class, 114, **114**, 125, 169
Junior Offshore Group, 107–8

K

kahikatea, 52, 60
Kahurangi, 13
kaikawaka, 52
kauri, 52, 59
keelers **125**, 128, 130, 136
keels, 131, 149
Kendall, Barbara, 94, **148**
Kendall, Bruce, 6, 147–8, **148**
Kenwood Cup, 127, 147
Kevlar, 149, 167. *see also* sails, Kevlar
kickers, 54, 56–7, **84**, 84–5, **85**, **104**
Kirby, Bruce, **79**, 145, 170
Kitten, 165
Kitty, 165
Kitty class, 165
Kiwi, 37, **37**
Kiwi Magic, **127**, 160–1
Koch, Bill, 94, 150, 160, 162
Kohimarama club, 172
Kouros Cup (1990), 148
Kurrewa V, **157**
Kuttel, Paddi, 152–3
KZ5, 159
KZ7, 159

L

ladies committee, 94
laminar flow, 83–4
la quintessence, **139**
Laser class, **79**, 80, **97**, 99, 106, 170
    national women's championships, 170
Laser II class, 106
Leander Trophy, 25–6, 116
Lester, Peter, 6
Lidgard, Don, 6, 80, 172
Lidgard, Heather, 6
Lidgard, John, 134
life jackets, **65**, **82**, 96
Life Savers, **103**
lightness, 30, **30**
Line 7 clothing brand, 95
Linge, Jan, 174
Lion New Zealand, **150**, 152, **152**, 154
Little America's Cup, 165
Logan family, 6, 10, **10**, **87**
Logan Memorial Trophy, 170
Longobardi, 138
Loraine, **66**
Louis Vuitton Cup challenger series (1992), 159–60

M

Macky, Sarah, 94
Mad Max, 135
Magic Bus, 140, 146
Maiden, 153
mainsheets, **56**, **104**, 110
Makura, 21, 22, 23
Mammoth, 137, 171
Manaia, 87, **87**
Mander, David, 106
Mander, Graham, 6, 34, 64, 73–4, 104, 105, 106, 109, 173
Mander, Peter, 65, 104, 106, 107, 109, **109**, 114, 116, 117, 124–5, 169, 173
Mander, Stan, 117
Manly Yacht Club, 114
Mark Foy starts, 93, **122**
Marks, Dave, 81, **81**, 172
Marten Marine, 138, 164
Mason, Sam, 112, 113, 168
masts, 53
    aluminium, 57, 123
    hollow, 69, 70
    marconi, 13, 57
Matariki, 23
match racing, 134, 148, 174
Maxi World Championships (1989), 138
Mayfly, 165
M-class, **32**, 135, 170
McNeil, Phillip, **98**
measurement debates, 62, 65
measurement templates, 65, **66**, 66–7, 72–3
Meiklejohn, Andrew, 26
Menai, 21, 22, 23, 24
Mercedes, 87
Merit, 153
Mighty Mary, 94, 162
Miller, Bob, 166
Miss Nylex, 165
Miss Stars Travel, 165
Mistral class, 114, **114**, 136, 170
mobile sailing schools, **49**
Moffat Cup, 33, 38, 39, **39**, 63, 64, **65**, 66, 67, 69, 70, 71, **73**, 87, 91, 95
Moonlight, 136
Morris, Len, 115, 171
Moth (Australian) class, 115, 171
Moth (British) class, 171
Moth class, **88**, **91**, 114–15, **115**, **122**, **124**, 137, 141
Moth (Classic) class, 166, 171
Moth (International) class, **79**, **115**, 137, 171
Moth (New Zealand) class, 115
Moth (Restricted) class, 171
    national championship (1966), 157–8, 171
Moth World Championships, **115**
Mr Bojangles, **113**
Mulgrew, Peter, 136
Mullet Boats, 134, 171
multihulls, 150–1, 163, 165
Murihiku, 31
Murray's Bay Father and Son class, 121, *121*, 173
Myth, **65**, 135

N

NACA sections, 88
Nada, 64
Naomi James Challenge Trophy, 94
National Classes, 67, 104, 108, 113, 116, 166, 168, 173, 175
national conferences, 62, 65, 66
national contests, 32, 47, 48, 49–50, 62, 63. *see also* Cornwell Cup; Moffat Cup; Sanders Cup; Tanner Cup; Tauranga Cup
National Moth Boat Association, 171
New Plymouth Anniversary Day Regatta (1961), 118, 175
Newspaper Taxi, 140
New York Yacht Club, 139
New Zealand, 159
New Zealand Boating World, 136, 157, 160
New Zealand Company, 8, **8**
New Zealand Half Ton championships, 135
New Zealand Monotype Cup Championship, 105
New Zealand Moth Owners Association, 114–15, 171
New Zealand Optimist Dinghy Association, 172
New Zealand Sailing and Motor Yacht Federation, 97
New Zealand Trailer Sailer Association, 175
New Zealand Yachting Association, 9
New Zealand Yachting Federation (NZYF), 67, 70, 104, 106, 108, 111, 112, 113, 116, 124, 156, 166, 167, 168, 173
Ngaroma, **10**
Noelex 22 class, 175
Norlin, Peter, 85
Norrie, Ian, 168
Northerner, 123
Novak, Skip, 152–3
NZI Enterprise, 152, 152, 153, 155
NZL-39, 139, 162

O

offshore racing rules
    changed to counter Bruce Farr, 137, 146–7
O'Hara, Bill, 111
OK Dinghy class, 60, 70, 172
    national championship (1963-64), 172
Olsen, Knud, 172
Olympic Games (1956), 104, 107, 109, 109, 111–12, 114, 127, 140, 147–8, 164, 166, 167, 169, 173, 174
Olympic points system, 69, 93
Olympicsail '92, **148**
Olympic trials, 109, 112
one-design classes, 43–4, 118
Onerahi Regatta, 55
One Ton Cup, 135, 136, 142, 145, 146, 147
on-the-wind starts, 50
ooching, 167
Open Sanders Cup, 169
OPNI, 133
Optimist class, 127, 172
Oram, Mark, 138
oregon, 59, 67
Otago Cruising Club, 94
Outsider, 141
Outward Bound, 135, 152

P

Pajot, Yves, 146
Pall Mall Trophy, 112, 167
Paper Tiger class, 165
Papps, Cliff, 165
Paprika, **148**
Pardon, David, 81, 122, 132
Paremata Easter Regatta, **65**, 105
Parnell Sailing Club, 10
Party Pro, 141, **141**
Pathetic, 81, **81**
Patiki class, **10**, 10–11, 12, **13**, 14, **14**, 32, 123, 134, 136
Patrick, Joe, 39
Patterson, Mark, 105
P-class, **28–9**, 33–5, 43, 44, 47–8, **49**, 52, 55–8, **58**, 70, 82, **82**, **84**, 91, 95, **104**, **105**, 118, 125, 127–8, 132, 136, 139, 174
    age restriction, 47
    aluminium masts, 104
    carbon-fibre masts, 105
    construction, 55
    construction diagrams, **55**
    construction tolerances, 57
    cost, 56, 104
    crew, 53
    fibreglass construction, 104
    first woman to win, 162
    kitset, 104
    national contests, 57–8. *see also* Tanner Cup; Tauranga Cup
    plywood construction, 104
Peacemaker, 141
Pearse, Richard, 11
Pedersen, Helmer, 6, **55**, 114, 114–15, 174
Peet, David, 165
Peet, John, 165, 174
Peggy, 41
Pendragon, 135, **135**
Peterson, Doug, 160, 161
Phase II class, **46**
Pied Piper, 145
Pig Hunter, 141
pigrooting, **28–9**
Pinkie, 112, 113, 168
planing, **13**, 31, 59, **75**, **100–1**, **102**, **113**, **120**
    definition, 11, 12–13
    definition of sustained, 11
    history, 10–12
    hull shape, 5, 149
    P-class, 104–5
plywood *see* construction, plywood
Poole Bay Olympic Training Regatta, 121
Poole, Hugh, **66**, 67, **72**, **74**, 74, 85
    effigy **106**
'Populars', 9
Pretty Boy Floyd, **140**
Prince of Wales Cup, 107, 109–10, 169
Pritchett, Paul, 172
Proctor, Ian, 175
professionalism, 98–9, 119–20, 142
Prospect of Ponsonby, 145

pumping, 167
pumps
 hand-operated plunger, 82–3
 lever-action, 83
Puriri design, 171
Pursuit, 21, 22–3, 24

Q

Q-class, 102–3, 120, **120**, 164, 172
 owners association, 172
Quarter Ton Cup, 140, 143, 145, 146
Query, 80
Quarter Ton Cup class, **146**

R

race control, 62
Ragtime, **133**
Rainbow II, 142
Ranger, **128**, 133
Rank Xerox, **6**
Rank Xerox, **98**
R-class, 26, 54, **54**, 83, **102**, 102–3, **116**, 116–17, **120**, **122**, 125, 131, 173
Real, Ivan, 96
Red Duster, 157
regatta, 7–8
Reid Shield, 38, 62, **62**
Resolute Salmon, 145
restricted classes, 44, 118, 120
Ricochet, **63**
Rietschoten, Cornelis van, 151, 152
rigging
 gaff, 13, 57, 59
 galvanised steel, 53
 gunter, 37–8, 59, **59**
 stainless steel *see* stainless steel
Riley, Dawn, 94
Robb, Arthur, 157
Roberts, Clive, 6, **111**, 172
Roberts, Ralph, 6, 106, 107, 109–10, 112, 167, 169
rocking, 89, **89**, **111**
roller reefing, **115**
Rona, **39**, 40–1, 72
Rona-Jellicoe boats *see* X-class
Rongomai, 37, **37**
Ross 40 class, 140
Ross 780 class, 140
 national championship (1989), **140**
Ross 930 class, 140
Ross, Bill, **34**
Ross, Murray, 140, 160
Rothmans, **27**
Rothmans, 112, 121, 167, 173
Rothmans Father and Son class *see* Murray's Bay Father and Son class
Round Australia Race (1988), 150
Royal Hawaiian Ocean Racing Club, 147
Royal Hobart Regatta, 16
Royal New Zealand Yacht Squadron, 94, 174
Royal Yachting Association (RYA), 63, 108
rudders, **88**
Ryan, Barry, 165

S

Sabot class, 127
sailing clothing, 95–6
sailing schools, 93
sailmaking, **156**, **157**
sails
 adjustment, **129** *see also* cunninghams; kickers
 batten lengths, 67
 breaking in, 17–18
 care, 17
 cotton, 16–17, 53
 Dacron, 17, 54
 japara, 53–4, 67
 Kevlar, **2–3**, 54, **149**
 nylon, 65, 67, 123
 Terylene, 17, 54, 67, 118, 123
Sanders Cup, 31, **31**, 40, **41**, **44**, 63, 72, 73, 74, 87, 91, 104, 118, 119, 139, 167, 168
sandpaper, 'wet and dry', 83–4
San Francisco big boat series, 147
Saracen (A-class), 165
Saracen (Spencer 37), 133
Sarby, Rickard, 112, 167
Saunders Roe (boatbuilders), 11
Scandal, 59, **59**
Scat, 165
Schnackenberg, Tom, 6, 154, 160
Scimitar, 123, 133
Scully, Barney, **66**, **69**, 113, 132
Scully, Ken, **69**
seamanship, 30, 125, 128, 130, **130**
Sea Spray, 6, 16–17, 17–18, 19, 34, 50–1, 73, 77, 78, 79–80, 81, 82, 83–4, 85, 87, 88, 92, 94, 95, 96, 97, 98–9, 107, 108, 116–17, 119, 119–20, 123, 124–5, 132, 138, 146–7, 150–1, 153, 157, 159, 172
'Selects', 9
Sellers, Rex, **6**
Serene, 136
seven-footer *see* P-class
Sharpie class *see* International Sharpie class
Shearer, Jan, 94, **94**
Shearwater class, 165
sheets, 54
Shepherd, Gordon, 83–4
Shingana, **10**
Shirley, 61
Shockwave, **147**
Silver Fern class, 139
Slipaway, **60**
Slipaway Revival, **75**
sloop, 7
Smale, Geoff, 6, 107, 109–10, **110**, 110–11, 111, 169, 173
Smirnoff, **76–7**
Smirnoff vodka, 146
Smith, Peter, 19–25
Soling class, 174
Soper, Leanne, 94
Sopranino, 117–18
Southern Cross Cup, 158
Sowry, Glen, **98**
Spencer, John, 6, 59, **64**, 67, **68**, 69, **69**, 74, 105, 106, 108, 109, 113, 114, 123, **132**, 132–3, 137, 166, 168, 169
spinnakers, 35, 63, 67, **142**
sponsorship, 4, 98–9, 119–122, **120**, 146–7, 157
 tobacco, **119**, 120–22, 157
Staccato, **56**
Stagecoach, 26, **26**, **120**
stainless steel
 solid-drawn, 67
 solid-wire, 53
 stranded-wire, 53
Stanley, Margaret, 170
Stanton, Graham, 165
Starlight, 136
Starling class, **85**, **86**, **93**, **123**, 174
St. Clair Brown, Don, 120, 147
Steinlager 1, 150
Steinlager 2, 138, 153, 154
stepping-stone classes, 29, 43, 45, 47, 48, 52, 64, 66, 75, 77–8, 101, 102, 103, 116, 118–19, 132
Stewart 34 class, 134, **134**, 148
Stewart, Barry, 172
Stewart, Bob, 123, 134, 136
Sunburst class, 123, **123**, 174
surfing, 11, 15, **105**
Swuzzlebubble V, **138**
Sydney to Hobart race, 152, **157**

T

Taka see Z-class
Takapuna Boating Club, 35, 60
Takapuna One Design class, 60
Talisman, 21, 22, 24
Tamaki Yacht Club, 114, **132**, 165, 170
Tamariki, **14**
Tanner Cup, 34, 47, 58, 64, 94, 162
Tanner Cup (1945), **34**
Tanner, George, 34
Tatariki, **35**
Tauranga class *see* P-class
Tauranga Cup, 34, **42–3**, **46**, 47–8, 58, 63, 64, 94
Tauranga Regatta (1924), **56**
Tauranga Yacht Club, 105
Taylor, Digby, 135, 152
T-class, 19
Team New Zealand, 161
Telford, Ross, 91
Tempest class, 175
Tempest, Don, 119–20, 157
Termanto Foam, **87**
The Guru, 26
Thier, Brett de, 165
Thom, Murray, 105
Thorneycroft (boatbuilders), 11
Three-Quarter Ton Cup, 135
Thunderbird, 147
tiller extensions, **45**, **79**, 86–7, **87**, **88**, 104
Timms, Chris, 6, 147–8
Titus Canby, 144
Ton Cup, 127
Ton Cup classes, 144
Tonga, **7**
Topaz, **83**
topsides, flared, 141, **141**
Torbay/Taiotea Yacht Club, 94
Tornado class, **80**, 147–8, 165
Townson 32 class, 136, **136**
Townson, Des, 105, 114, 136, **136**, 170, 174
trailers, 49, **49**
trailer sailers, 107, **108**, 175
Jim Young, 139
 national championship, **125**
 national championship (1970), 175
trapezes, 55, **55**, **61**, **87**, 87–8, 91, **91**, **103**, **119**
Treleaven, Brian, 116
Treleaven, Ian, 119, 120–1
Turner, Ted, 145
Tutukaka South Pacific Yacht Club, 162
twelve-footers, **90**, **103**, 141
twelve-foot skiffs, **120**, 172
twelve-metre class, 158
world championship, 159
Twilight, 136

U

UBS Switzerland, 152–3
Urban Cowboy, 140

V

Valet, **19**
Valiant, 21
Vallings, Alex, 26
Vamp, 16
vangs *see* kickers
Varasi, Gianni, 138
Vaudrey, Jan, 94
venturis, 54, **54**, 83
Victory, **45**
Viper, 32, **32**
VPP computer programs, 138

W

Waddilove, W W, 56
Wagstaff, Hal, 6, 117, 171
Wagstaff, Warren, 106
Wai Aniwa, 136
Wakatere Boating Club, 168, 174
Wall, Brian, 116, 131, 173
weight distribution, 138
Wellington Anniversary Regatta, 8–9, **9**, 41, 63
Wellington Provincial Yacht and Motor Boat Association (WPYMBA), 38, **64**, 70, 71
Wellington Provincial Yachting Association, 61, 62
Wellington R Class Squadron, 116, 173
wetboots, 95–6
wet-weather gear, 96, **143**
wetsuits, 96
Wherat, Toby, 15
Whitbread 60 class, 138, **154**, 154–5
Whitbread Round the World, 6, **85**, 135, 138, **150**, 151, 152, **152**, 153–4, **155**, 158
 design studies, 138
White Heather, 139
White Lines, **141**
Whiting, Paul, 6, 140, 145, 146
Whiting, Penny, 6, 94
Whittenbury, Roy, 16–17
Why Not, **69**, 132
Wiig, Gary, 113
Wilkinson, Bill, 39
Willcox, Hamish, **143**, 164
Williams, Leslie, 151
Williamson, Bob, **60**, **63**, 106
Wilson, Barry, 95
Wilson, Brin, 173
Wilson, Graeme, 116
Windex, **45**
Windhover, **51**, **65**
Windhover II, **49**
Windhover III, **50**
wind indicators, **82**, 85–6, **86**, **104**. *see also* Windex
Wing, Neil, 109
Winkelman, Henry, 32, **39**
Women's World Sailing Championship (1990), 148
Woodroffe, Graeme, 114, 169
World 18-footer Championships, 5
Worser Bay Boating Club, **26**, 37, 50, 92, 111, **116**, 169

X

X-class, 31, **31**, 32, **32**, 39–41, 43, 44, **71**, 71–5, **73**, 78, 82, 91, 104, 118, 119, 135, 139
 change to restricted status, 72
 construction, 71
 crew, 53
 fibreglass construction, 73–4, 104
 national championship *see* Sanders Cup
Xies *see* X-class

Y

Yachting, 170
Yachting New Zealand, 156
Yachting World class, 165
yachts, definition, 7, 27
 history, 18–19
Yamaha, 138
Yamaha, 154
Young 11 class, 139, **139**
Young 88 class, 139, **139**
Young America, 139
Young, Greg, 163
Young, Jim, 6, 137, 139, 141, 145, 160
Young Nick, 136

Z

Z-class, 31, 35–6, 37, 43, 52, 59–60, 61, 71, 73, 78, 82, 91, 95, 118, 125, 132, 139, 174
 age restriction, 47
 construction, 59
 crew, 53
 demise, 59–60
 marconi masts, 105–6
 modern revival, 106
 national championship *see* Cornwell Cup
 plywood construction, 105–6
 World Championship, **75**, 106
Z-class Monotype Cup, 106
Zeddie *see* Z-class
Zeehaen, 7, **7**
Zephyr class, 118, **118**, 136, 175